Folkestone A Third Selection

IN OLD PHOTOGRAPHS

ALAN F. TAYLOR

Alan Sutton Publishing Limited
Phoenix Mill · Far Thrupp · Stroud
Gloucestershire · GL5 2BU

First Published 1995

Cover photographs: front: The Stade and weather-boarded buildings, 1920s; back: The west end of the Leas, Clifton Crescent and Madeira Walk, c. 1895.

British Library Cataloguing in Publication Data.
A catalogue record for this book is available from the British Library.

ISBN 0-7509-0970-6

Typeset in 9/10 Sabon.
Typesetting and origination by
Alan Sutton Publishing Limited.
Printed in Great Britain by
Ebenezer Baylis, Worcester.

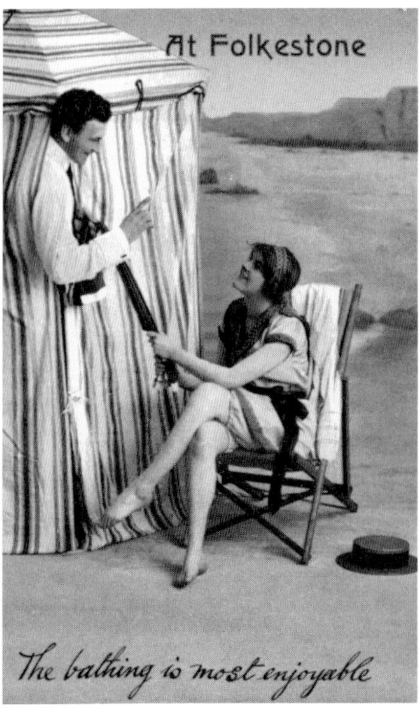

An Edwardian postcard sent from Folkestone in 1909, during the heyday of picture postcards. It illustrates the days when changing on the beach was not permitted, tents or bathing wagons being more common.

Contents

	Introduction	4
1.	Streets and Trade	7
2.	Harbour and Fishing	51
3.	Seafront	71
4.	Lifeboats and Shipwrecks	81
5.	The Leas	89
6.	The First World War 1914–18	97
7.	More Glimpses of Bygone Folkestone	111
	Acknowledgements	126

Introduction

I am pleased to be able to bring you this third selection of *Folkestone in Old Photographs*, compiled completely from my own collection and that of the late C.P. Davies. It is largely due to the success of the previous two books that the publishers have invited me to compile a third selection.

Due to recent purchases I am able to include a number of early photographs in this selection. Some of these are taken from stereographs. Stereographs consist of a pair of photographs of the same subject mounted on a piece of card 175 mm long by 85 mm wide. They are viewed through a stereoscopic viewer giving a 3D effect. From the mid-Victorian period most families of substance would have had a stereoscopic viewer and stereographs; the latter possibly bought while on holiday.

One of Folkestone's pioneer photographers, Mr William Venables, on coming to Folkestone first took a job as a wine waiter at the Pavilion Hotel. He started his photography business around 1856 and some of the early photographs in this selection were taken by him.

In this third volume I have included some of the sections which were most popular in the last selections. I feel it would not be complete without a section on the fishing industry as there are still many people in and around Folkestone whose ancestors were, in one way or another, connected with the industry. The subject is of great interest to me and one on which I have given illustrated talks. A reference to Folkestone for the year 1556 states there were 120 inhabited houses and 20 fishing boats; by 1767 there were 49 fishing boats and 800 men employed in the industry. English's *Guide to Folkestone, Hythe and Sandgate* for the year 1900 states: 'there are now about 50 large boats and many small ones constantly engaged in the fisheries'.

In November 1703 a disastrous storm wrecked the Stade, and, on 14 April 1710 a memorandum was made in the Common Assembly minute book to the effect that 'Whereas tis too well known to this assembly, that the Stade of this town is very much diminished, and likely to be lost, by the rage of the sea, and consequently the fishery, so beneficial to the towne and country adjacent, must withdraw from hence, and the great part of the towne be ruined, unless some speedy and effectual care shall be taken in the premises'. To this end William Markwich, the Romney Marsh engineer, was consulted. He surveyed the harbour and advised the building of three 'Knocks' of timber and stone, between the high and low water marks, to cost £600. For this purpose stone was taken from the quarry and a subscription was raised. The work was done, but a further storm on 17 December 1724 swept away a considerable portion of the new work and did damage to the extent of £1,100. This time the population was overwhelmed by the losses and, in April 1725, petitioned for state aid with a result that a Royal Brief was obtained and church collections made throughout the kingdom. What the results were of the collections does not seem to have been recorded. In 1766 an act of parliament was obtained to support and preserve the parish church, and the lower part of the town, from the ravages of the sea. By this act the coal dues paid from 1661 were appropriated for the repair of the old and the erection of the new sea-defence work.

In 1807 another act of parliament was obtained for the construction of a harbour. A subscription list was opened and £16,000 subscribed. The foundation stone was laid in 1808, and ultimately three stone jetties were built. The scheme failed, perhaps owing to lack of capital, and the harbour was moribund until bought for the South Eastern Railway Company by the Chairman, Mr Baxendale, for £18,000.

I have included another large section of Streets and Trade as this section was very popular. In 1776 Charles Seymour's *Survey of Kent* was published. This contains a good deal of information about the town and describes it as 'wealthy and populous'. There was a further manorial survey in 1782 and, as in the earlier survey, most of the houses lie in the area now represented by the Stade, North Street, South Street, Dover Street, High Street, The Bayle, Church Street and Rendezvous Street. It is rather difficult to envisage the lower part of the town as it was at this date owing to the changes made, not only in our own time, but by the two great nineteenth-century clearances. The first of these was when the tram-road was built around 1840; the second when Tontine Street was built through the valley around 1850. In 1782 the area at the bottom of the High Street was very much built up. South Street (then called Gulston Street) backed on to the Pent, as did Pent Buildings. These faced due east, and occupied the site later covered by the tram-road. Both Gulston Street and Pent Buildings ran down into Kingsbridge Street, which faced what is now the inner harbour. Dover Street (Harbour Way), then Dover Lane, and Great and Little Fancy Streets, later Fenchurch Street, were built and the area north of the Pent Bridge at the bottom of High Street (now the mouth of Tontine Street) was closely built up and covered by Ladd's and Nicholas's yards. Millbay provided the only direct communication between High Street and Dover Road (then Mill Lane).

A section on the Folkestone Lifeboats and Shipwrecks has been included. I give illustrated talks on Folkestone lifeboats and it is surprising how many local people don't know that Folkestone had a lifeboat station. The station had a comparatively short life from 1893 to 1930. It is possible that the RNLI would not have built a station at Folkestone if the first boat hadn't been sponsored by Miss Curling of Denmark Hill, London, who categorically insisted that the boat was to be stationed at Folkestone. The second factor behind the decision was the loss of the sailing ship *Benvenue* off Sandgate in 1891. This disaster caused much concern about the lifeboat facilities in the area and many people thought they were inadequate. Just eight days after the disaster there was a public meeting at the Folkestone town hall. A lifeboat committee was formed in accordance with the wishes of the local residents.

The wreck which caused the concern was the 2,033 ton sailing ship *Benvenue* of Glasgow, bound from London to Sydney with a general cargo. She was proceeding down the channel under tow of a tug on 11 November 1891. The wind had increased to hurricane force when they were off Folkestone. At 5 a.m. the tow parted and the stricken vessel was swept towards the shore. The captain dropped his anchors just off Brewers Hill, Sandgate. This halted the drift, but the seas cascaded over the vessel and she began to sink so the crew took to the rigging. The rocket apparatus was at once brought into use by the coastguards, but their efforts failed. One shot went over the vessel, but the rope had parted. In the meantime the Sandgate lifeboat *Meyer de Rothschild* had been taken to Hythe and was launched around 9.30 a.m., but after a short distance from the shore she turned completely over losing a crew member, Mr Fagg. Attempts with the rocket apparatus to reach the vessel continued all day until the supply of rockets ran out. By around 8 p.m. the wind had abated and a volunteer lifeboat crew from Folkestone finally reached the *Benvenue*; twenty-seven survivors were snatched to safety and taken to Folkestone harbour, where large crowds cheered their arrival. The captain of the *Benvenue* and an apprentice were both drowned. The wreck of the *Benvenue* still lays in four fathoms of water about 350 yards from the shore straight out to sea from Brewers Hill. It is still a hazard to fishermen's nets.

Quite a large section on the First World War has been included. Folkestone harbour played a major part during the war by embarking and disembarking troops to and from the Continent. To accommodate the troops four rest camps were set up in the town, many large blocks of houses were acquired and huts were built. Hotels and manor houses were also transformed into military hospitals. From the start of hostilities to the signing of the peace, the numbers embarking from and landing at Folkestone harbour were: British officers and men, 537,523; civilians engaged in Red Cross and other war work, 846,919; German prisoners of war, 3,592. Folkestone also had a large contingent of Canadians who came to Shorncliffe military camp in February 1915. Within a year there were 40,000 men training there.

England's first contact with the grim horrors of war was in Folkestone, around 20 August 1914, when boats came into the harbour crowded with Belgian refugees. These early arrivals came in fishing boats and coal carriers. The visitors were terror stricken, and many of them refused to leave the boats. The news of the coming of the Belgians was not made public until eight or nine days later, when it finally appeared in the press. So Folkestone played a major part during the war, with its rest camps and the transportation of troops to and from the Continent.

A.F.T.
Folkestone, February 1995

SECTION ONE

Streets and Trade

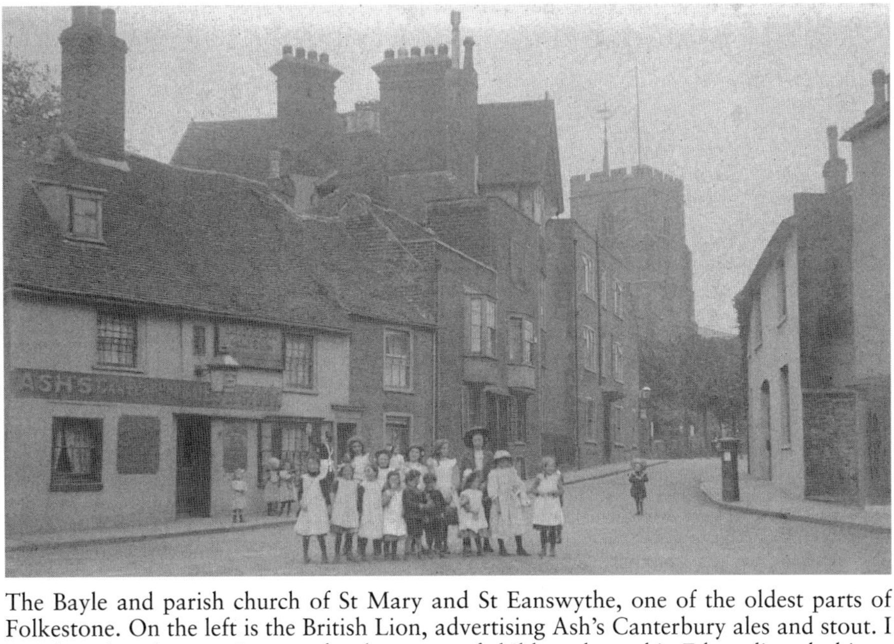

The Bayle and parish church of St Mary and St Eanswythe, one of the oldest parts of Folkestone. On the left is the British Lion, advertising Ash's Canterbury ales and stout. I wonder what the occasion was for the group of children dressed in Edwardian clothing.

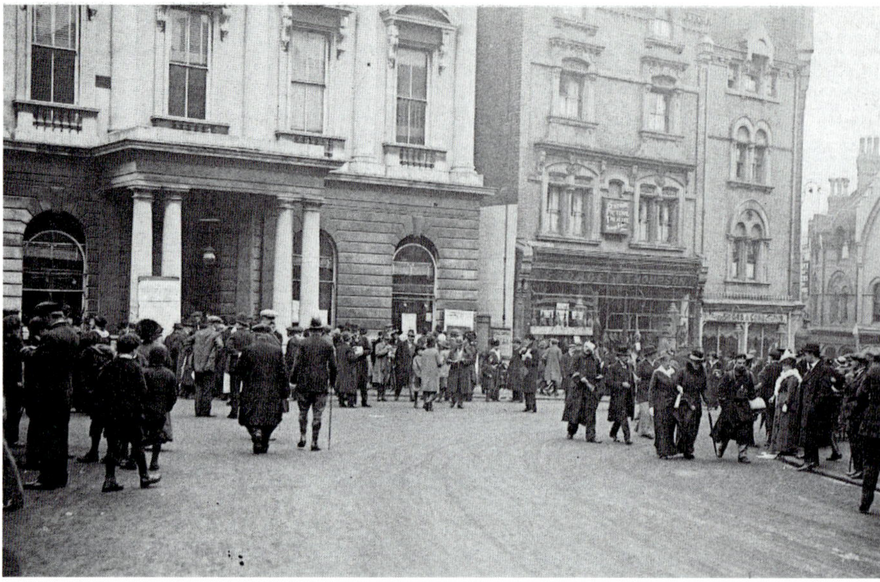

An animated scene outside the town hall, October 1914. The people have come to read the latest news on the First World War. This was posted outside the town hall daily.

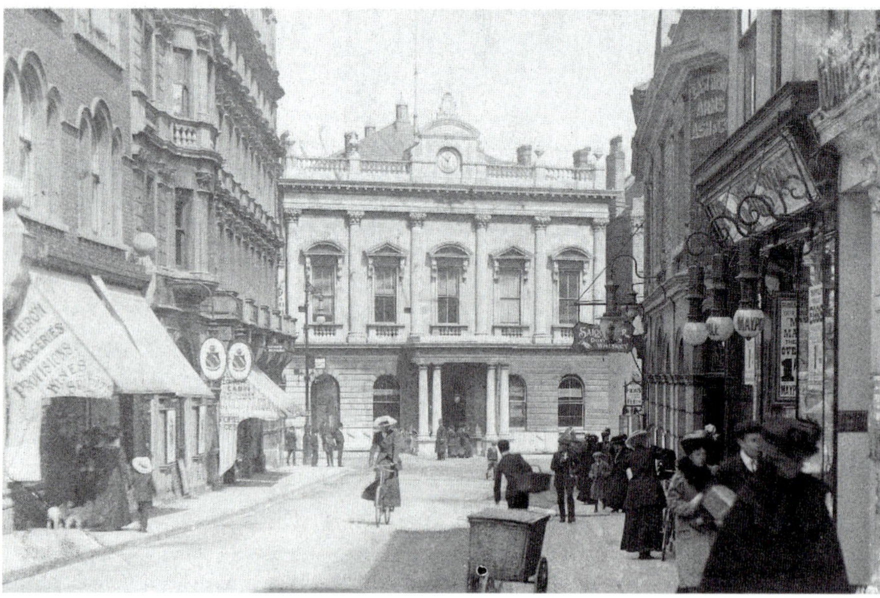

The lower end of Sandgate Road, 1910. In the left foreground is Heron's groceries and provisions, the Bodega wine and spirit merchants, Uncle Tom's Cabin – Thomas Wing (tobacconist), George Mount (florist), Mark Bradwell (umbrella manufacturer). The Queen's Hotel is in the centre on the corner of Guildhall Street. In the right foreground Maypole Dairy is followed by the East Kent Arms, proprietor Charles Major.

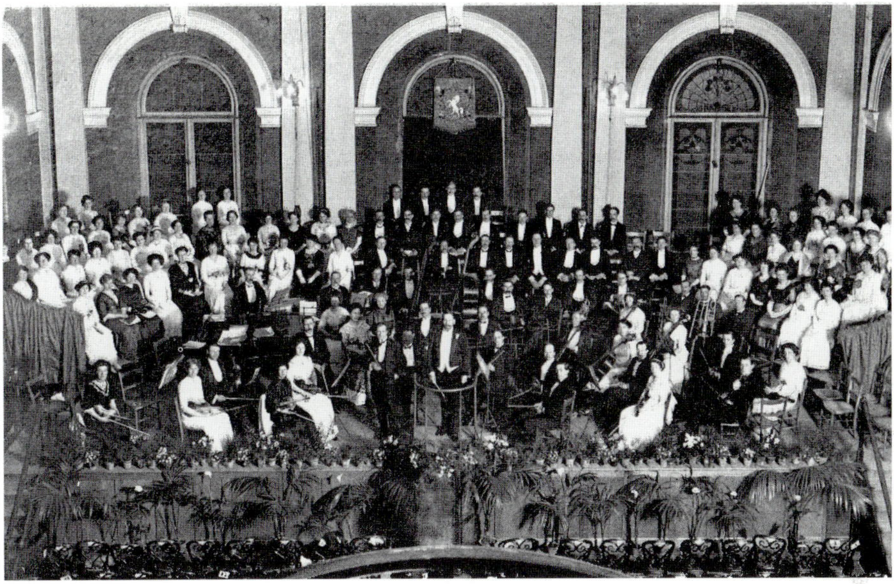

The interior of the town hall. Apart from housing the council chamber, town sergeant, coroner's office, police station, etc., the town hall had a concert room. On this occasion the Folkestone Philharmonic Orchestra is playing.

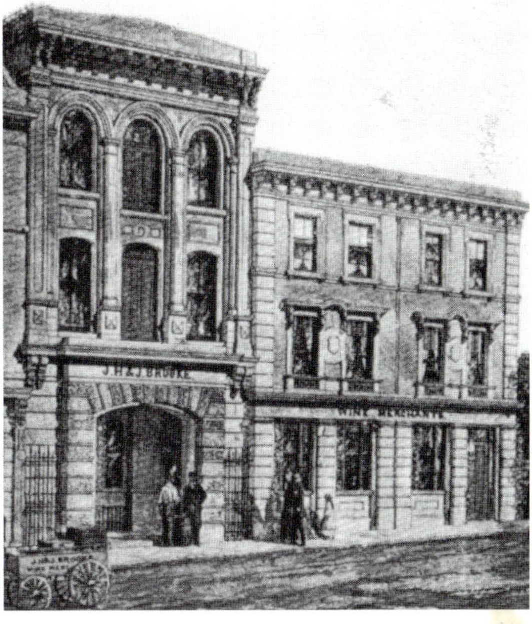

Messrs J.H. and J. Brooke, wine merchants, 25–7 Sandgate Road. Brooke's represents one of the oldest established wine merchants' businesses in Kent: this branch opened in July 1864. Around 1895 no. 27 became Oclee & Son, watchmakers, and no. 25 became J. Sainsbury, provision merchant, in 1909.

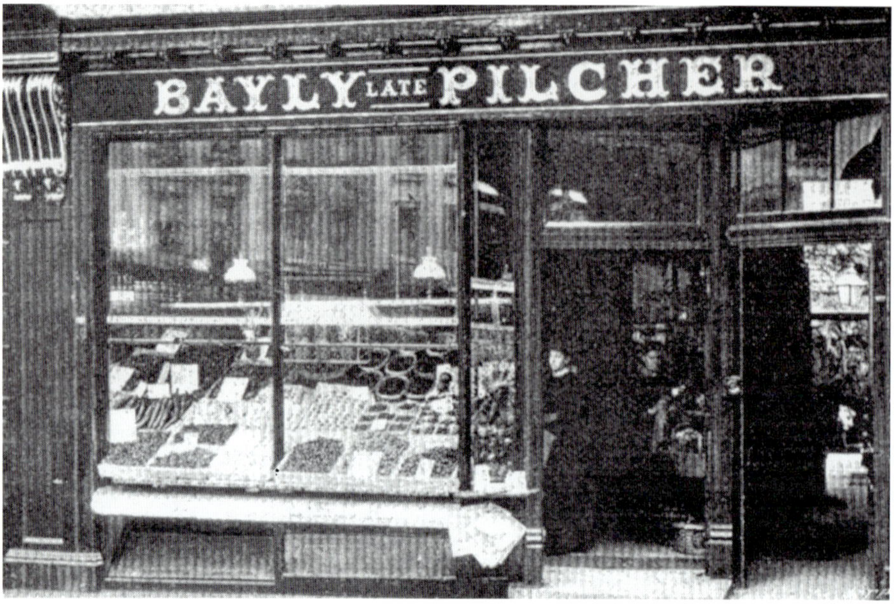

Messrs Bayly, greengrocers, British and foreign fruiterers, 7 Sandgate Road. The business was founded by Mr W.G. Pilcher and was taken over by the Bayly brothers in 1892, who traded there until 1909.

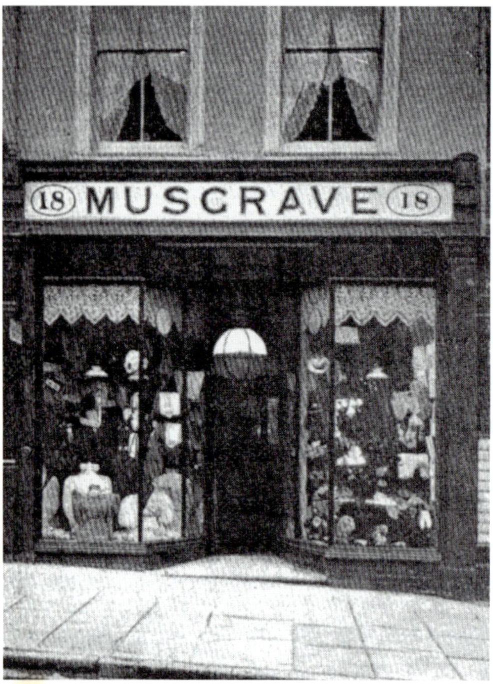

Mr Joseph John Musgrave established his draper, milliner and mantle makers business at 60 High Street. He moved to 18 Sandgate Road some time between 1874 and 1878 where the business remained until 1963.

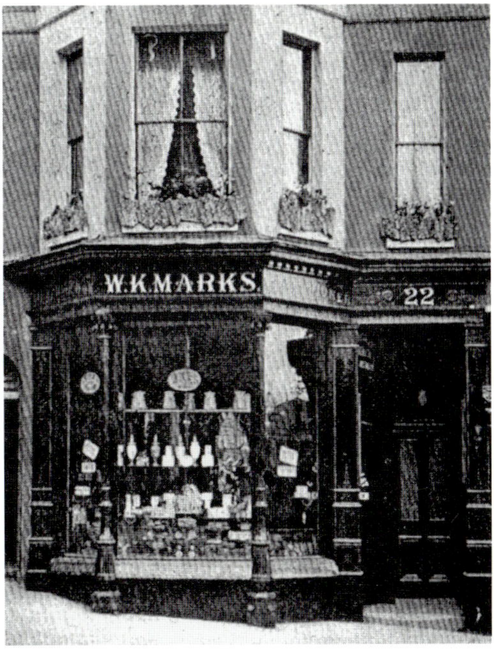

Mr William Marks, fancy bread and biscuit maker. The business was established at 43 High Street in around 1840. He moved to 22 Sandgate Road between 1878 and 1882 and remained there until 1934, when the business was taken over by Mr John Strickland.

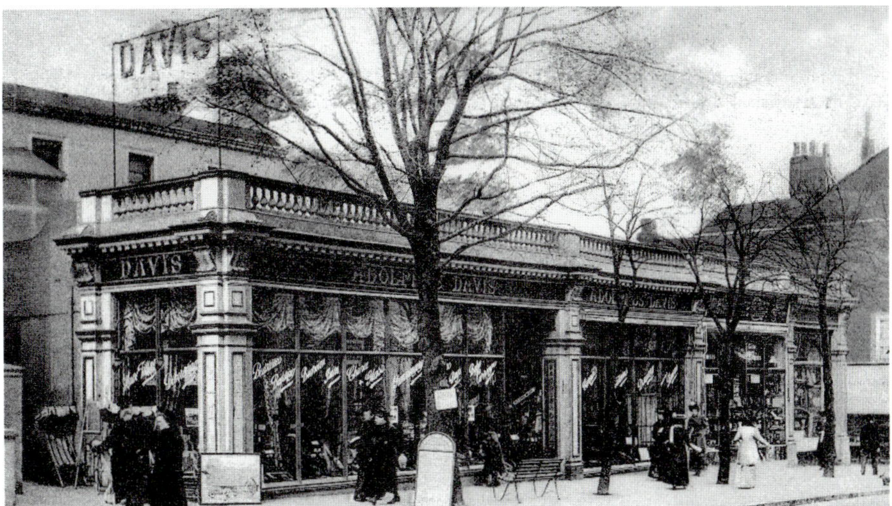

Mr Adolphus Davis, complete house furnisher and draper, Alexandra House, Sandgate Road. Mr Davis established his business in the High Street in 1870. He later took additional premises in George Lane. Shortly afterwards he took a long lease on the private house and grounds of the late Lewis Solomon Esq. at the corner of Sandgate Road and Alexandra Gardens. Mr Davis built this shop in the gardens fronting Sandgate Road. It opened on 19 February 1881 and he traded there until 1908. It is interesting to note that the trees in front of the shop were in Mr Solomon's garden.

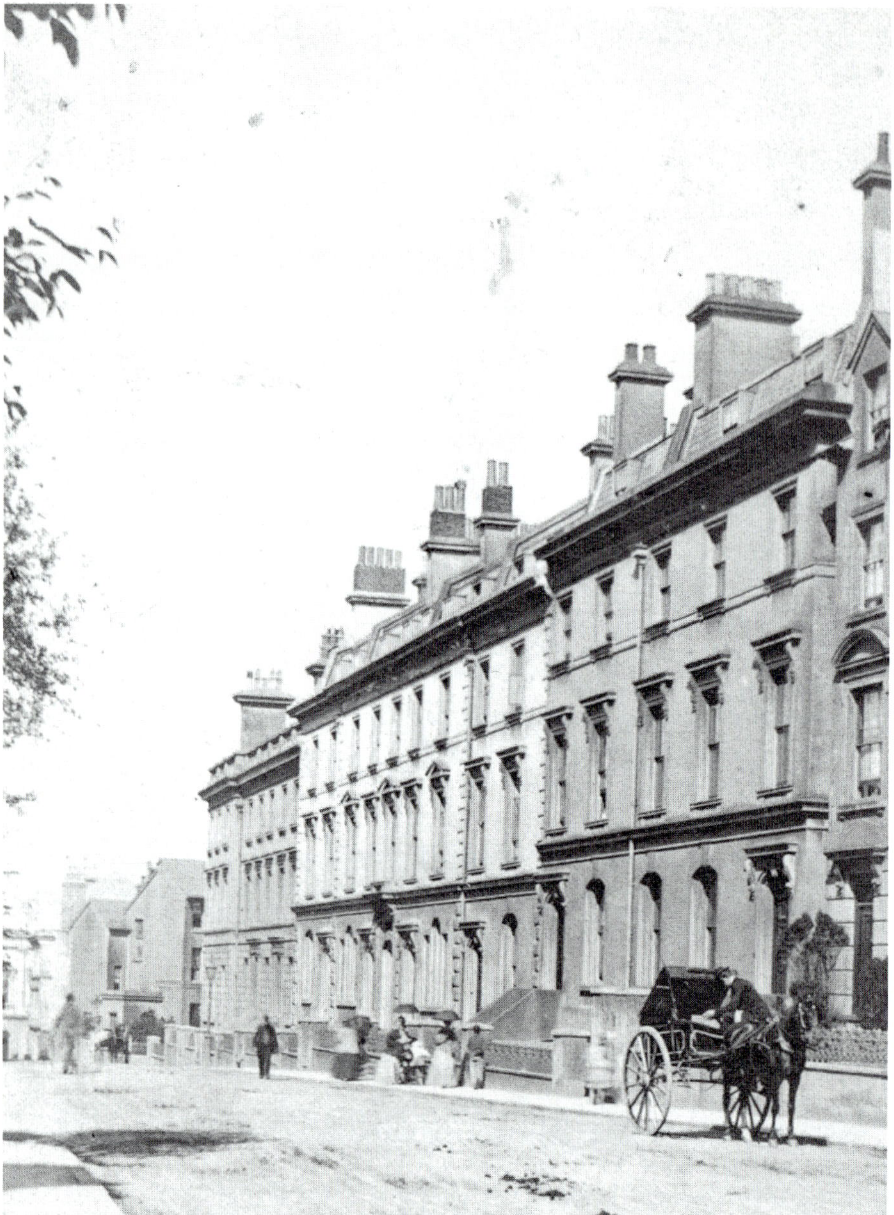

Sandgate Road looking down from Bouverie Place, *c.* 1870. Note that all the large Victorian buildings are private dwellings with walled gardens. The building at the extreme far end of the terrace is now Lloyds Bank and is the only one of these buildings still standing: the rest have all been demolished. Next to Lloyds Bank is West Cliff Gardens, on the other corner of which now stands Midland Bank. Here the site is occupied by houses.

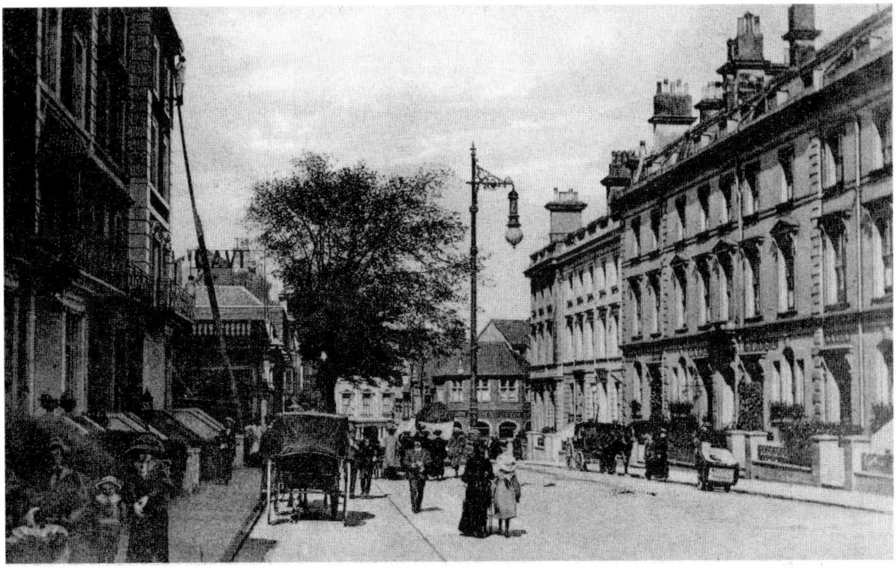

Sandgate Road looking down from Bouverie Place, *c.* 1906. On the left side are boarding houses followed by Mr Adolphus Davis, house furnishers. On the right side in the foreground is Bates's private hotel followed by a boarding house, dental surgeon, Lloyds Bank, West Cliff Gardens and Midland Bank.

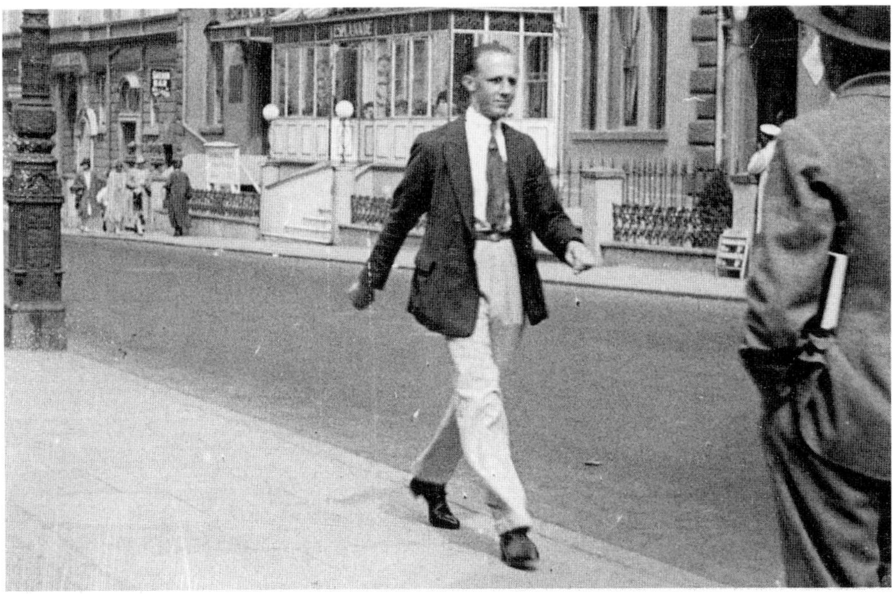

The briskly walking gentleman is Mr Eric Hadaway, 11 July 1929. Behind Mr Hadaway is the Esplanade Hotel, formerly Bates's. The Esplanade was sold for development and was demolished in 1972. The site is now occupied by four shops: Saxone, Dixons, Dewhurst and the NatWest Bank.

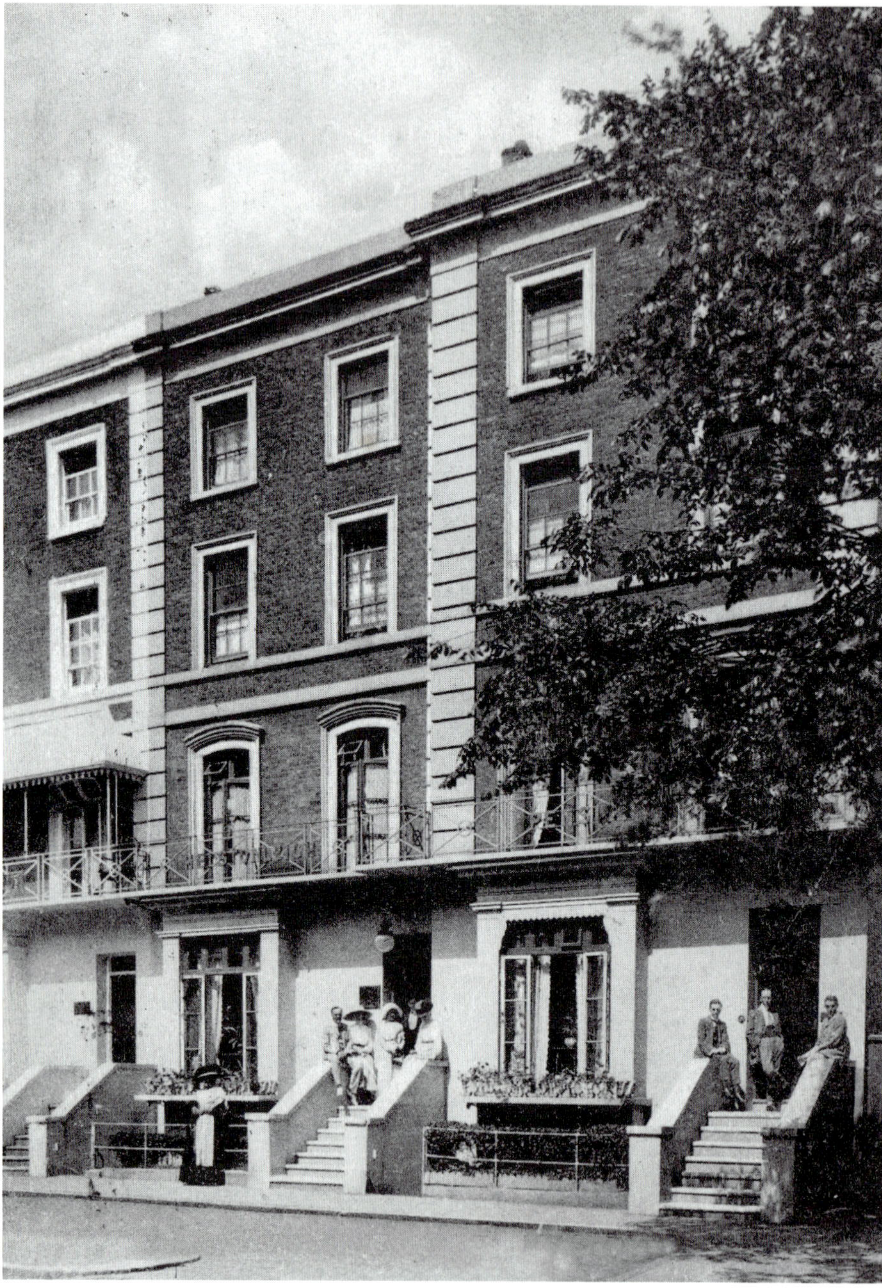

Boarding houses in Sandgate Road. They were demolished around 1922 to make way for Bobby's department store. During the First World War Messrs Bobby & Co. generously placed at the disposal of the Belgians a terrace of seven houses which included these two.

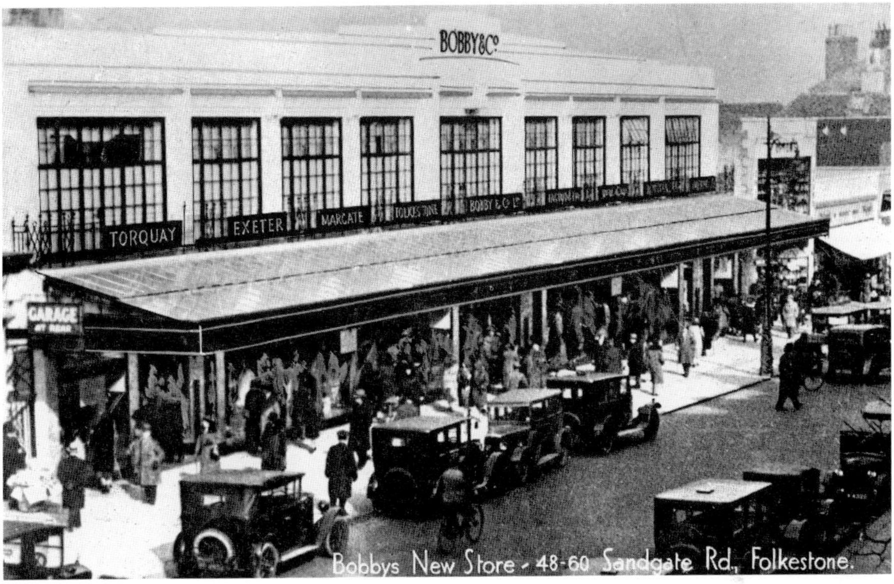

Bobby & Co., department store, Sandgate Road. In 1931 the store moved from Rendezvous Street to these purpose-built premises. In 1972 the business was taken over by Debenhams.

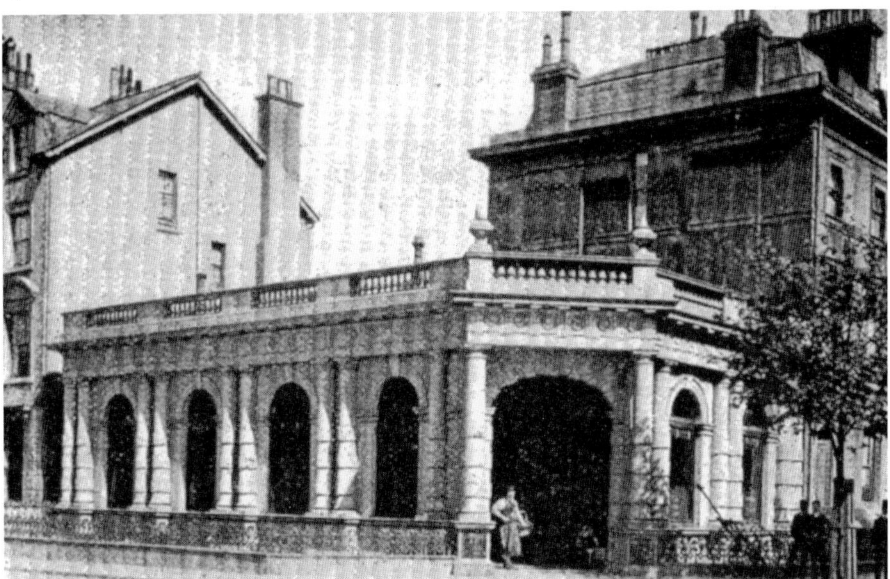

Messrs Underwood, Penfold & Co., wine and brandy importers, 53–5 Sandgate Road. The business moved to these premises sometime between 1866 and 1870, previously being in Tontine Street. The premises were taken over by Barclays Bank in 1930, when upper floors were added.

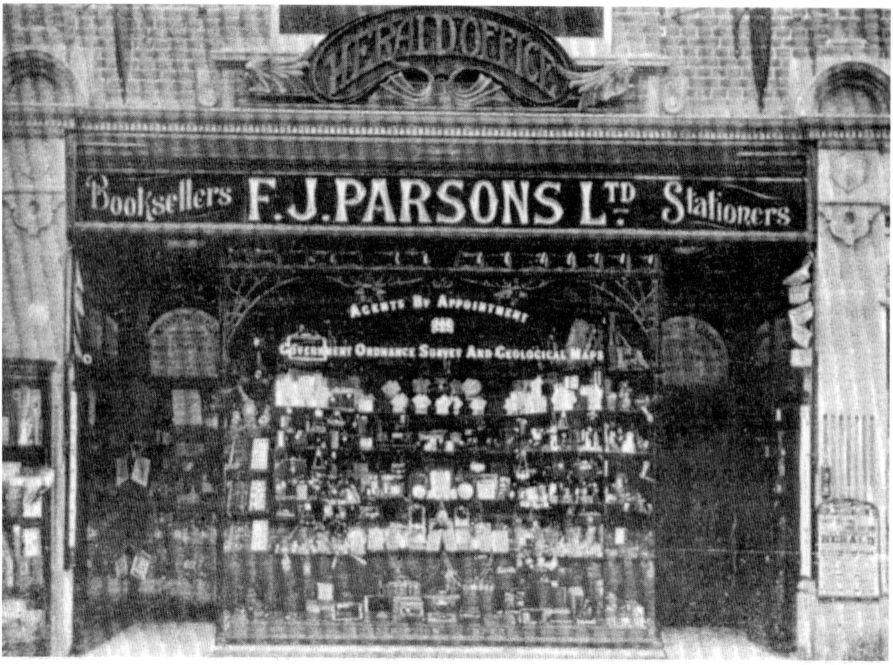

Mr F.J. Parsons, 66 Sandgate Road, booksellers and publishers of the *Folkestone Herald*, *c.* 1900. Mr Parsons was at these premises from 1896. In 1909 Sandgate Road was renumbered and Parsons became no. 86. The shop was taken over by W.H. Smith & Son in 1924 and is now Seeboard.

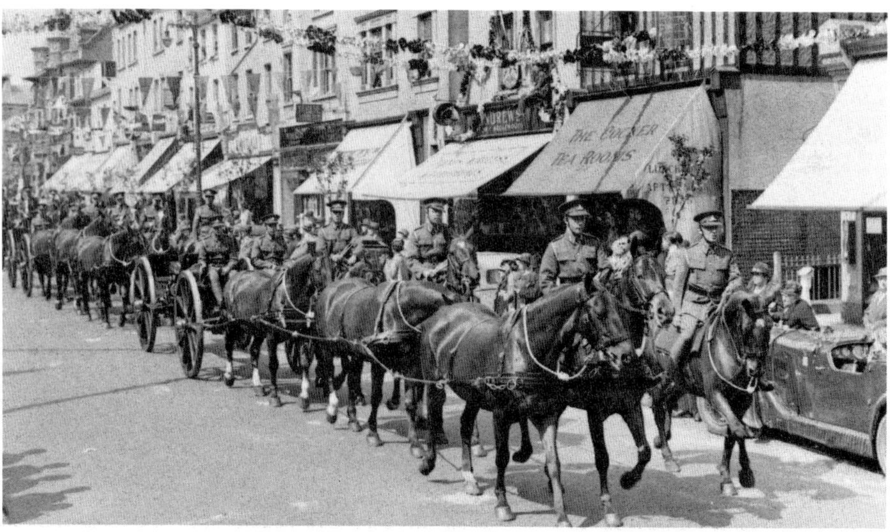

The royal artillery in Sandgate Road, 6 May 1935. They were present to celebrate the Silver Jubilee of King George V. The shops in the right foreground are the Cocker Tea Rooms and Andrews radio shop, both demolished in April 1975.

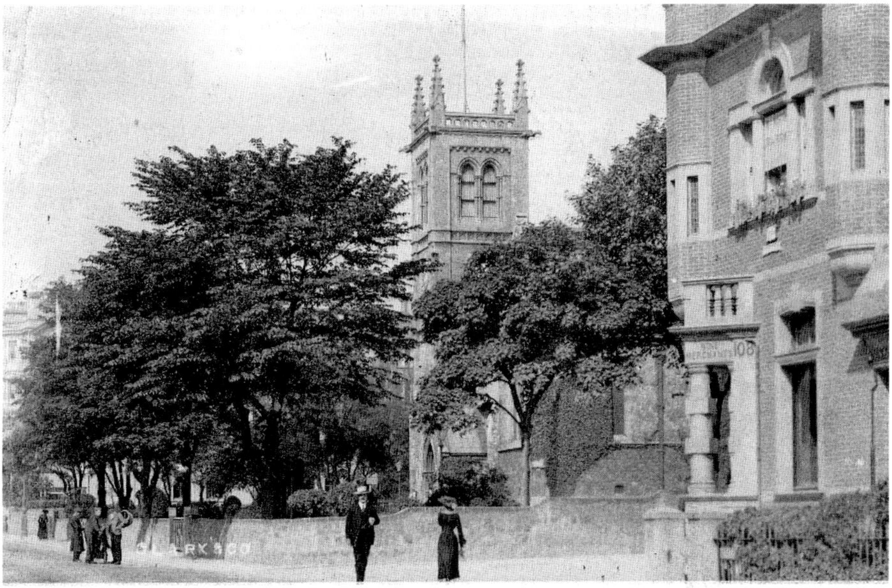

An unusual view of Sandgate Road, *c.* 1910. In the right foreground, on the corner of Manor Road, is Messrs J.H. and J. Brooke, wine merchants. On the other side of Manor Road is Christ Church. Brooke's opened this branch in 1903 and continued trading there until around 1968.

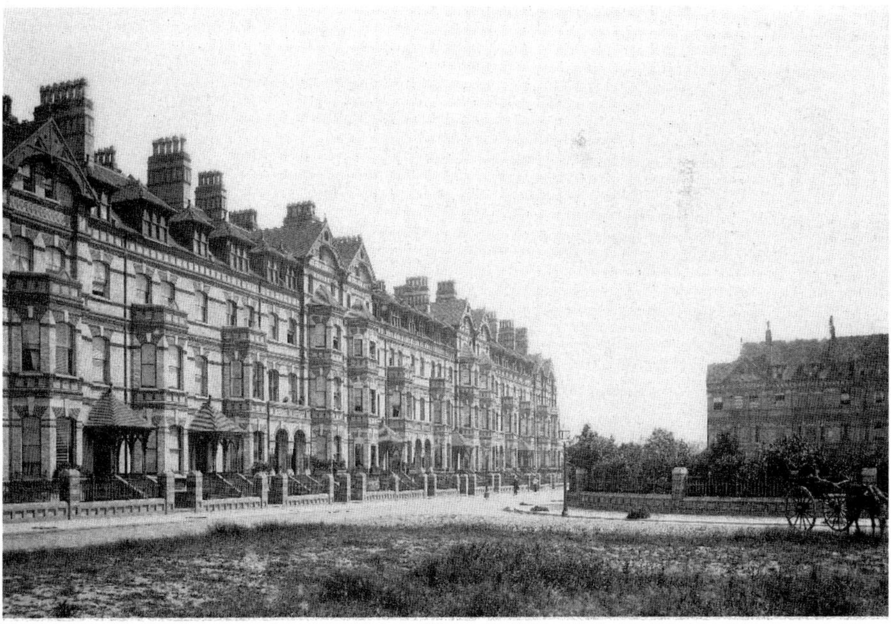

A rare view of Westbourne Gardens looking east. The photograph was taken before the west side was built, hence the grass in the foreground.

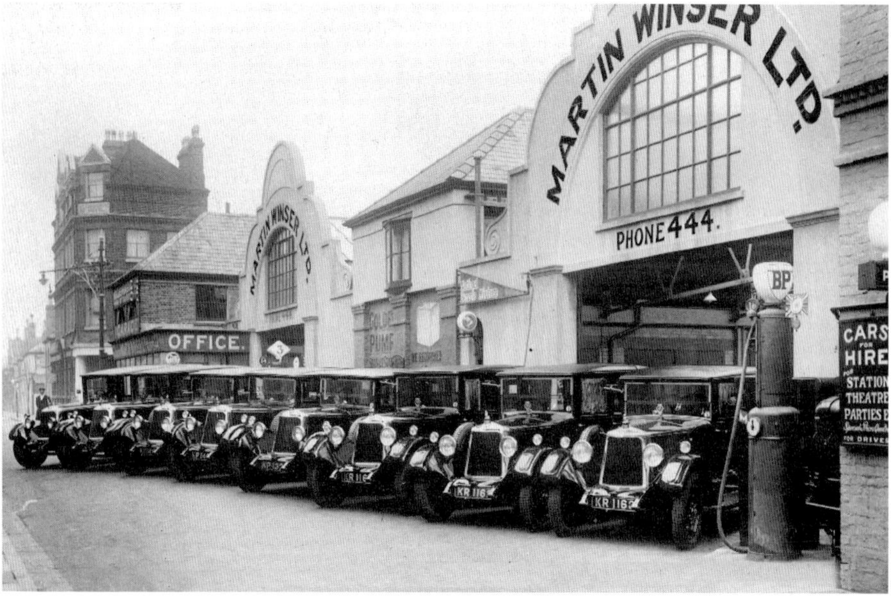

Martin Winser Ltd, 8–10 Bouverie Road West. A fleet of Armstrong-Siddeley landaulettes was for hire. The rates were: minimum fare (2 miles) 1*s* 6*d*, thereafter 9*d* per mile; shopping (limit 5 miles) 5*s* per hour.

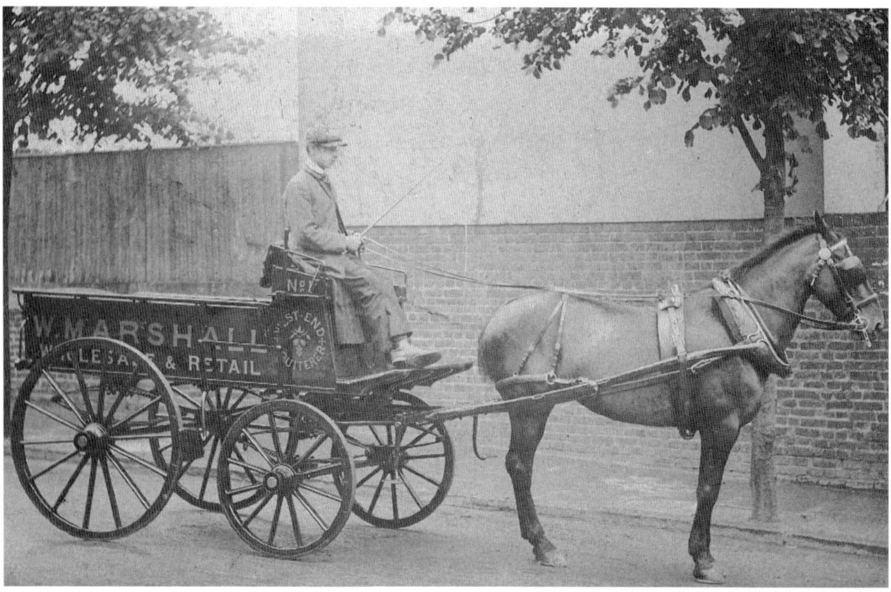

Mr W. Marshall's delivery vehicle. Mr Marshall was a greengrocer, fruiterer and florist and started his business at 18 Bouverie Road West in 1898.

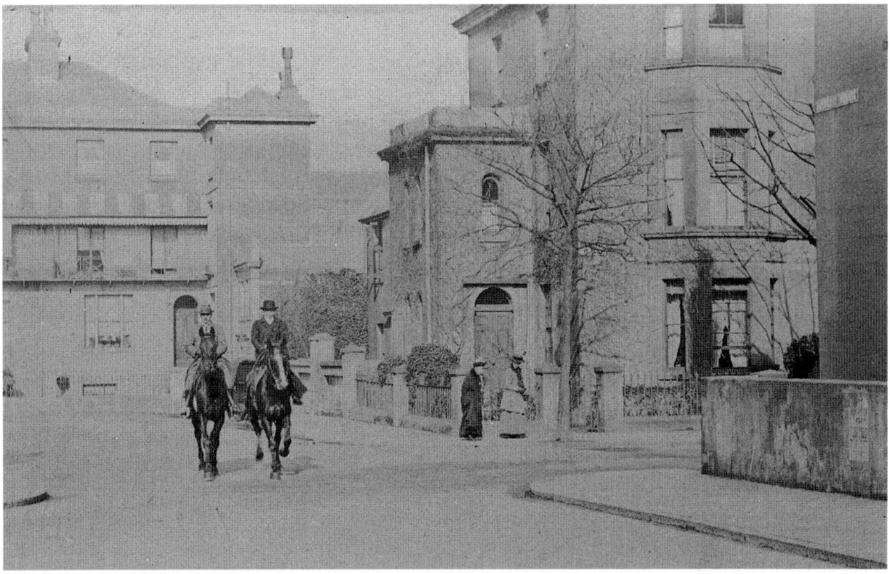

Bouverie Square at the junction of Bouverie Place, *c.* 1906. All the buildings in this photograph have now been demolished.

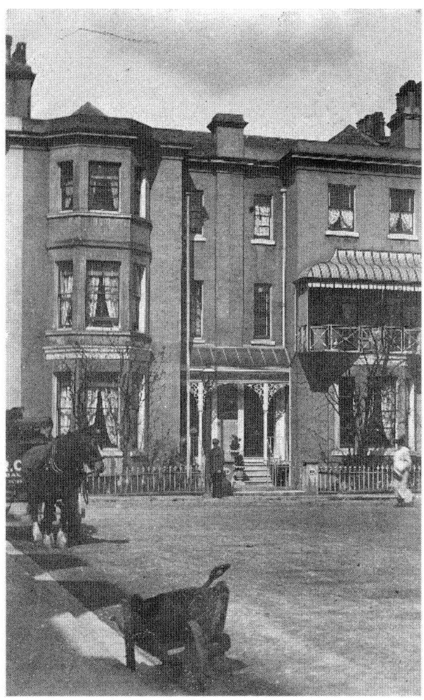

Bouverie Square (now Middleburg Square) looking towards the north side. These buildings are nos 25 and 26 and were demolished in 1972 for road widening. Part of the site is now occupied by Saga offices. The horse-drawn vehicle belongs to Mr R. Court, coal merchant, of 78 Tontine Street.

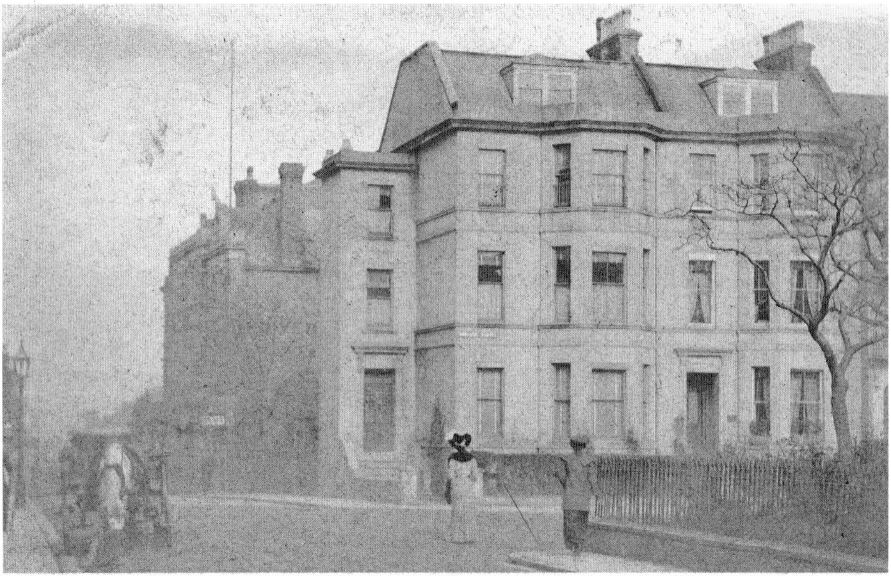

Bouverie Square looking down Bouverie Road East, *c.* 1907. In the right foreground are the railings round the gardens. The latter were done away with to build the bus station which opened in 1955.

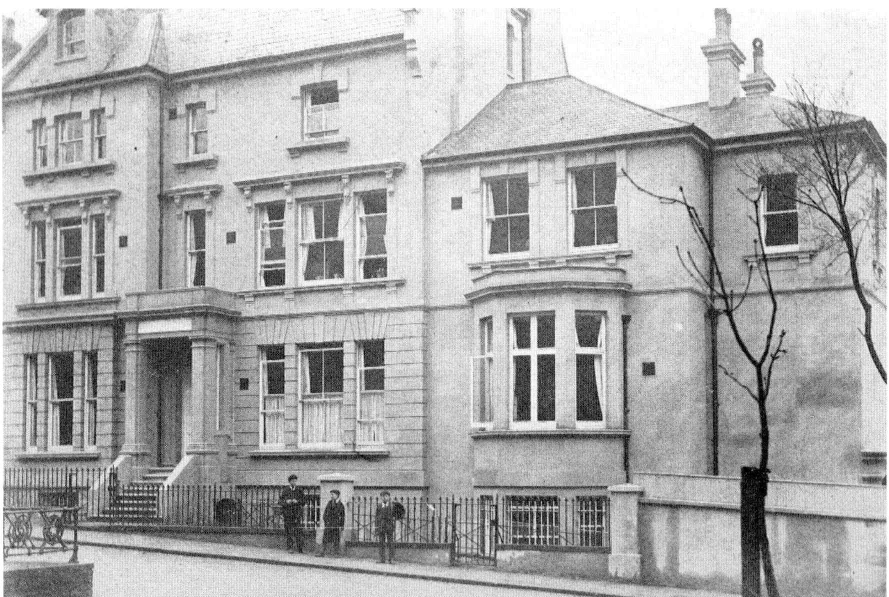

Bouverie Road East. The County School for Girls started in three rooms at the Masonic Hall, Grace Hill, in 1905. It moved to this building in Bouverie Road East in 1906. The school remained here until 1922 when it moved to Penfold House, Cooling Lane.

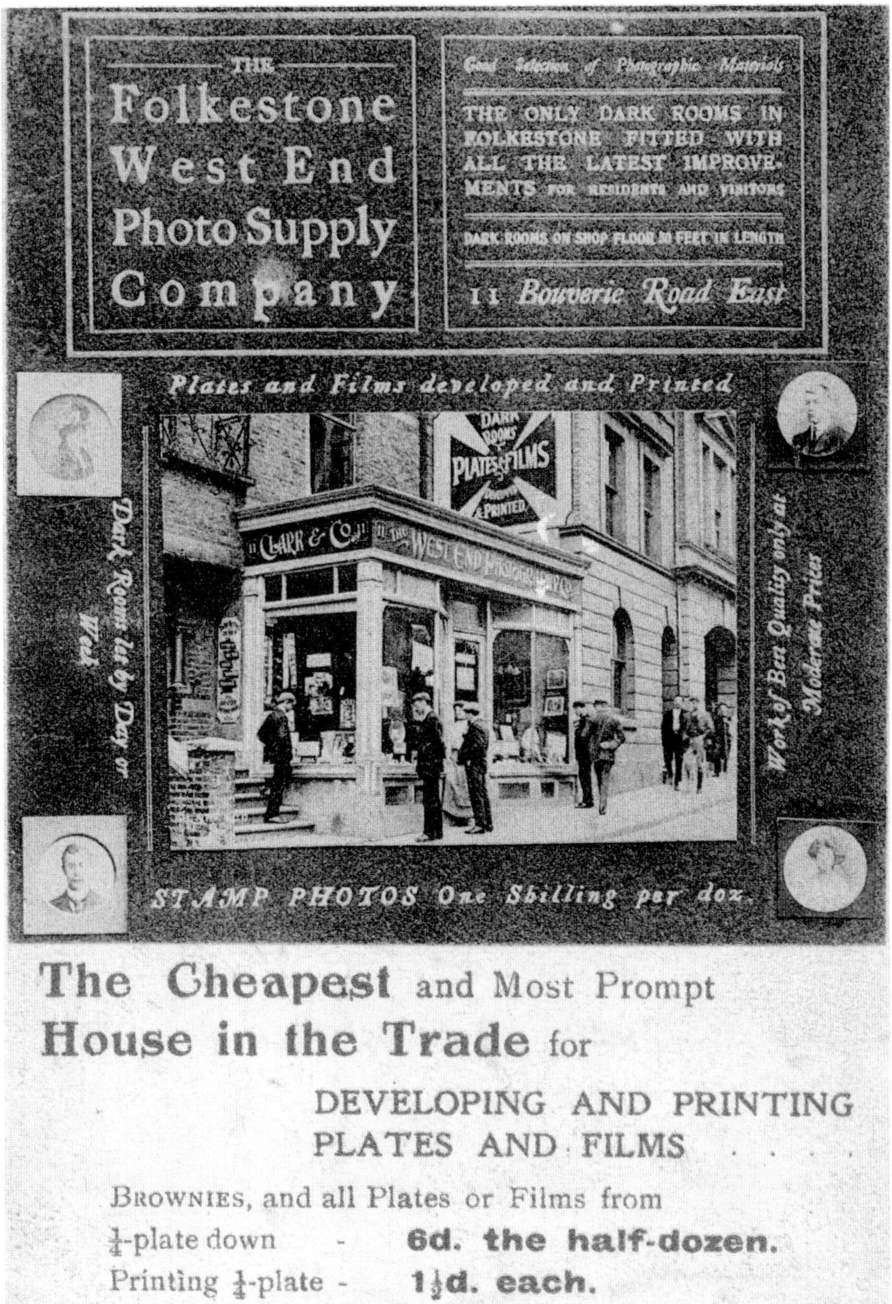

Advertising card for The West End Photo Supply Company, 11 Bouverie Road East. Mr Clark started his photographic business at 9 Church Street before moving to these premises. Until recently the shop was Gale's café.

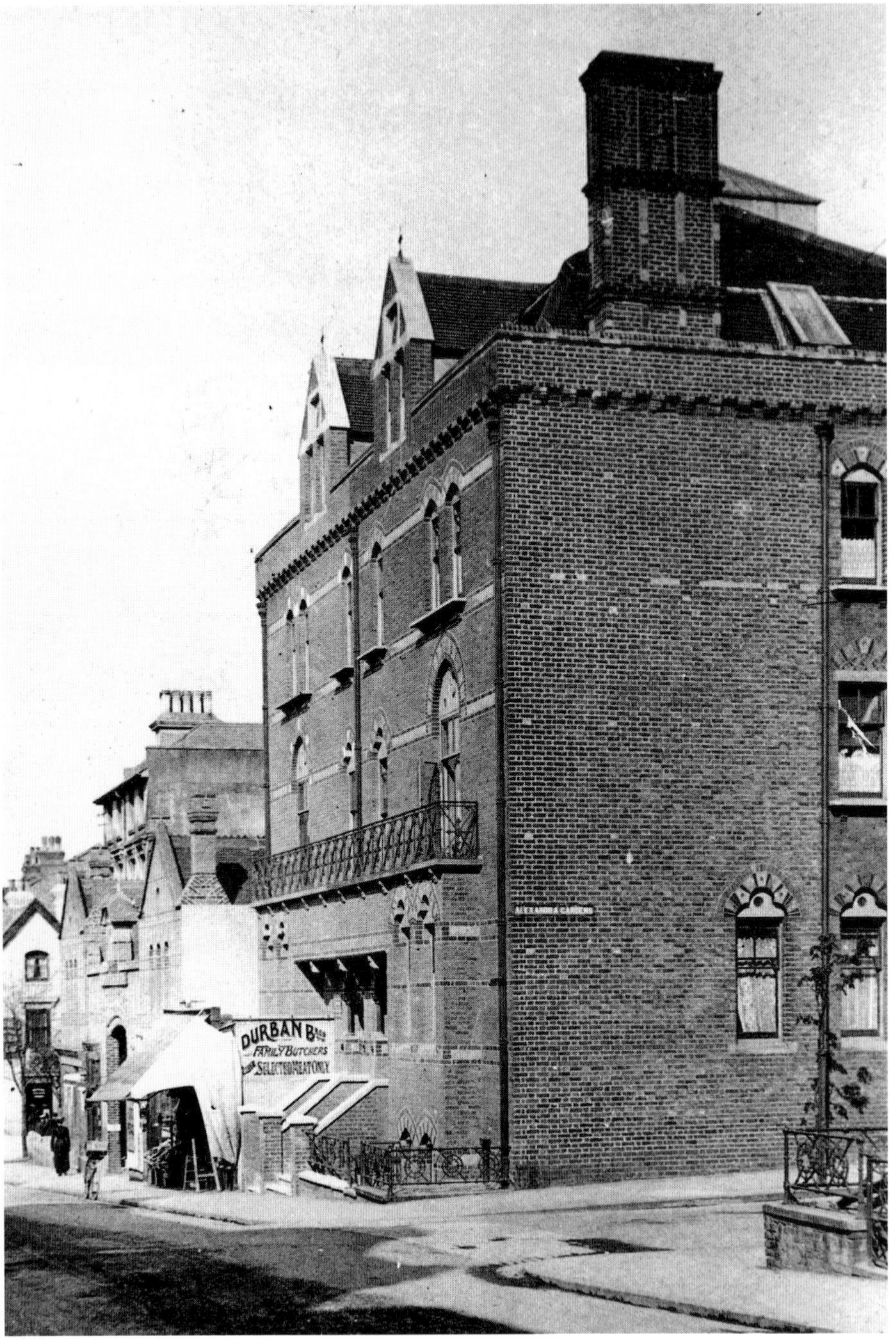

Looking down Bouverie Road East from Alexandra Gardens to Gloucester Place, *c.* 1908. All these buildings were demolished in 1973 for road widening.

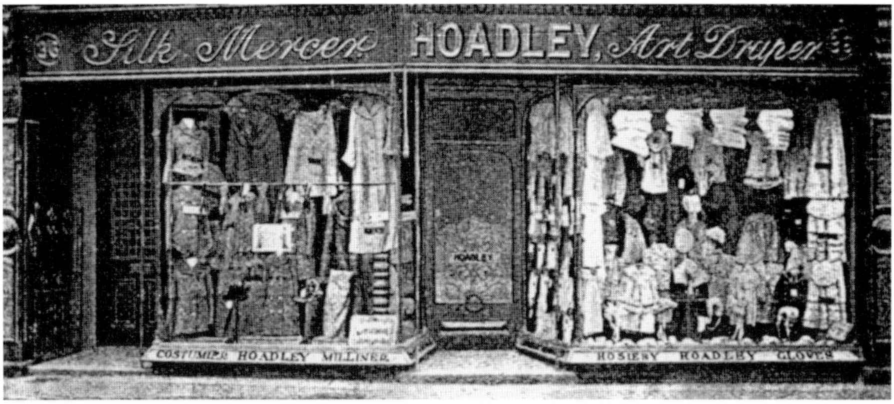

Mr William Hoadley, silk mercer and art draper, 36 Guildhall Street. Mr Hoadley traded at these premises from 1899 until 1906 when the business was taken over by Mr James Gray.

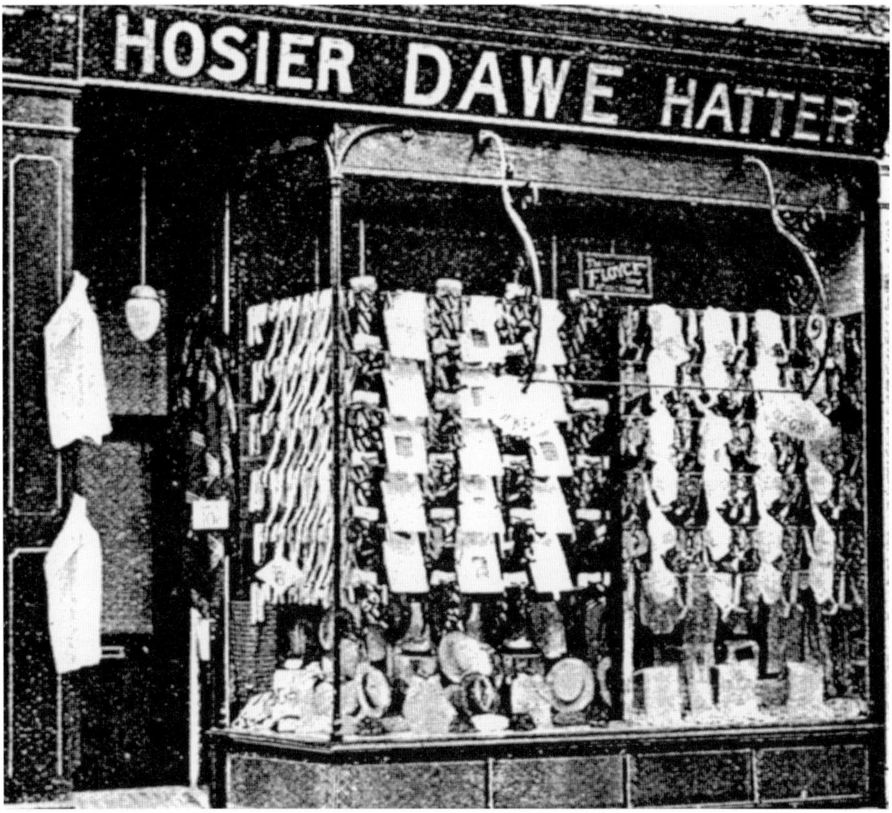

Mr Frederick George Dawe, hosier, hatter and glover, 7 Guildhall Street. Mr Dawe established his business at these premises in 1900, and continued trading here until around 1952.

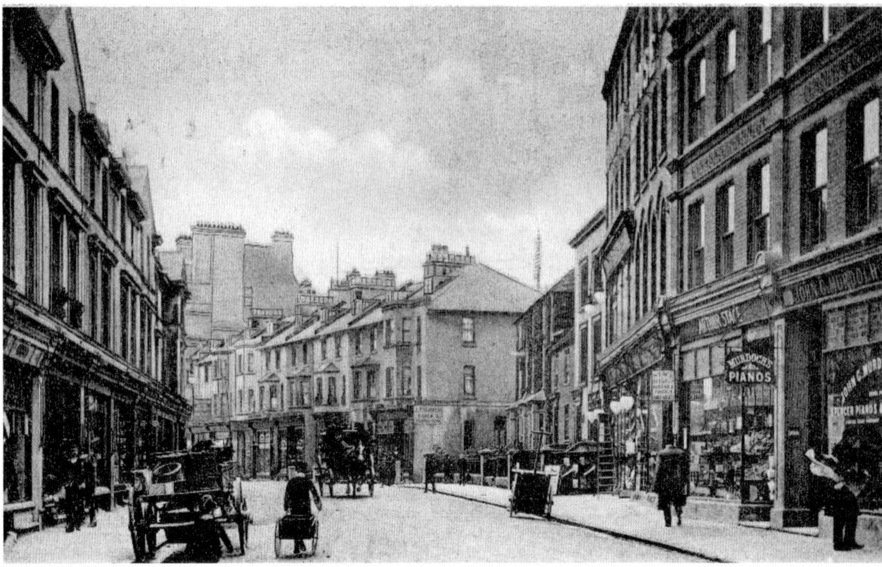

Guildhall Street looking towards the Town Hall, 1905.

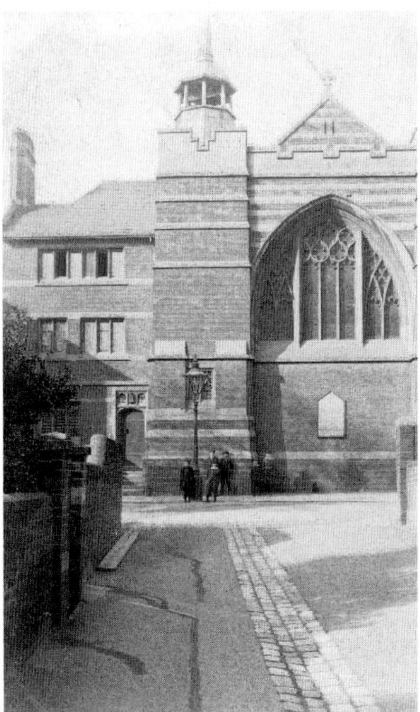

The Catholic church, Guildhall Street, between 1905 and 1911. The photograph has been taken from the alley-way which ran between the backs of the houses in Shellons Street and Copthall Gardens.

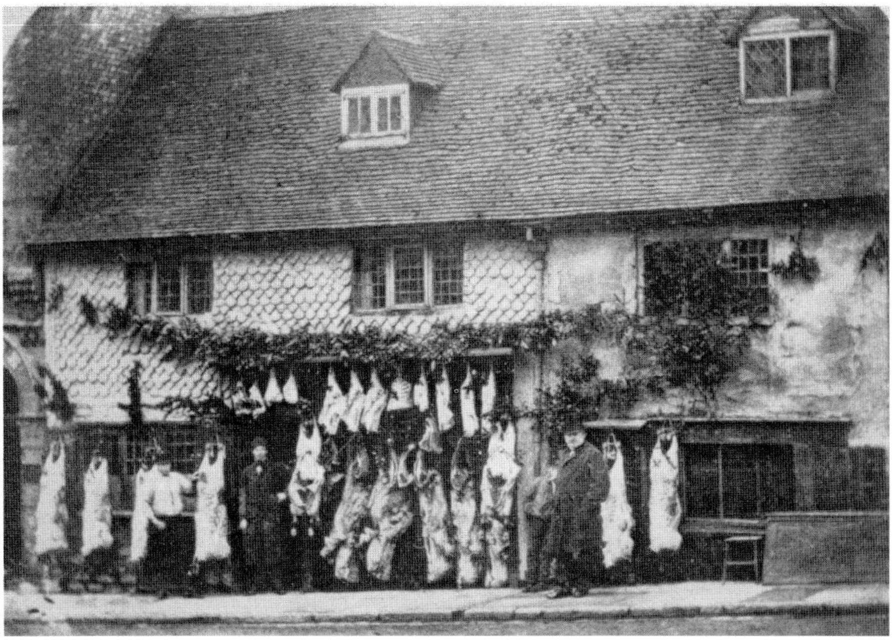

Mr John Castle, butcher, 4 and 6 Rendezvous Street. Mr Castle established his business between 1855 and 1858. The photograph was taken between October 1866 and February 1867. The site is now occupied by Impacts clothing store.

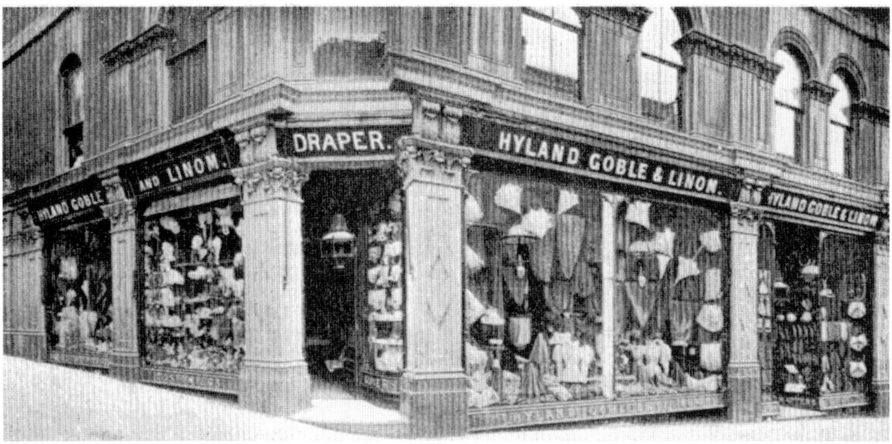

Messrs Lewis, Hyland, Goble & Linom, general drapers and silk mercers, milliners, costume and mantle makers, and carpet salesmen, 19 and 21 Rendezvous Street and Market Place, 1898. The business was founded in 1834 by Mr George Alexander Lewis. Improvements to the building were made chiefly in 1867. Mr Lewis had many partners: by 1874 the business was known as Lewis & Stapley; 1882 Lewis & Goble; 1887 Lewis, Hyland & Goble; 1891 Lewis, Hyland & Linom; until, by 1918, the business had adopted its familiar name of Lewis & Hyland. They were taken over by Whites of Kent in 1972.

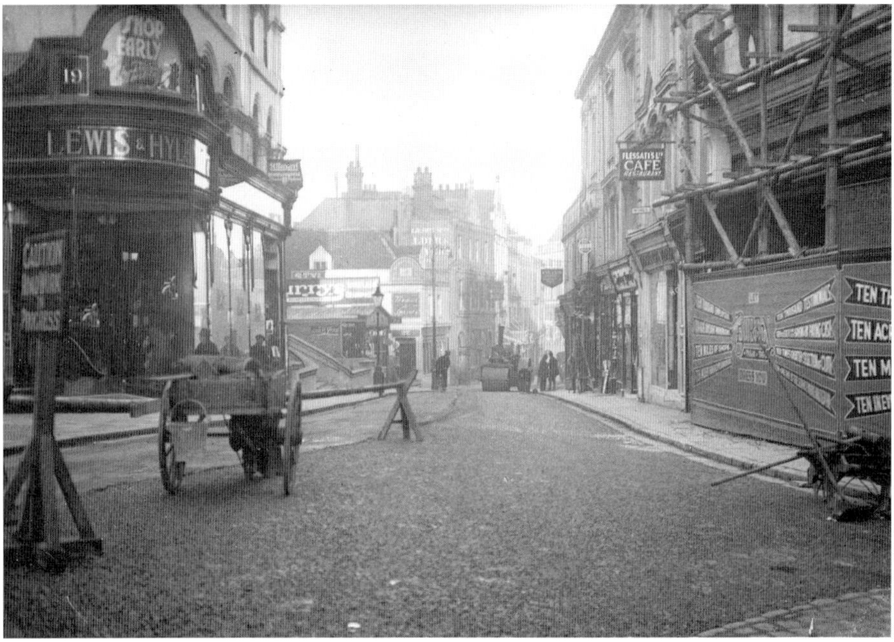

Looking down Rendezvous Street, 6 December 1928. The road is in the process of being resurfaced; in the distance can be seen the council's steamroller. In the right foreground Burton's men's outfitters shop is being built by the local builder, Mr Otto Marx.

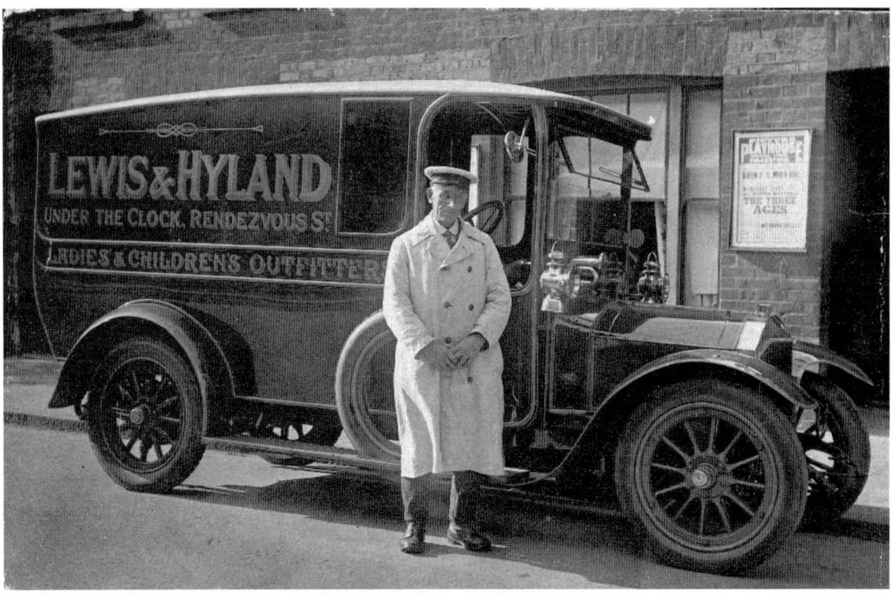

The delivery vehicle of Lewis & Hyland, general drapers, *c.* 1920. The photograph was taken outside 28 Mead Road.

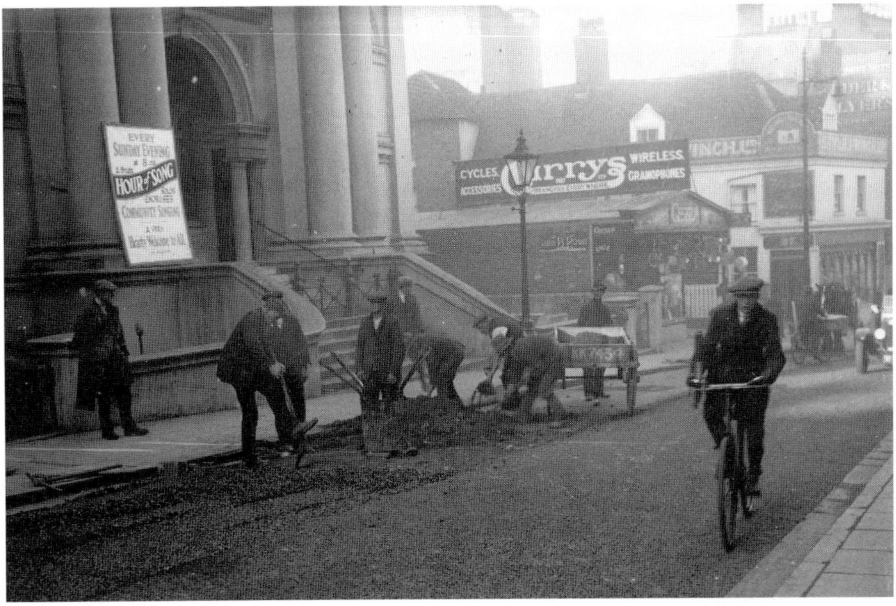

Roadworks outside the old Baptist church, Rendezvous Street, 6 December 1928. Curry's were at the premises next to the church from 1927 to 1936. Next to Curry's is Style & Winch Ltd, a brewery office, followed by the Prince Albert Hotel.

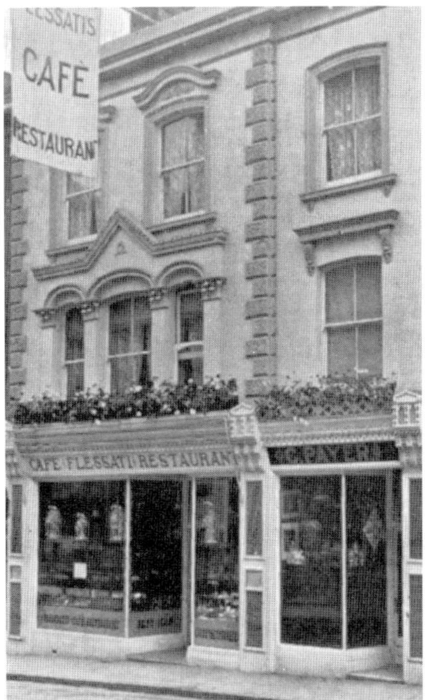

Flessati's café restaurant, 28 Rendezvous Street. Flessati's was a biscuit manufacturer, baker and confectioner which traded at these premises from 1905 to 1929 when the name changed to Savoy Café.

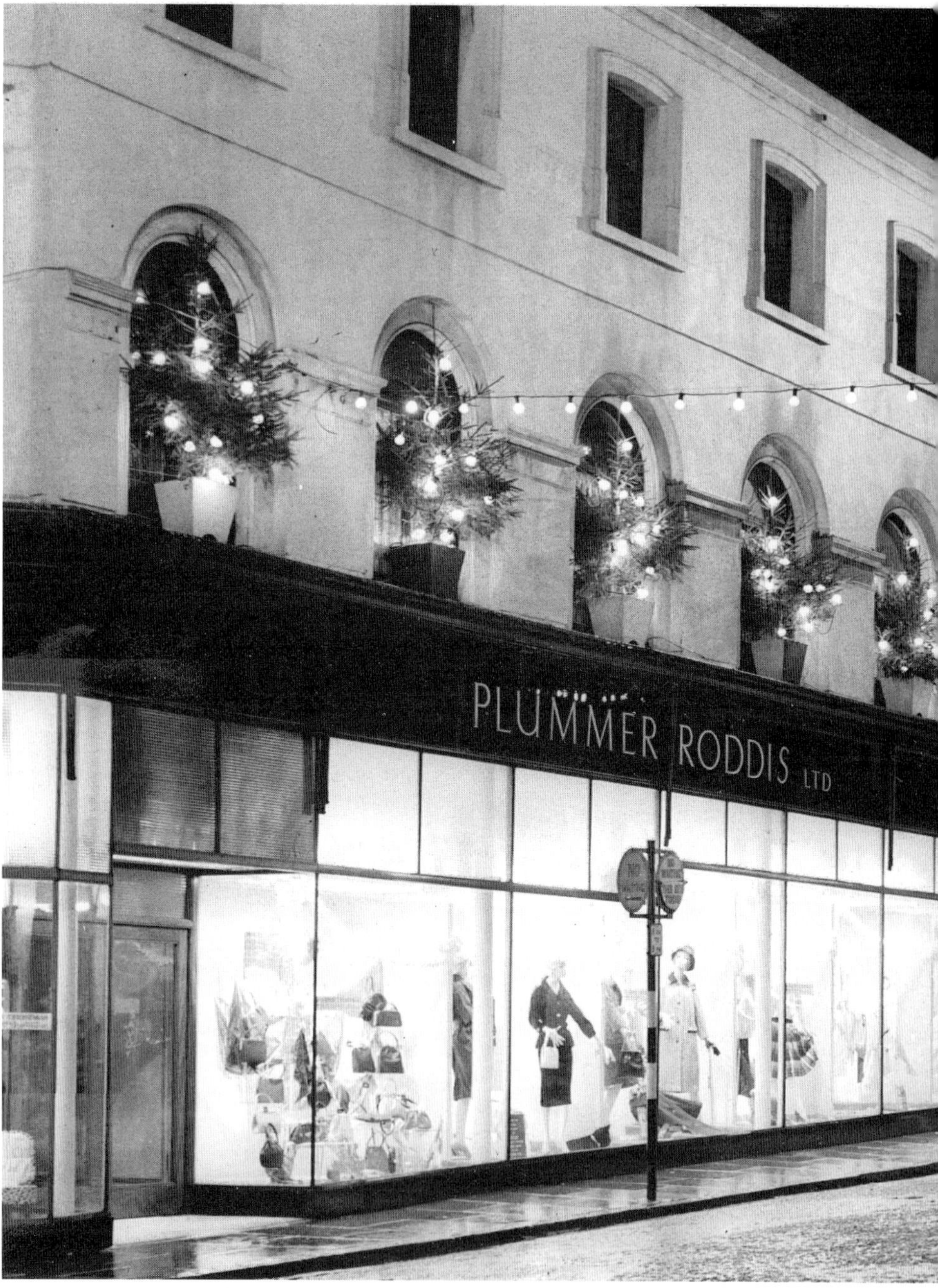

An evening scene at Christmas time in Rendezvous Street, 1960s. The popular shop of Plummer Roddis, drapers, milliners and costumiers, dominates the left-hand side of the photograph. The business was established in 1889 at 4 High Street. Over the years the

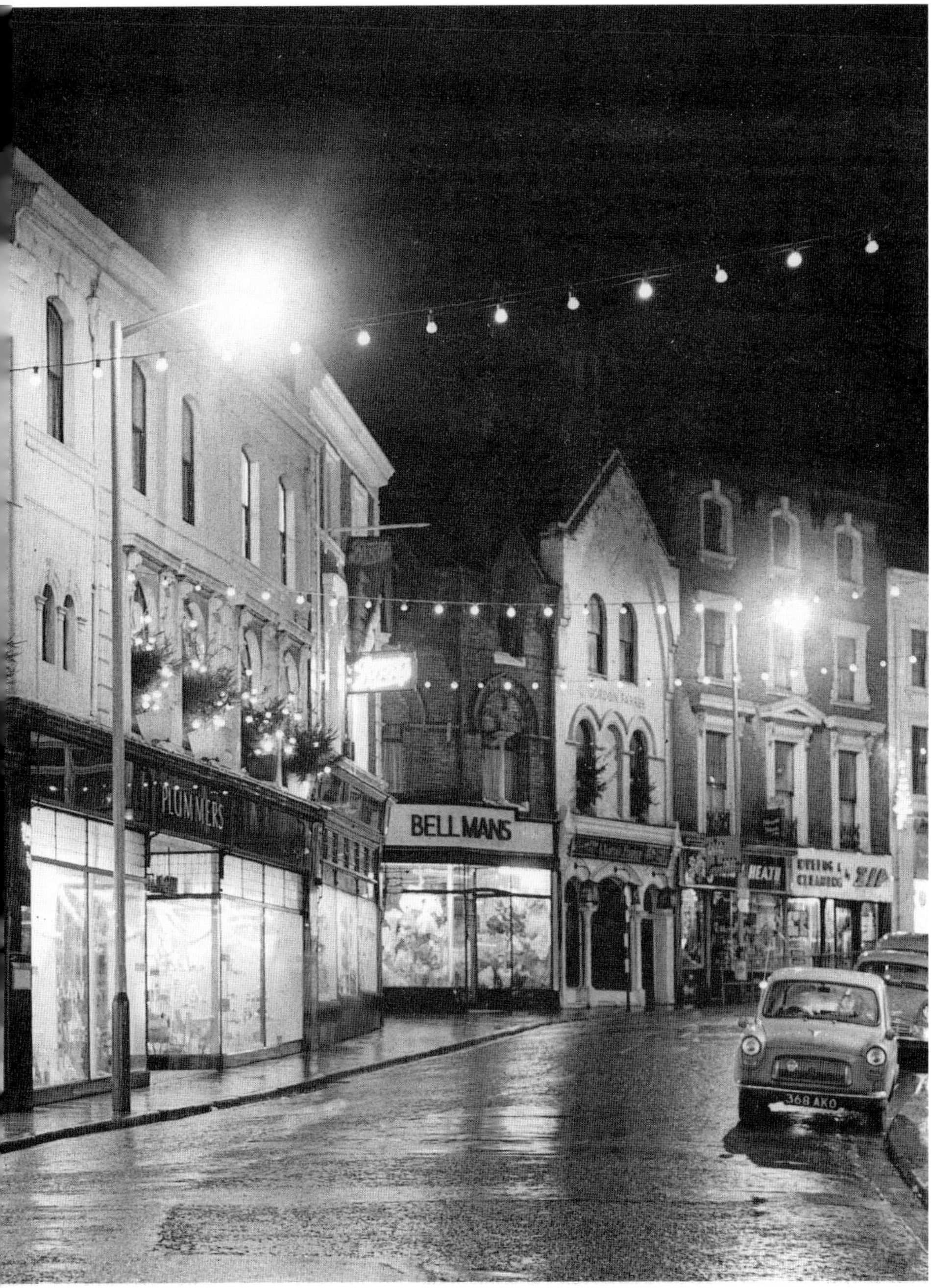

business expanded so that, by 1921, it occupied 2–4 High Street and 16–22 Rendezvous Street. Plummer Roddis closed in 1972 and the premises remained empty until they were demolished in 1984.

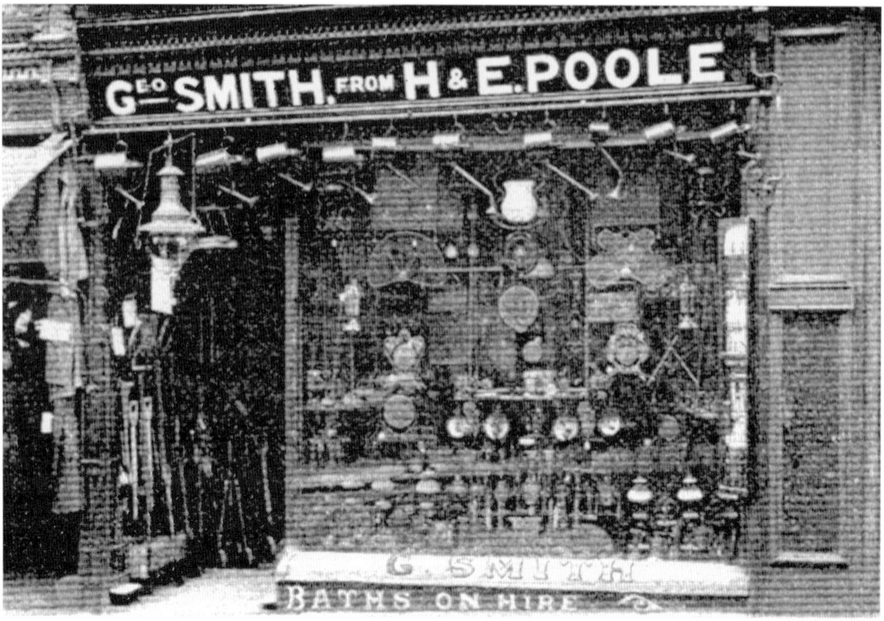

Messrs H. & E. Poole established their business in Folkestone about 1860. Mr George Smith worked for the Poole brothers for seventeen years. On their retirement in 1893 Mr Smith opened this ironmongery shop at 30 Rendezvous Street where he traded until 1897.

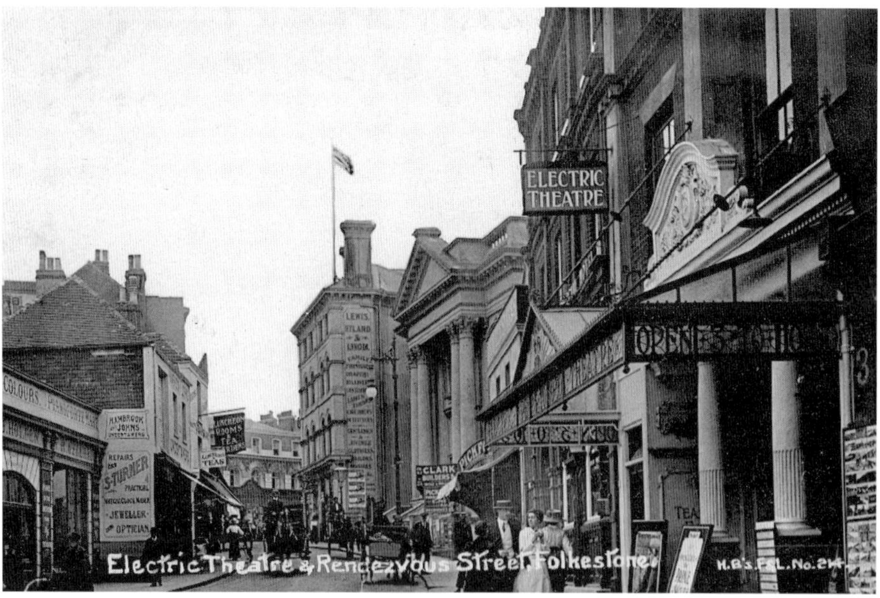

Rendezvous Street, 1912. In the right foreground is the Electric Theatre which opened on Tuesday 3 May 1910. It was renamed the Savoy in 1928 when equipment to show talking films was installed. The Savoy closed in 1963.

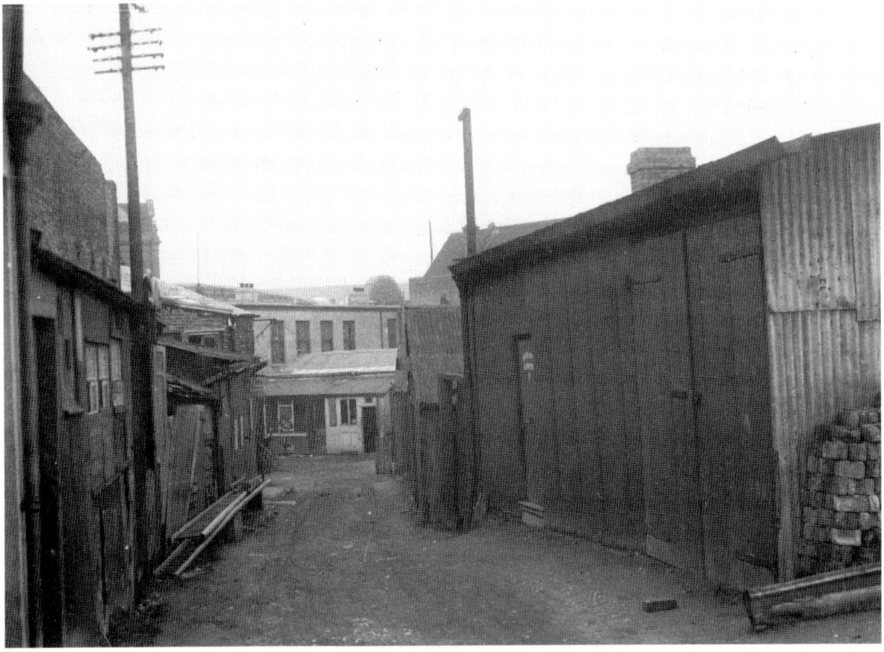

Park Lane, 1928. Park Lane ran from 12 Dover Road to 29 High Street (the gap by the Earl of Grey Inn). In 1928 there were fourteen businesses trading there. Park Lane was known as Payer's Park and this site is now Payer's Park car park.

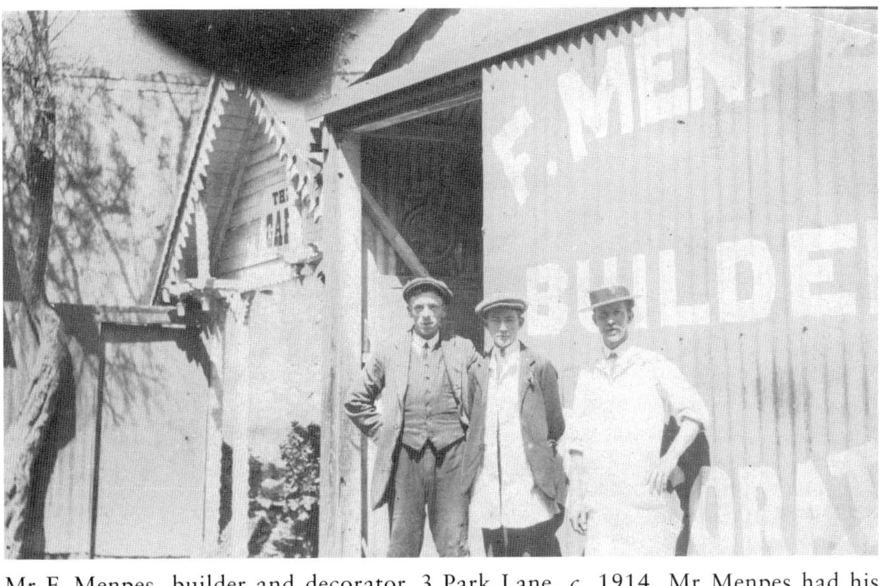

Mr F. Menpes, builder and decorator, 3 Park Lane, *c.* 1914. Mr Menpes had his workshop here in Park Lane and lived at 31 Queen Street.

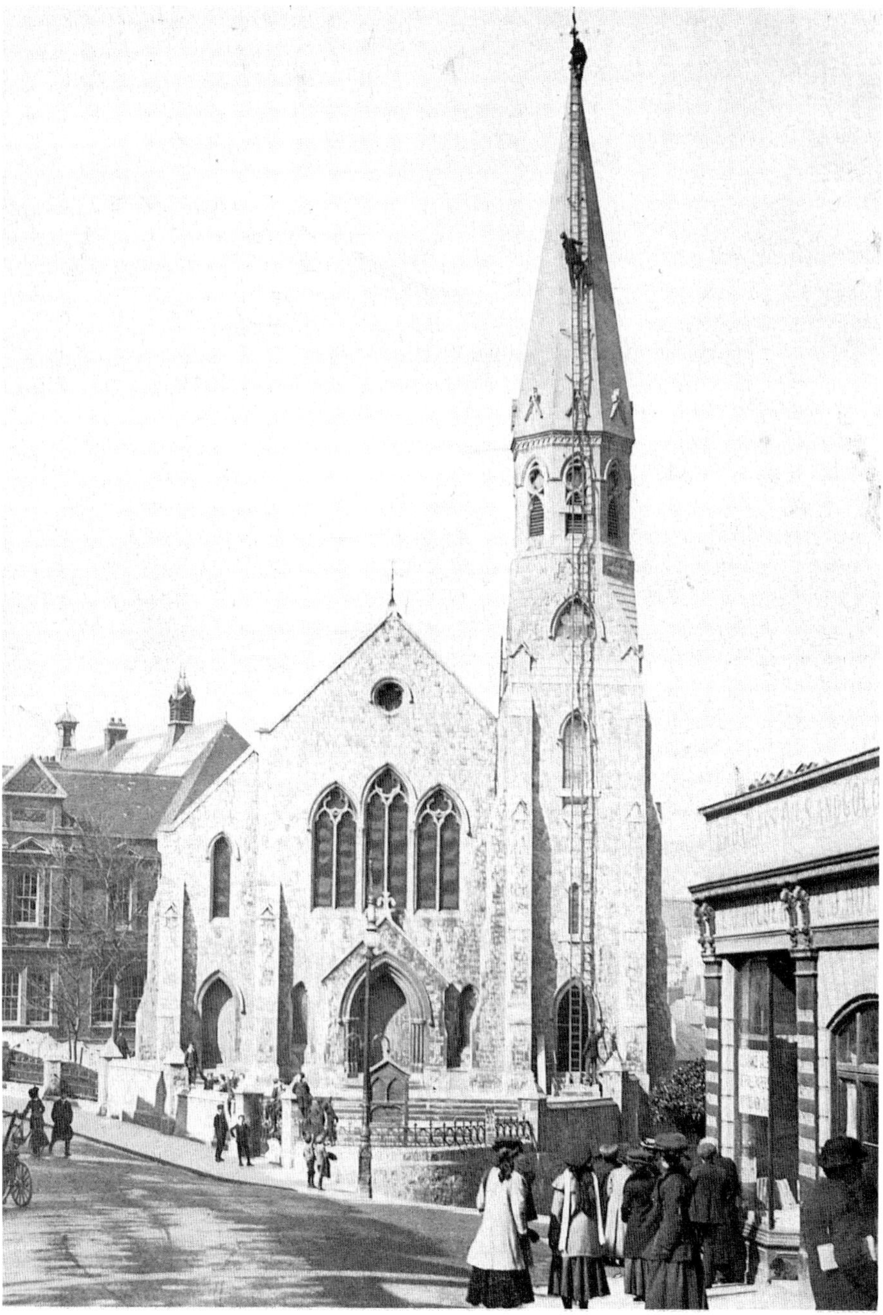

Wesleyan church, junction of Grace Hill and Dover Road, *c.* 1907. Note the people looking on as the steeplejacks climb the ladders to the top of the steeple. The church was demolished in 1976. The site is now occupied by Grace Court.

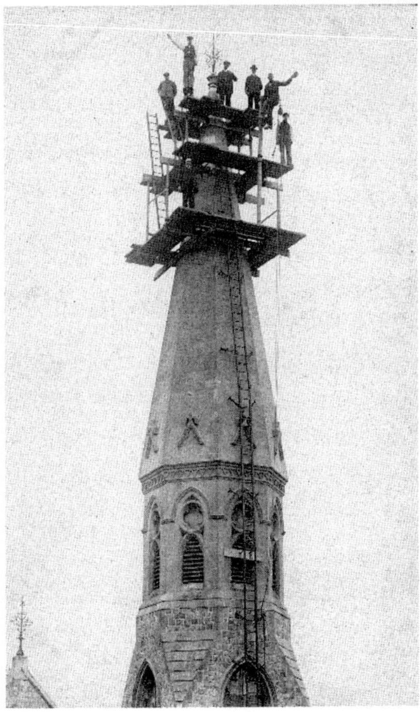

The Wesleyan church steeple, *c.* 1907. The steeplejacks have built a scaffold round the steeple and have taken time out to pose for the camera.

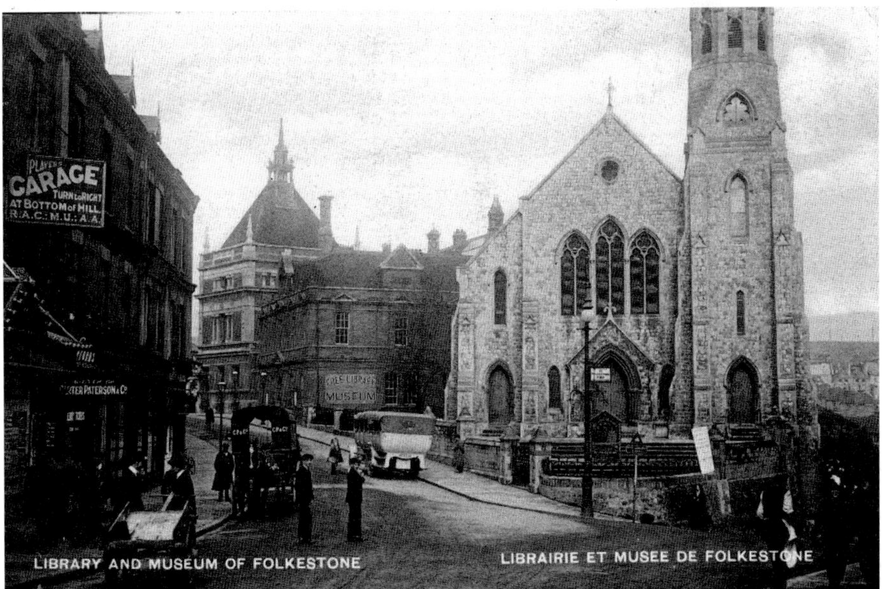

Grace Hill, 1916. On the right is the Wesleyan church followed by the library and museum. The church was built in 1865 and the library and museum were opened in 1888 by Sir Edward Watkin.

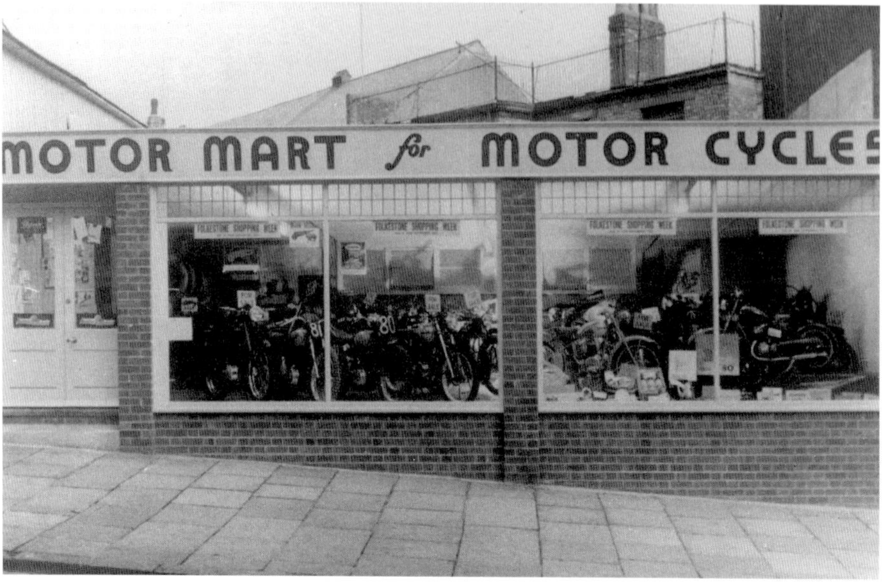

Motor Mart, 6–8 Foord Road, proprietor Mr Jack Canini. Mr Canini was in business at these premises from 1946 to 1957.

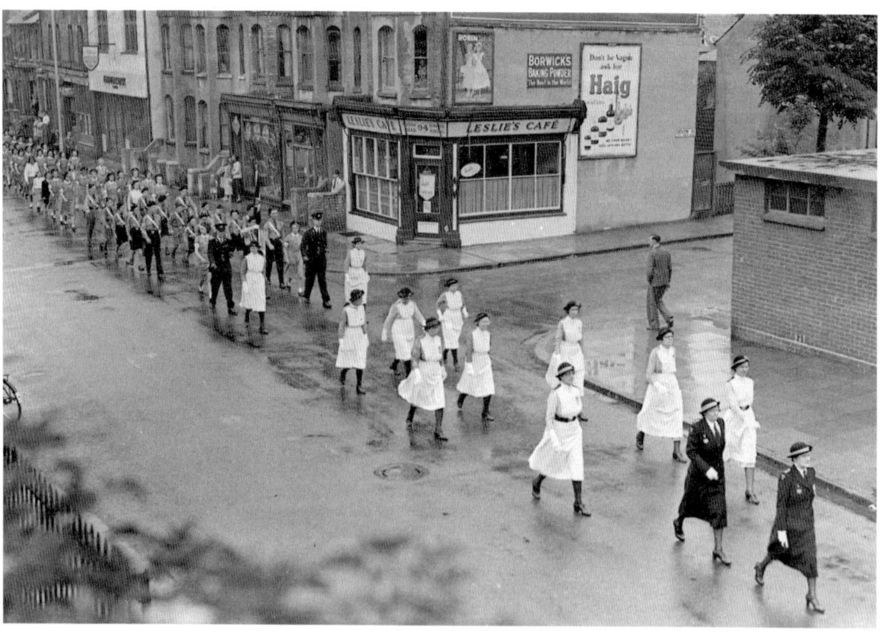

Foord Road at the junction with Devon Road. The occasion is the St John Ambulance church parade, either 1950 or 1951. Leslie's café and all the shops the eye can see are now part of Doves Group.

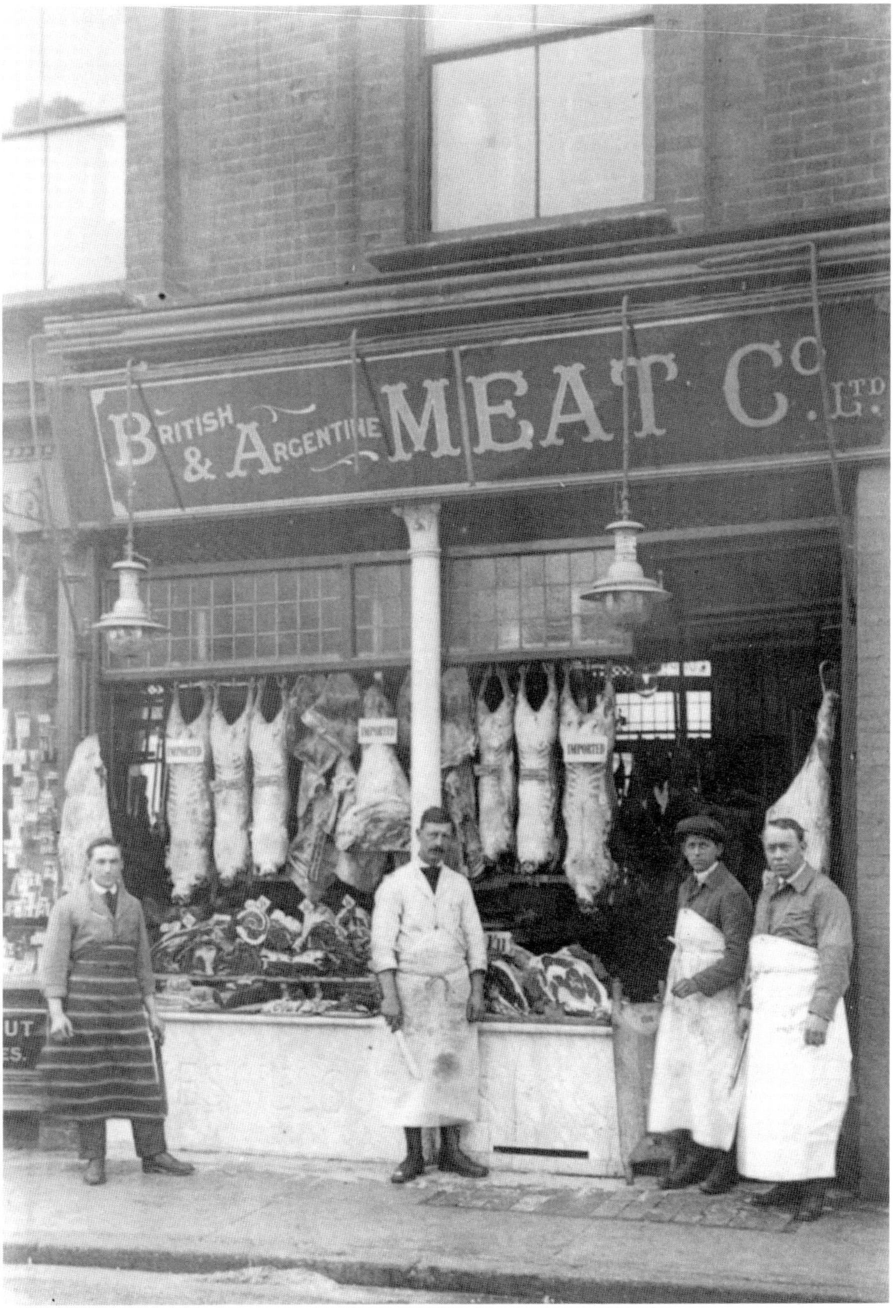

British & Argentine Meat Co., 20a Black Bull Road, corner of Bradstone Avenue, 1920. The British & Argentine Meat Co. was in business at these premises from 1914 to 1954. The gentleman with the striped apron is Mr Arthur Wells.

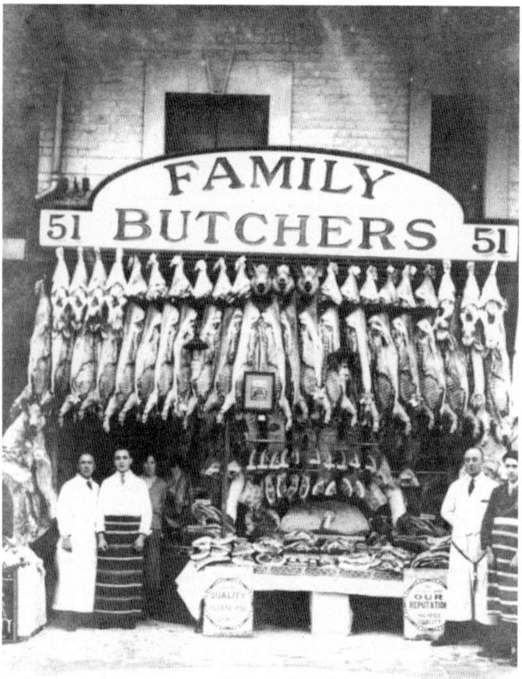

Coleman & Wells, family butchers, 51 Black Bull Road. Mr Coleman and Mr Wells opened this business in 1919. The photograph is of a Christmas display around 1925. Left to right are Mr Albert Victor Wells, Mr Frederick George Horan, Miss Rose Orris, Mr Sidney Coleman and Mr Reg Savage.

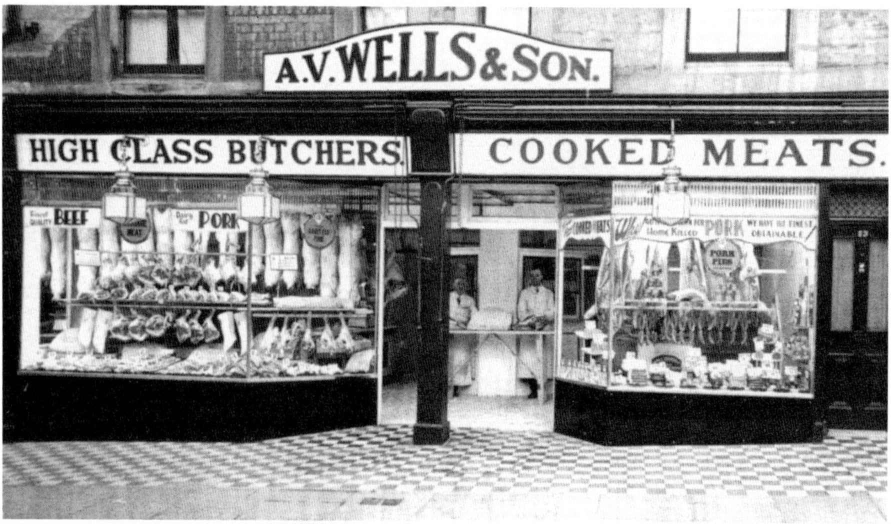

Mr A.V. Wells & Son, 51 and 53 Black Bull Road. Mr Wells ran these two shops from 1935 to 1967 and just no. 51 from 1967 to 1979 when the business closed. Left to right are Mr Albert Wells and Mr Bill Punyer.

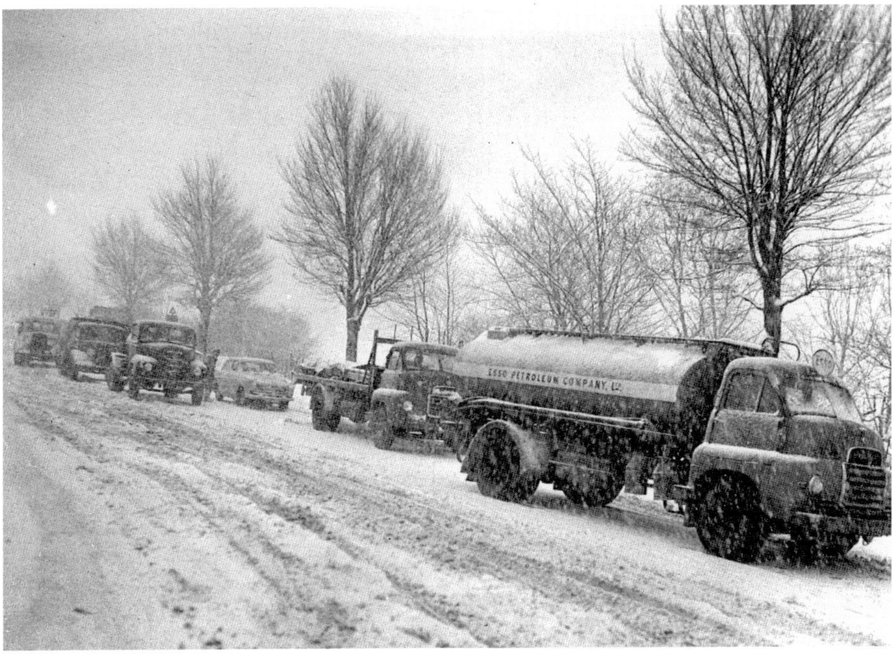

Dover Hill, 1963. This was a very long and hard winter and there were freezing conditions for three months.

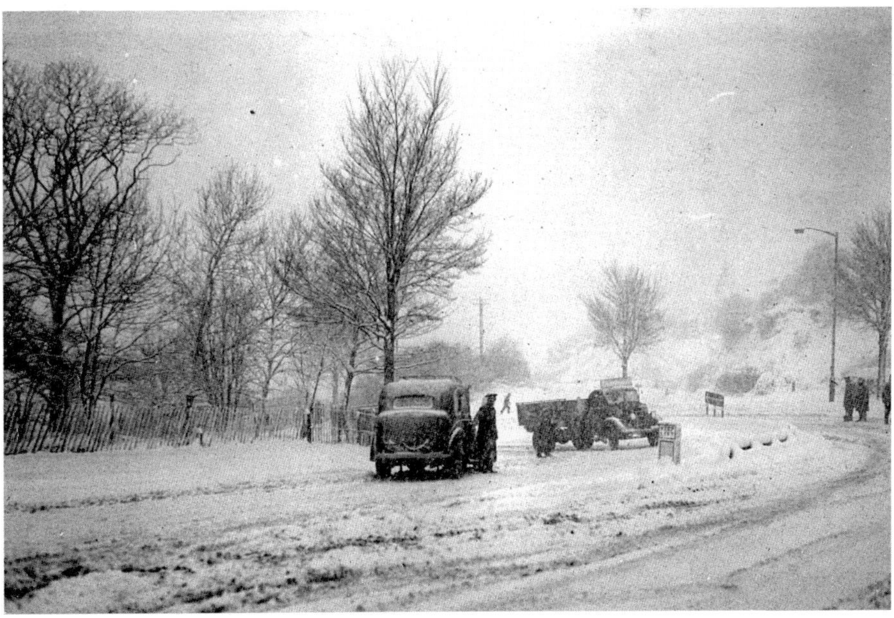

Another snow scene on Dover Hill, 1963. The vehicles are negotiating Killick's corner.

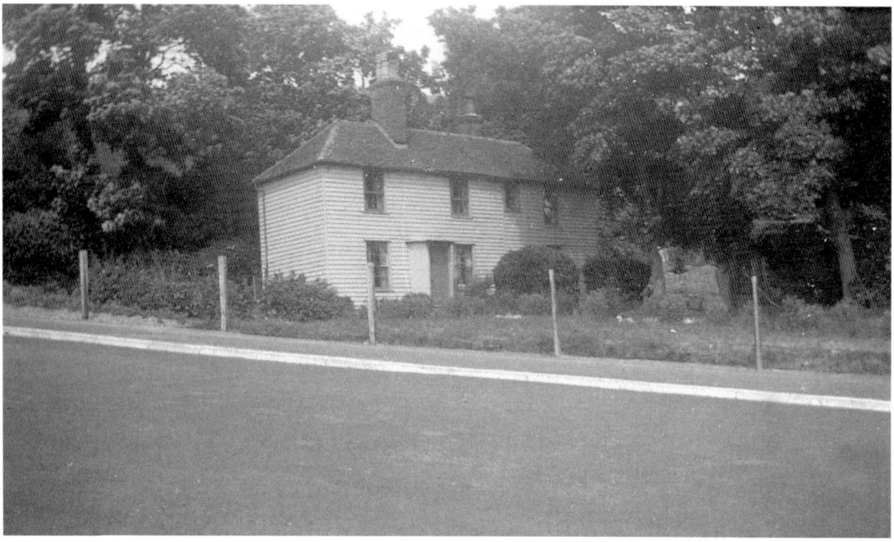

Lime Kiln Cottage, Dover Road. This weather-boarded cottage stood at the top of Dover Road just below Killick's corner. It was last occupied by Mr Richard Fagg who worked for Mr Aird, Martello Dairy Farm. Mr Fagg lived at Lime Kiln Cottage from 1919 to 1938. The cottage originally belonged to Lime Kiln Farm, Dover Road.

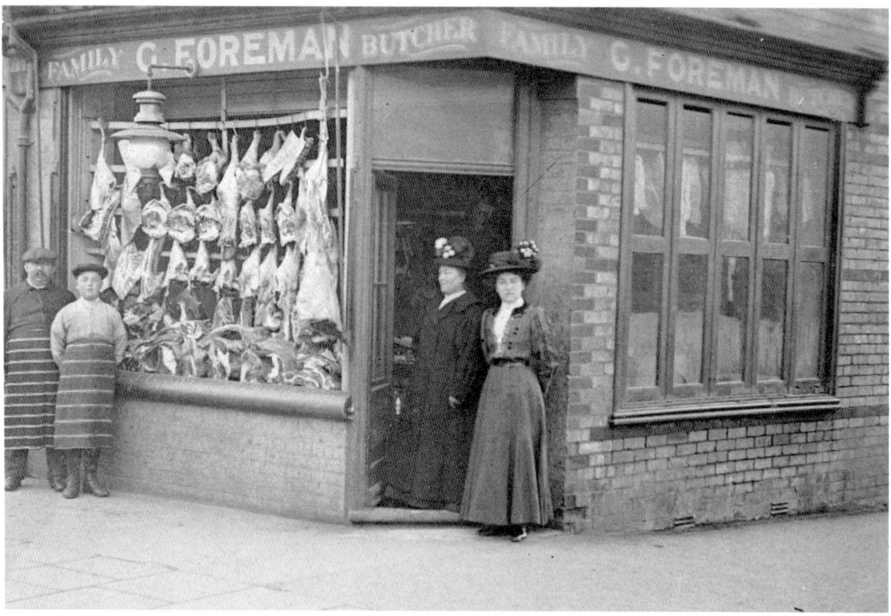

Mr Geoffrey Foreman (far left), butcher, Dover Road, on the corner of Grove Road. Mr Foreman was in business at these premises from 1896 to 1911. The shop was later a cooperative butchers and is now Paula's fruit and vegetable shop.

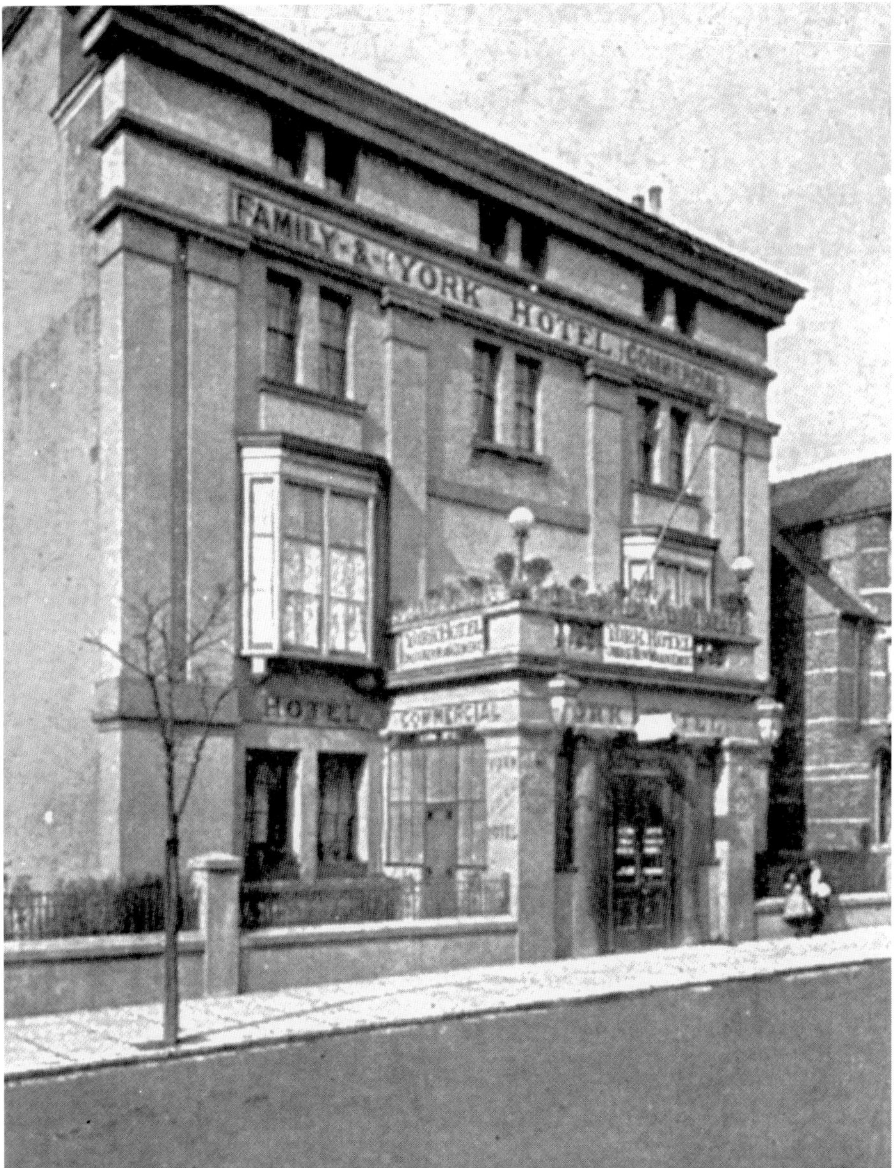

The York, a commercial and family hotel, 139 Dover Road. The hotel was built in 1902 and traded as a hotel until 1920 when it became Pickford's furniture depository. In 1938 it was taken over by Thompson & Son and in 1957 by Newman & Son, both furniture depositories. It became Chilton Court in 1969 and was later demolished to make way for five town houses.

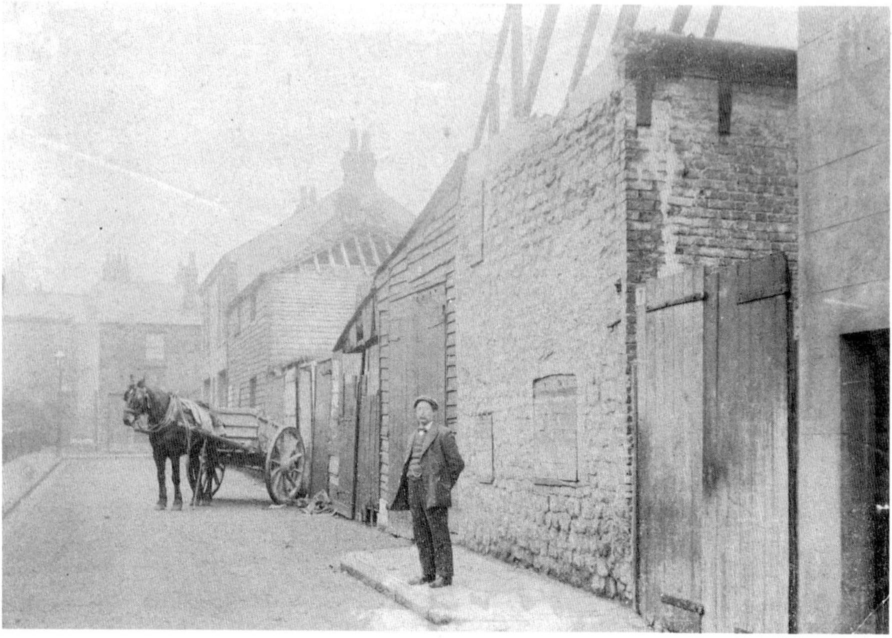

Peter Street between 1912 and 1913. The gentleman is Mr F. Menpes, builder.

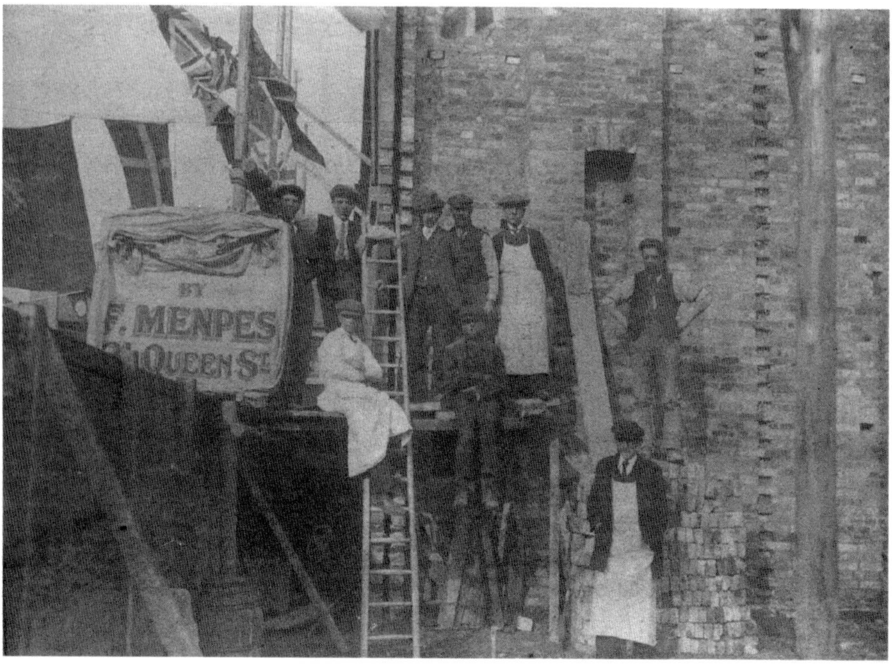

The staff of Mr F. Menpes, builder, 1913–14. They are building new houses on the site of the old buildings seen in the previous picture.

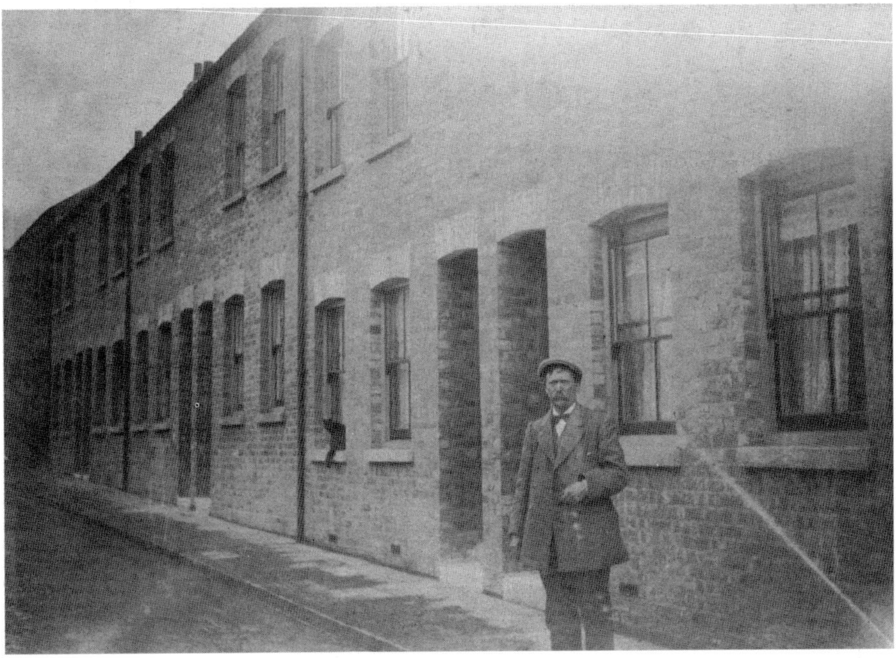

The new houses in Peter Street: compare this picture with the one opposite. Mr Menpes is posing for the camera, obviously proud of his work.

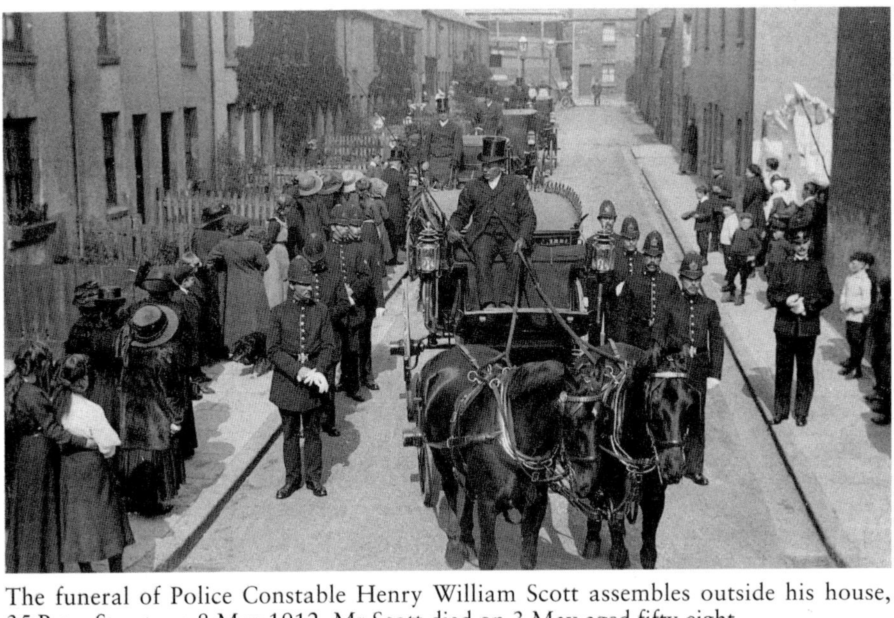

The funeral of Police Constable Henry William Scott assembles outside his house, 35 Peter Street, on 8 May 1912. Mr Scott died on 3 May aged fifty-eight.

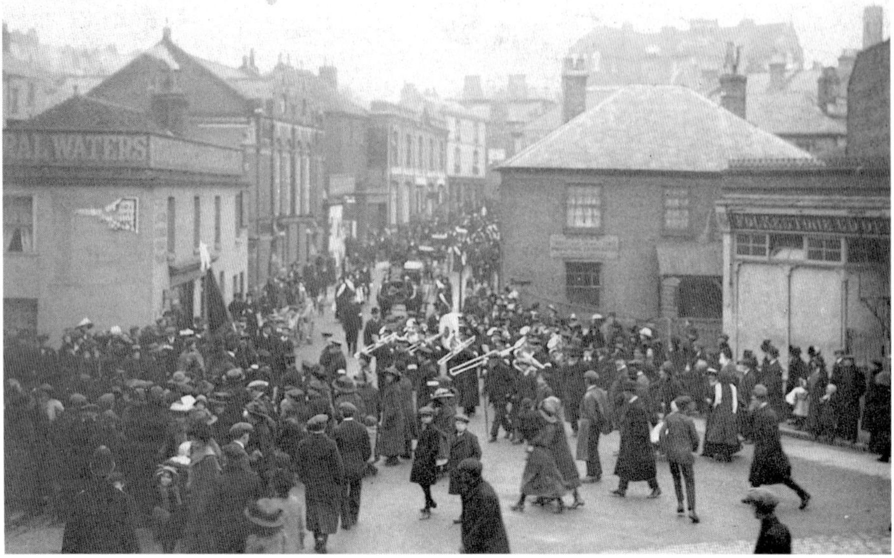

The funeral procession of Police Constable Henry William Scott, led by the Salvation Army, makes its way down Dover Road.

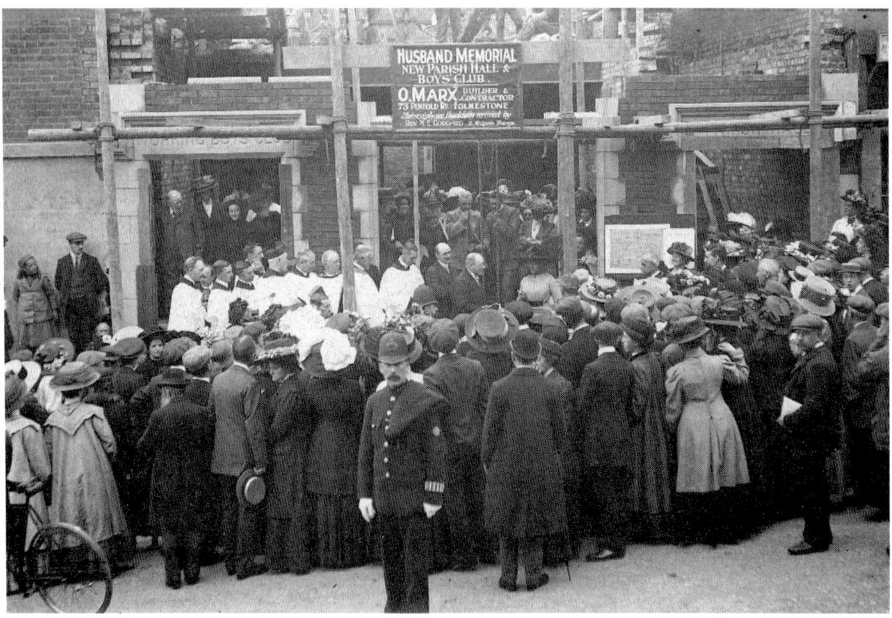

Edward Husband Memorial Parish Hall and Working Boy's Club. The picture illustrates the ceremony of the laying of the foundation stone by Lady Lumb on 12 September 1910. The building became St Augustine's Mission Church around 1956, after St Michael's Church was demolished.

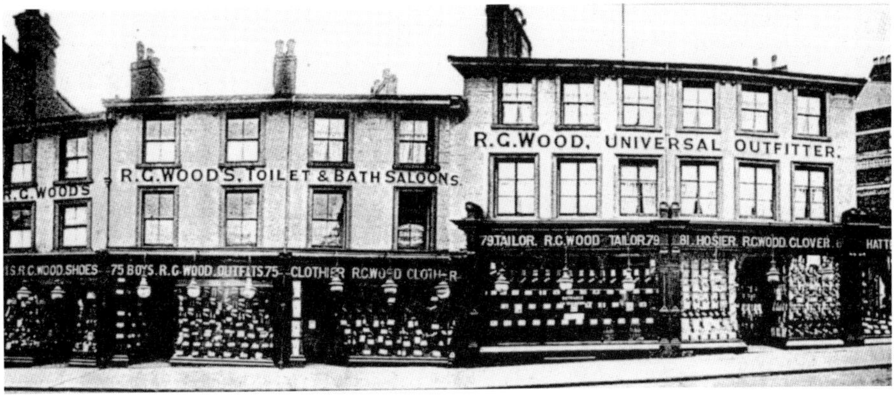

Mr Reginald G. Wood, merchant tailor and universal outfitter, 73–81 Tontine Street. Mr Wood took over the business at these premises from Mr T. Logan in 1904. The business continued trading until 1955. Mr Wood was the mayor of Folkestone from 1919 to 1922.

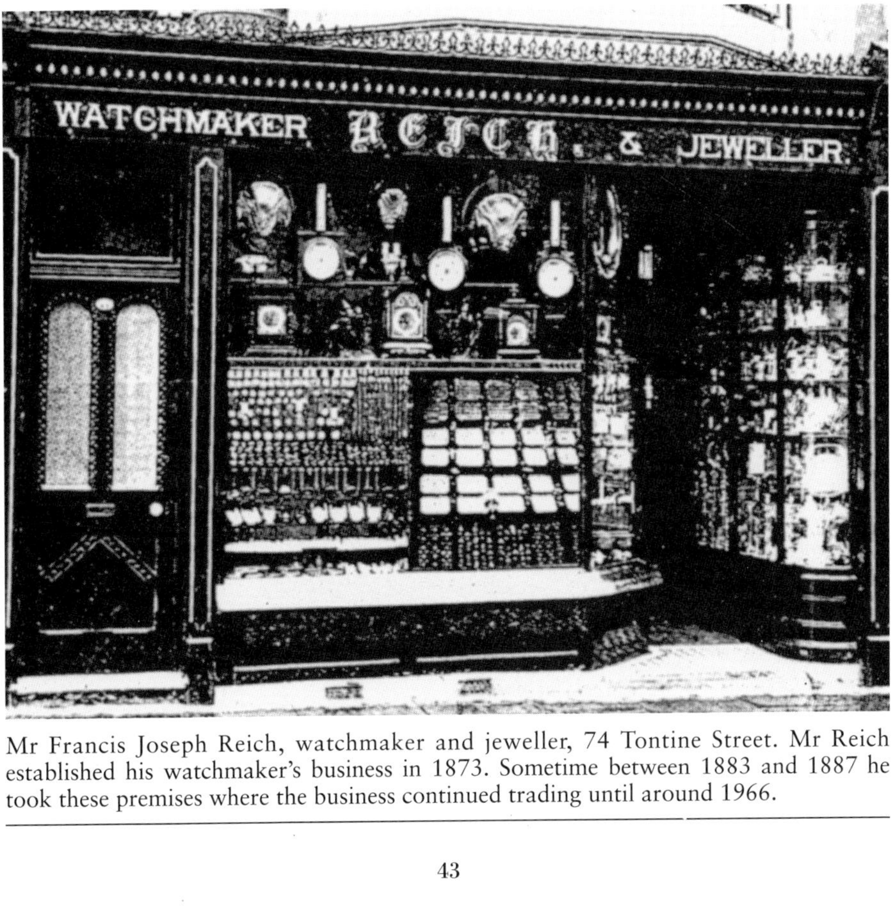

Mr Francis Joseph Reich, watchmaker and jeweller, 74 Tontine Street. Mr Reich established his watchmaker's business in 1873. Sometime between 1883 and 1887 he took these premises where the business continued trading until around 1966.

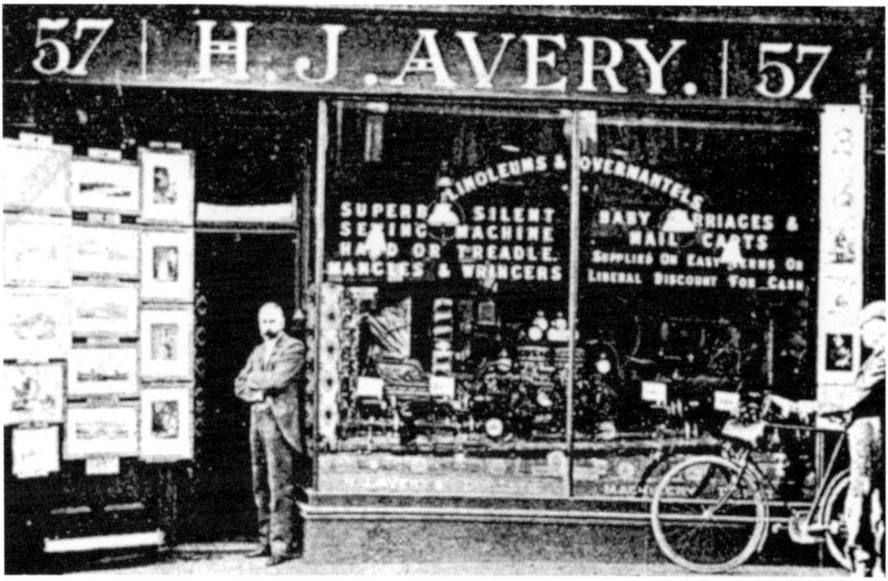

Mr H.J. Avery, 57 Tontine Street. He was in business with a partner at these premises from 1895 to 1899 when he became sole owner and continued trading until 1908. Mr Avery sold a variety of items including baby carriages, linoleums, overmantels, watches, clocks, mangles and sewing machines. He also had a large assortment of engravings and oil paintings.

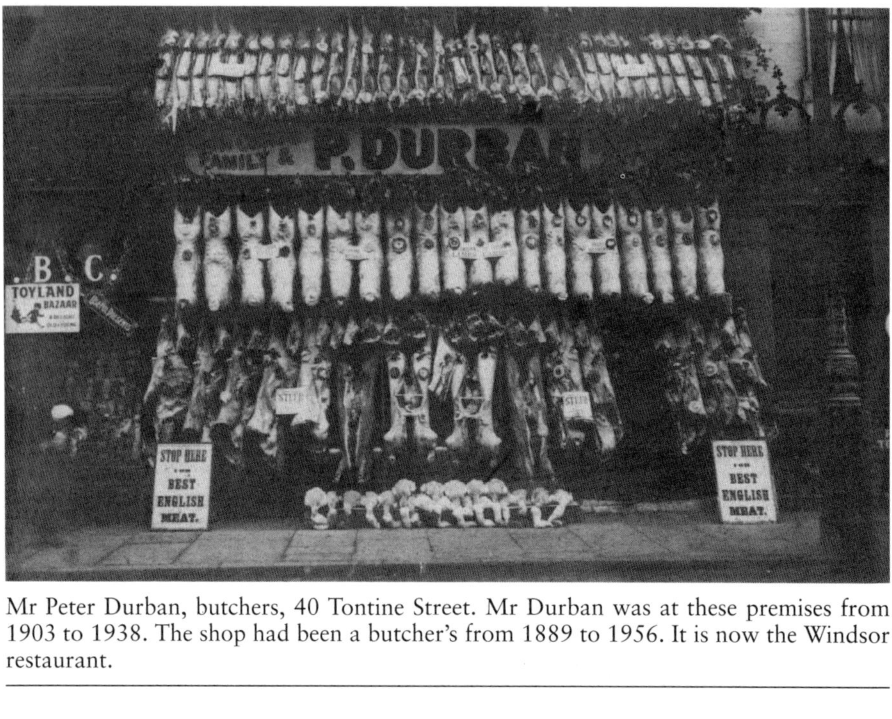

Mr Peter Durban, butchers, 40 Tontine Street. Mr Durban was at these premises from 1903 to 1938. The shop had been a butcher's from 1889 to 1956. It is now the Windsor restaurant.

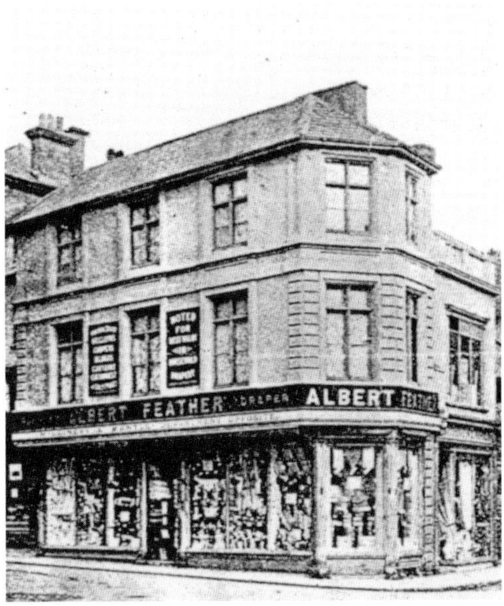

Mr Albert Feather, general and fancy draper and milliner. Mr Feather traded at these premises from 1895 to 1904. The premises are now occupied by Jolson's bar.

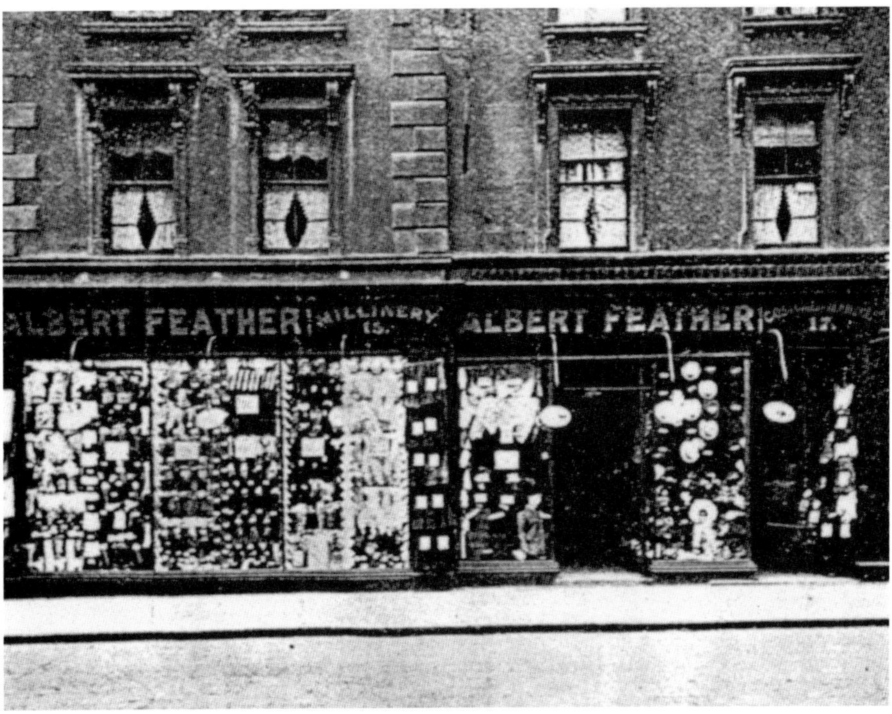

In 1896 Mr Feather opened a second branch to his drapery business at 17 Tontine Street and, in 1898, he also took no. 15. He traded at these premises until sometime between 1919 and 1922.

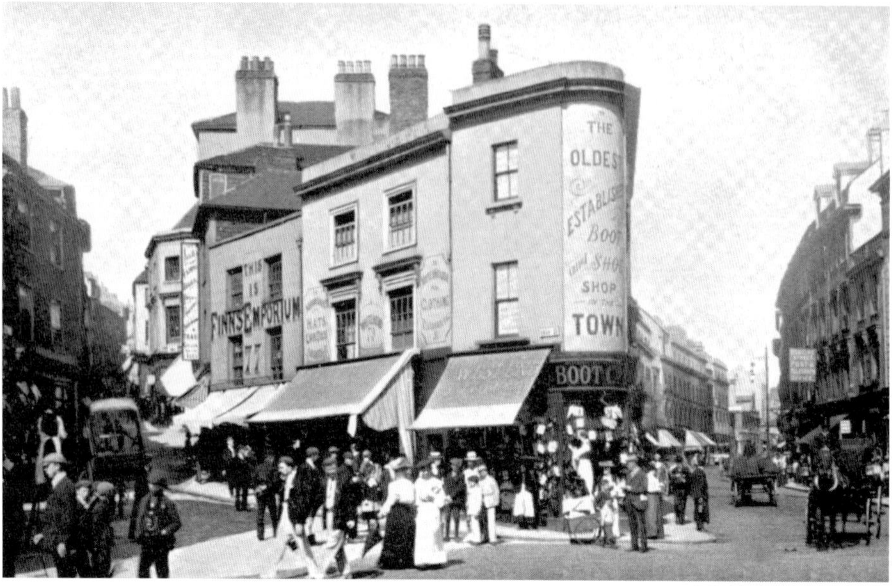

Junction of High Street and Tontine Street, *c.* 1910. These were the days when this part of the town was the main shopping area. Note the two ladies in the centre in their Edwardian dresses and hats.

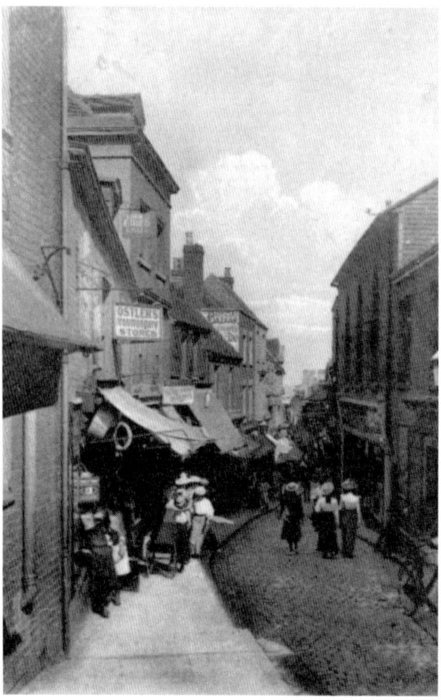

The old High Street looking downwards. The writing on the shop wall proclaims Bayfield's Bazaar: cheapest in town.

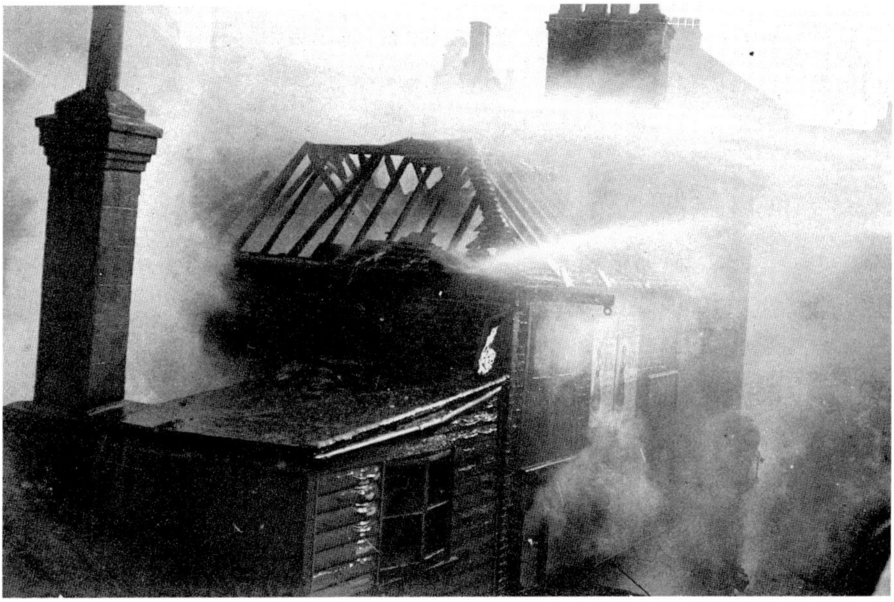

Mr George Mence Smith, grocer, oil and hardware dealer, 8 High Street. This terrible fire was on 26 April 1909; Mr S.J. Smallfield was manager at the time.

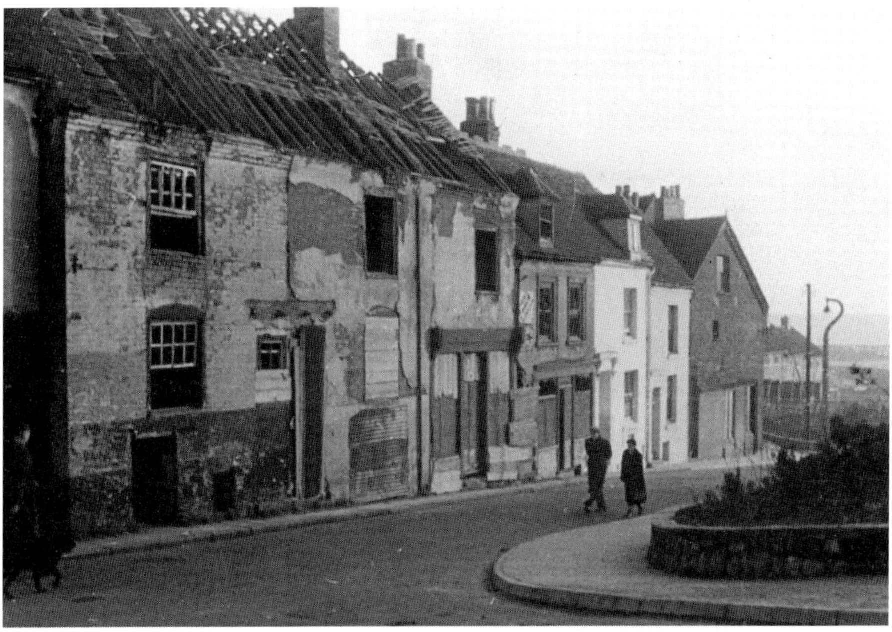

Harbour Way, formerly Dover Street. The street was gradually demolished from the bottom of the hill after a compulsory purchase order in 1956. On the right in the far distance can be seen some of the newly built houses.

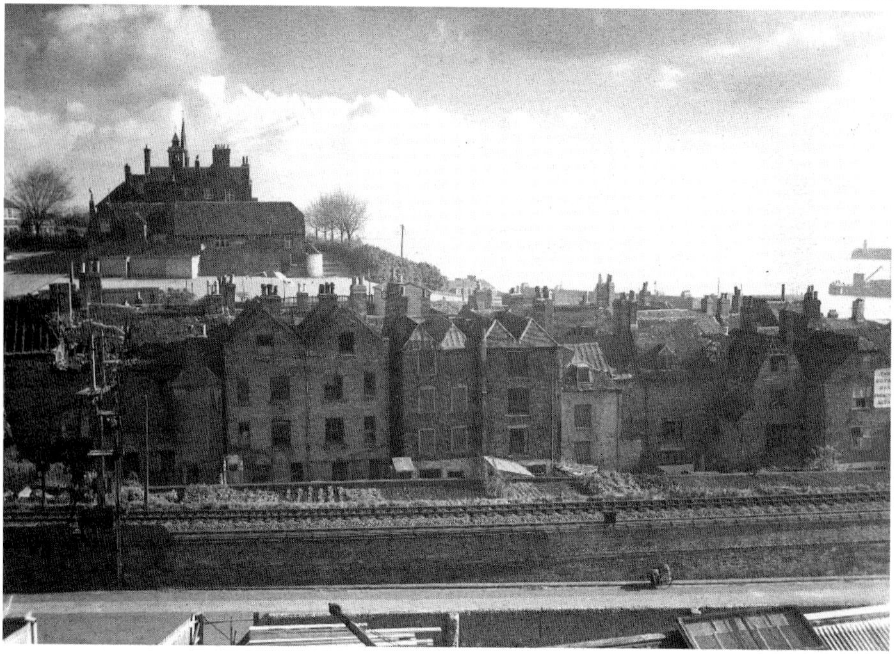

The backs of the buildings in North Street as seen from Saffron's Place, 1947. All these buildings in North Street, apart from four at the top of the street, were pulled down in 1953. The sign on the building to the far right of the picture says the Royal Oak, Fremlins Ales.

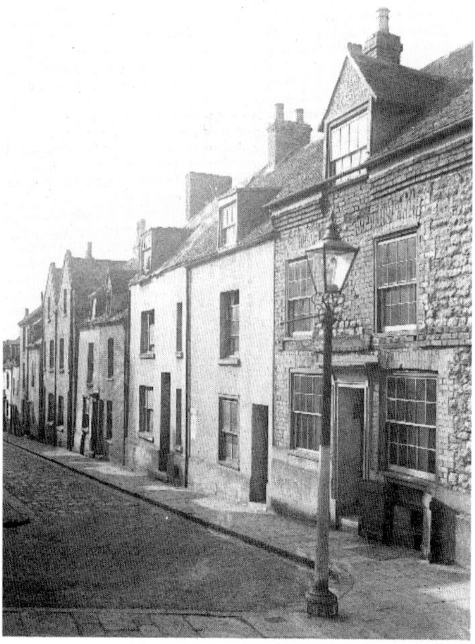

North Street looking down from the left-hand bend. Most of these houses were pulled down in 1953. The Lifeboat Inn is on the left corner.

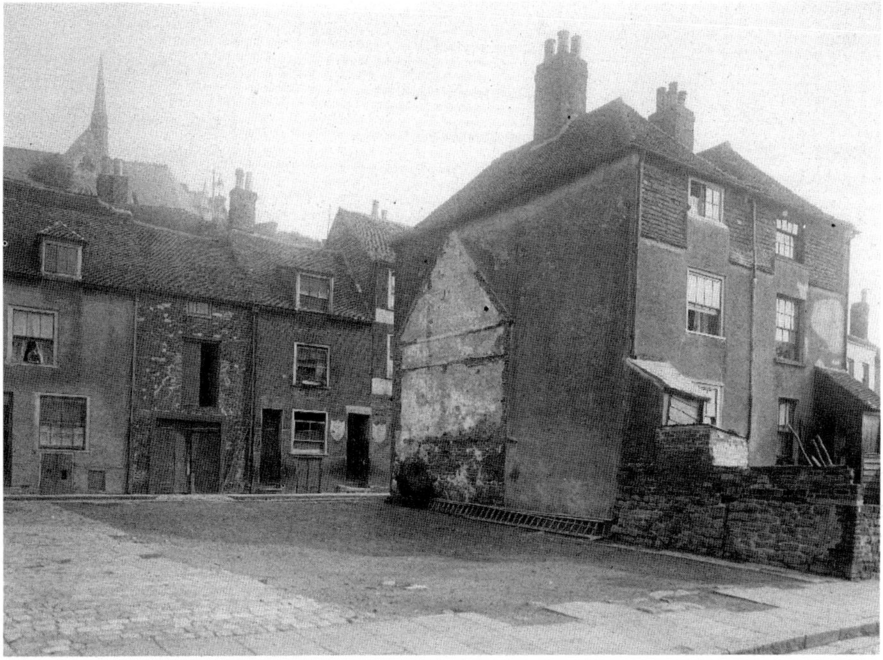

Radnor Street from the Stade, 1927. Some houses have been demolished exposing the north side of Radnor Street.

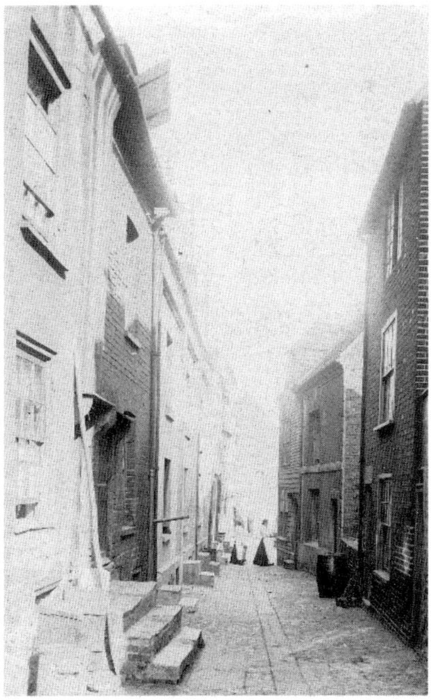

East Street, 1904. This is the west end of East Street which ran behind Radnor Street. It was demolished in 1935.

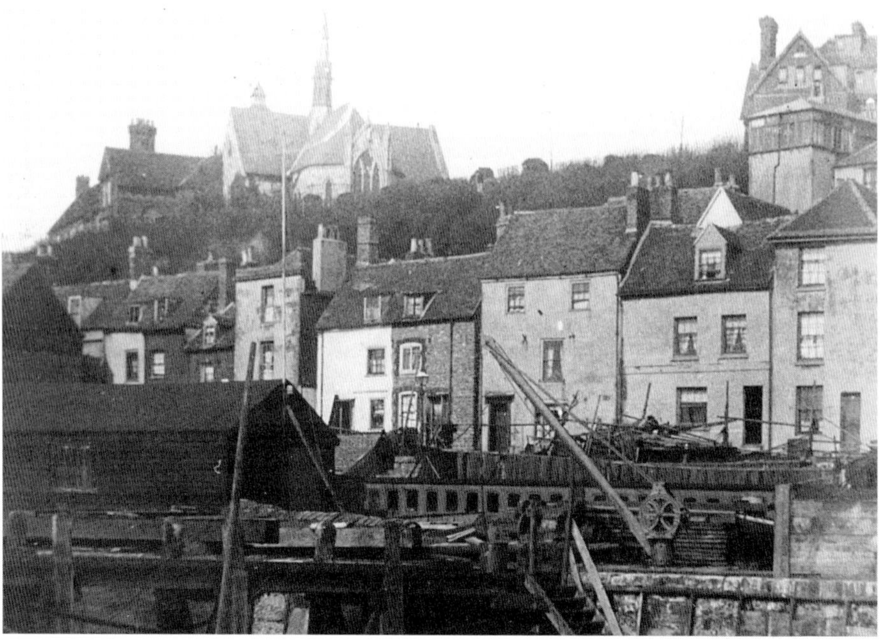

The Stade and some of the houses in East Street, *c.* 1900. In the foreground is the South Eastern and Chatham Railway's workshops and jetty.

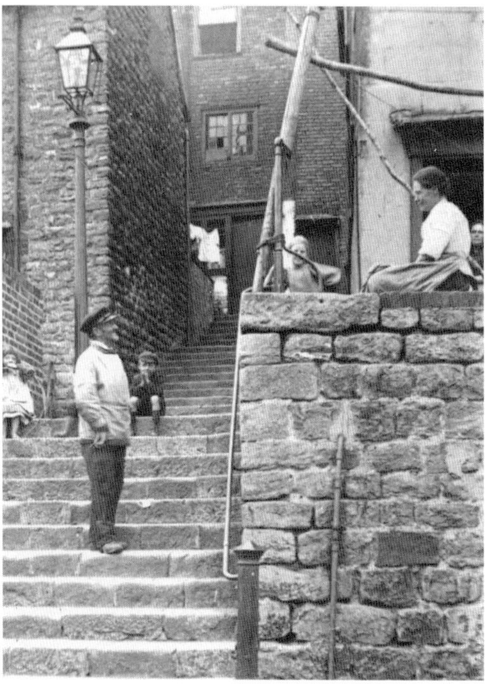

The steps from the Stade to East Street and leading on up to East Cliff. The present-day steps leading to East Cliff are in the same position.

SECTION TWO

Harbour and Fishing

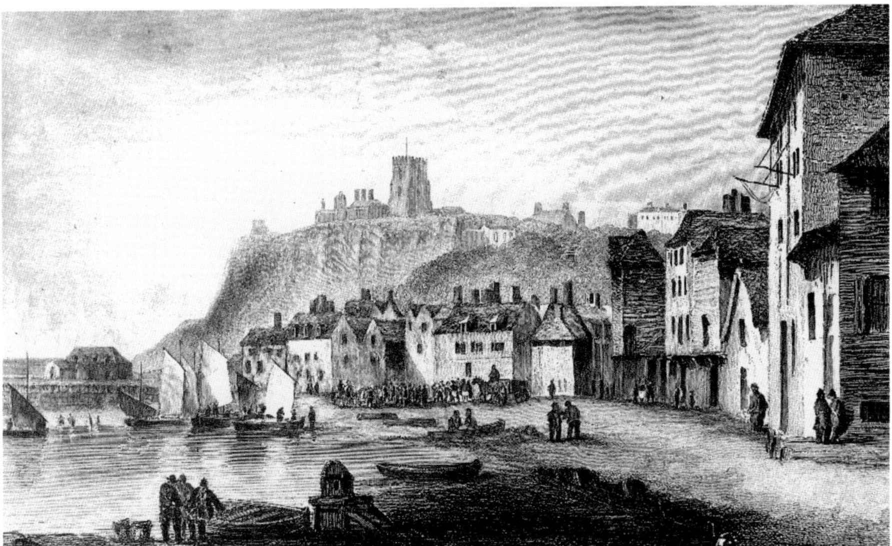

Folkestone harbour and the Stade at low water, 1840. The people gathered in the middle background are at a fish auction. The fish were laid out on the sand and the fishermen selling them would pick up a small stone and hold it at arm's length. He would offer the lot at a top price, from which he would descend until a bid was made. When the stone was dropped a bargain was concluded. Note the capstan in the foreground which was used for pulling boats up the beach. In 1783 the rent for keeping a capstan on the beach was 2*s* 6*d* per year; in 1788 the rent was reduced to 1*s*.

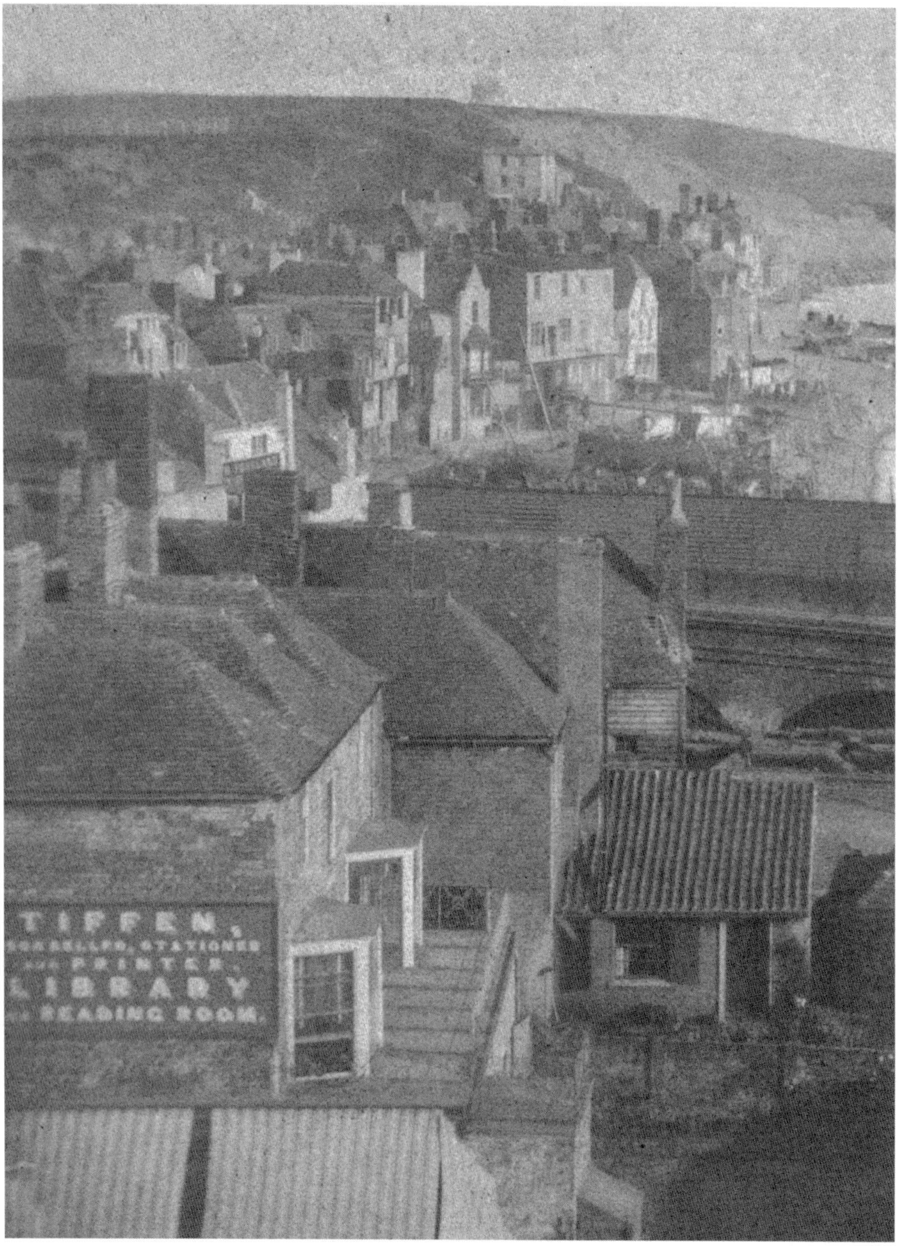

The inner and outer harbours, *c.* 1858. In the foreground is Mr William Tiffen's shop, bookseller, printer and stationer. Mr Tiffen had a shop at both Sandgate and Hythe and he opened this branch in about 1846. Beach Street, formerly Kingsbridge Street (where the whelk barrows stand), has not yet been built. The quay along the Stade in the outer harbour is also missing.

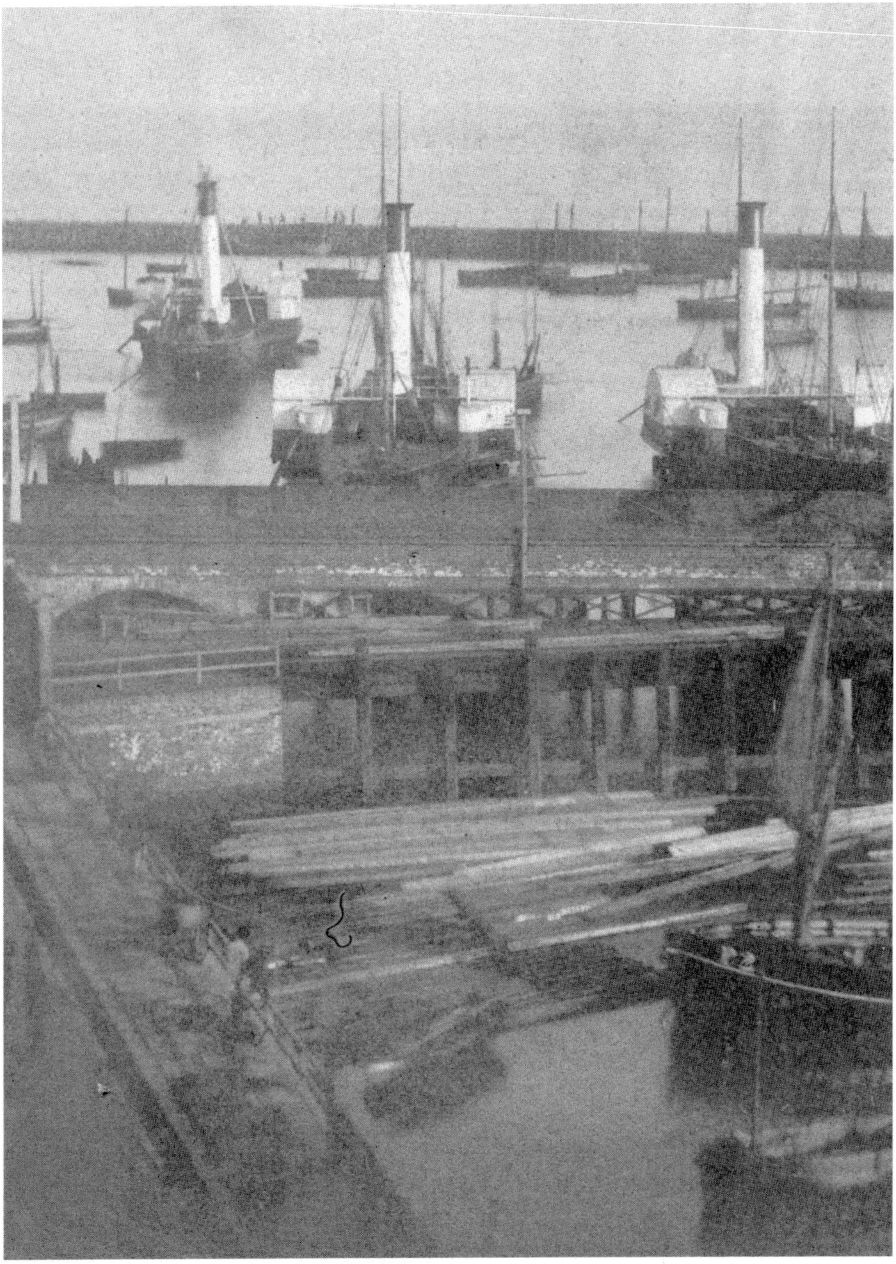

The inner and outer harbours, *c*. 1860. In the left foreground is the newly built Kingsbridge Street with two men looking over the railings. In the outer harbour there are three early cross-channel paddle steamers, built between 1844 and 1847.

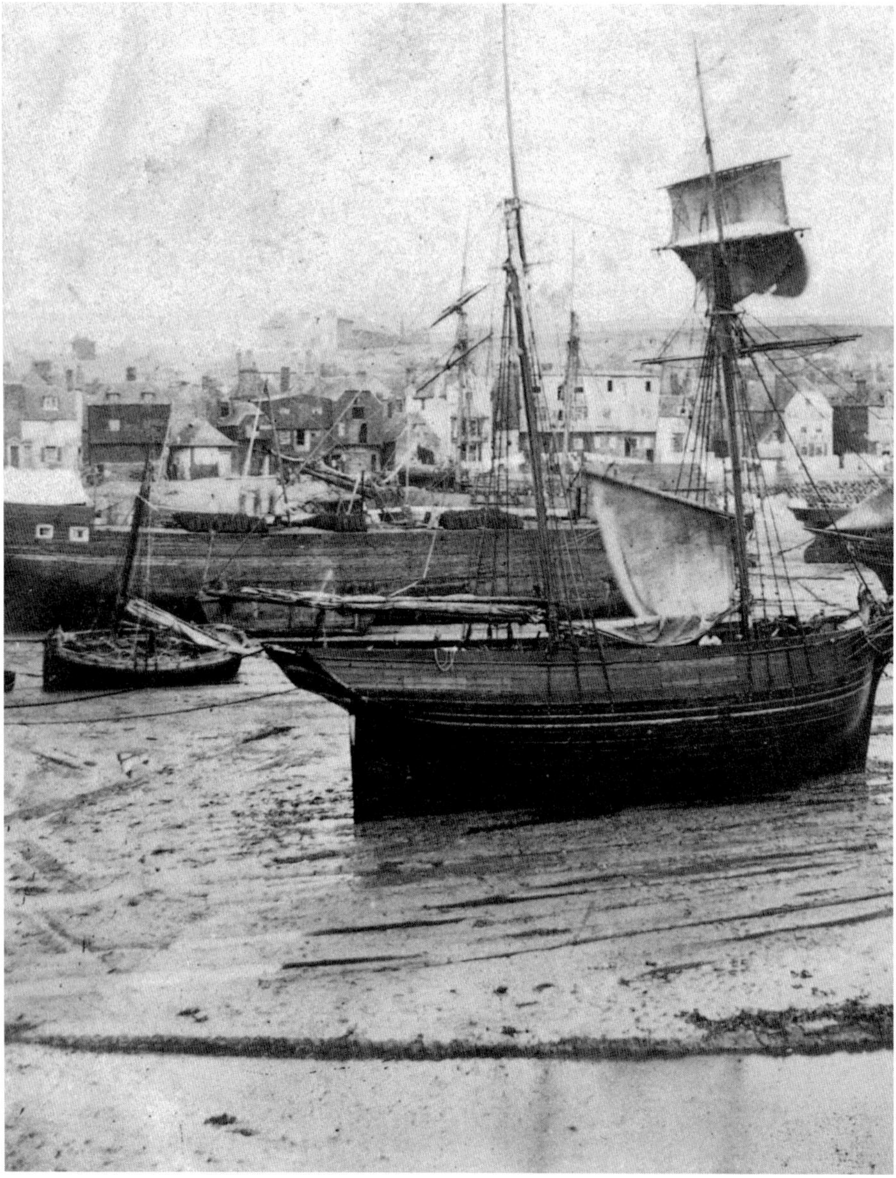

The outer harbour looking towards the Stade, *c.* 1858. The ship moored in the foreground carried cargoes of coal, timber or ice into Folkestone and possibly left with a cargo of chalk. The quay along the Stade has not yet been built; it came in 1860. At the right-hand end of the Stade can be seen a rock groyne, a prominent feature in the painting by R. Kerr which was shown in the first selection of *Folkestone In Old Photographs.*

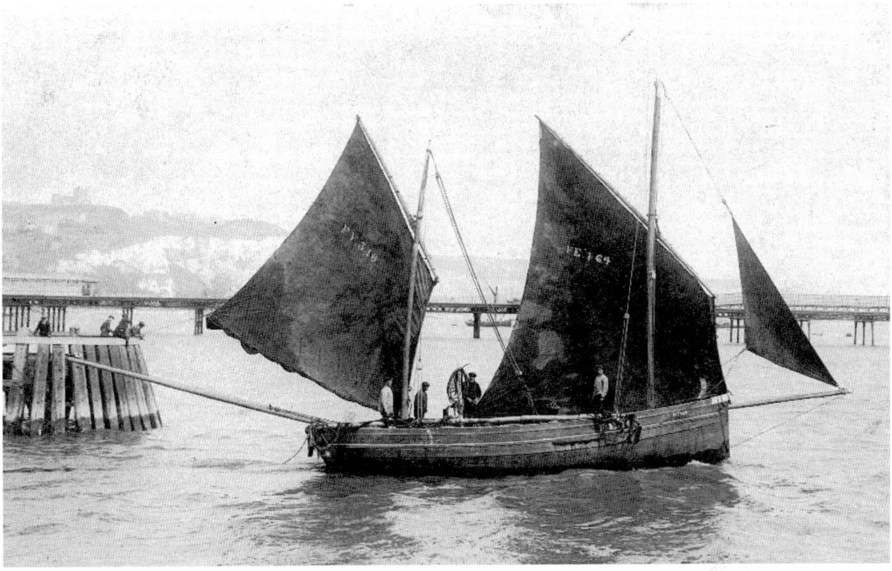

A fine example of a Folkestone lugger, *Alfred*, sailing out of Dover harbour. Her skipper is Mr William Gale (senior). FE 164 is her Folkestone registration. On her mizzen or aft sail is FY 346, the registration for Fowey, which was possibly the port from which she originally came.

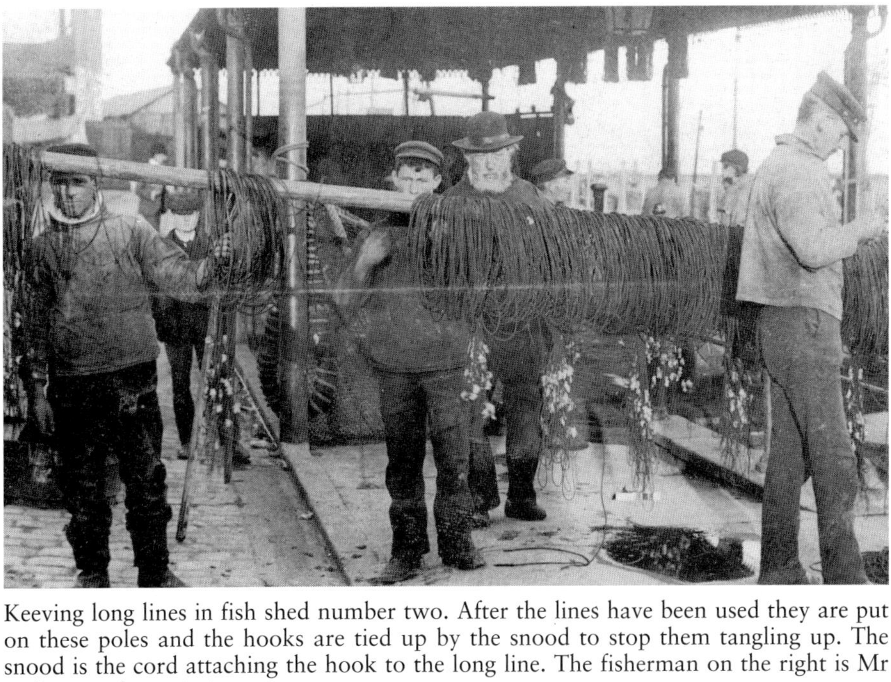

Keeving long lines in fish shed number two. After the lines have been used they are put on these poles and the hooks are tied up by the snood to stop them tangling up. The snood is the cord attaching the hook to the long line. The fisherman on the right is Mr William Gale (senior).

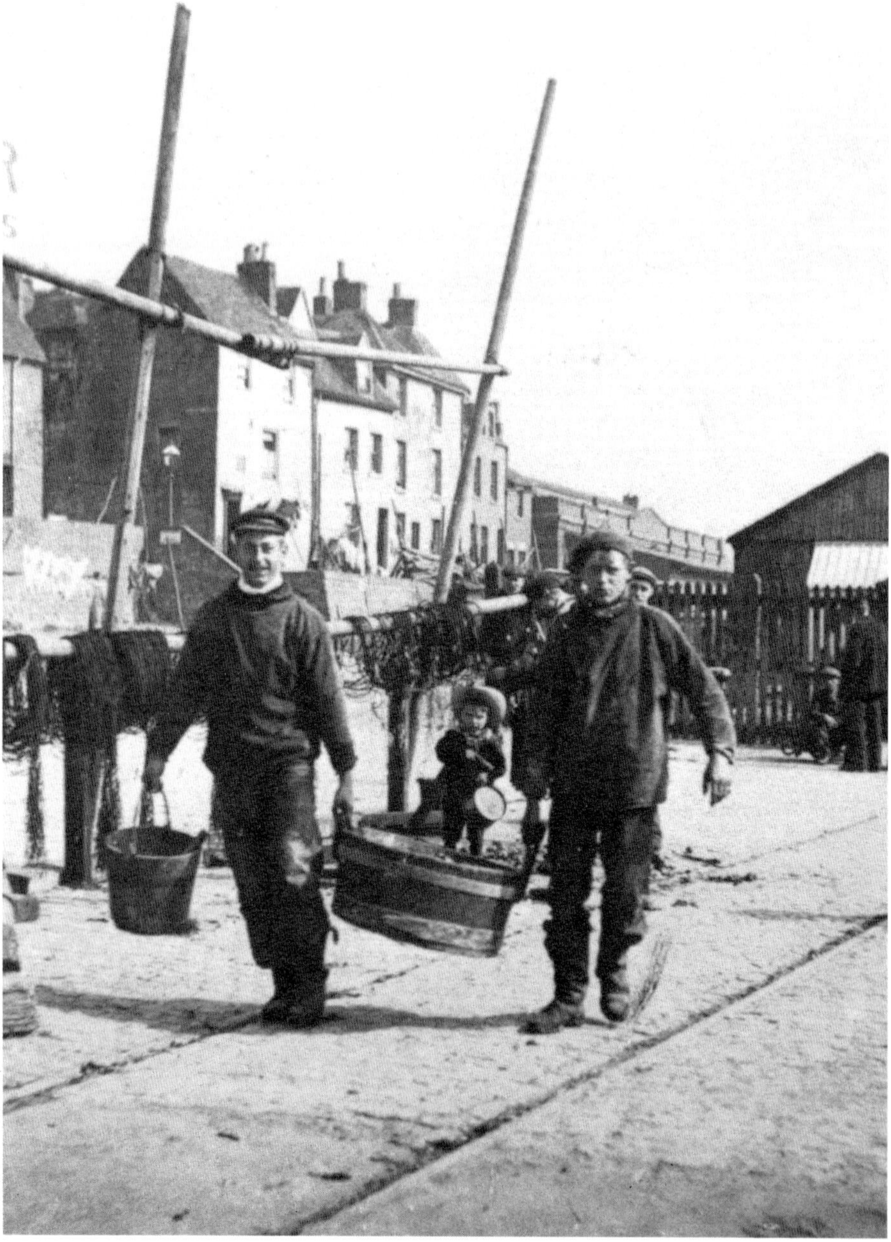

Two fishermen carrying a tub along the Stade. These wooden tubs were used for baiting long lines in and carrying fish. They were succeeded by galvanized baths. Behind the men are long lines hanging out to dry on keeving poles.

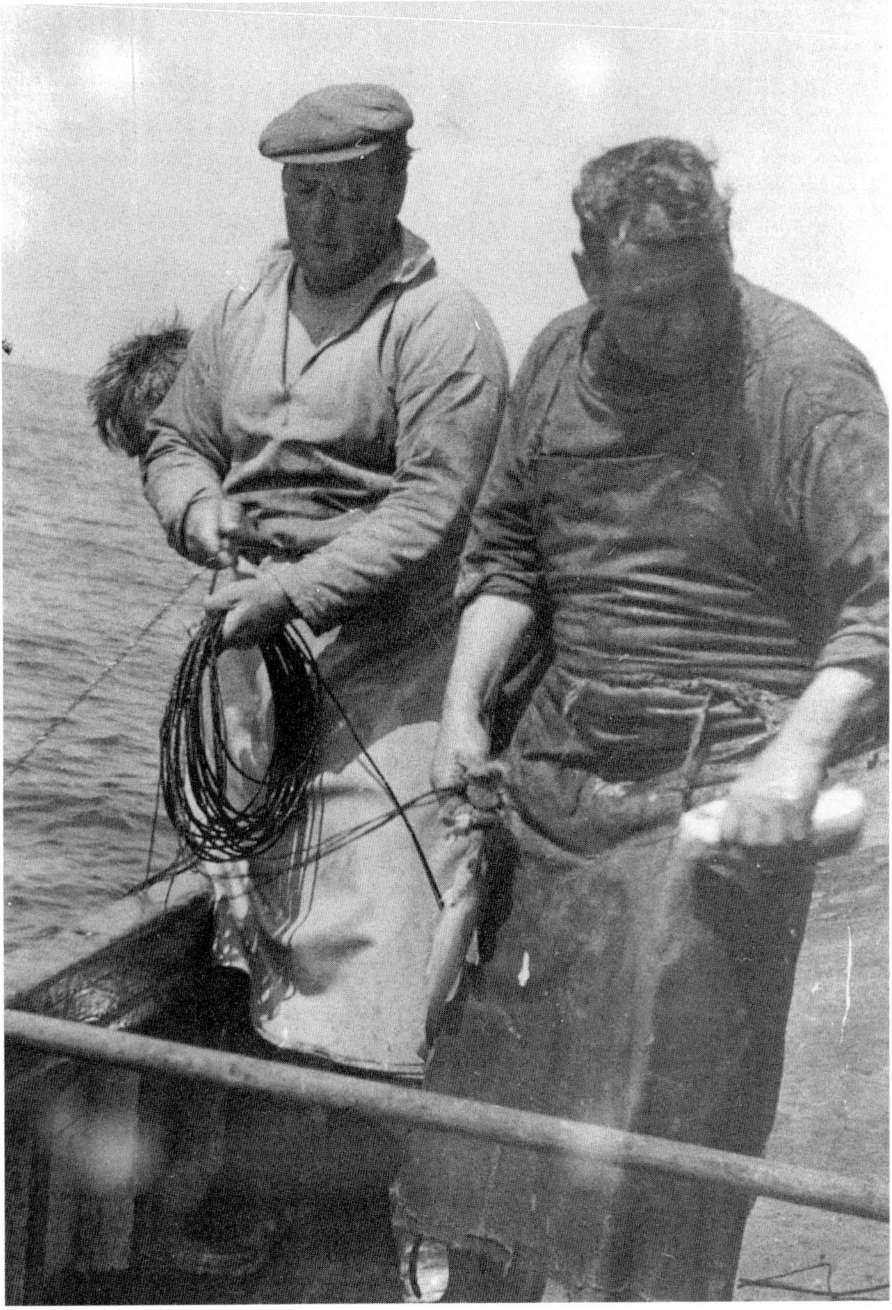

Mr George Neal hauling a long line, while Mr Albert 'Nobby' Taylor takes off the fish, aboard FE15, *c.* 1958. This method of long-line fishing, a hard and tiring task, is unique to Folkestone.

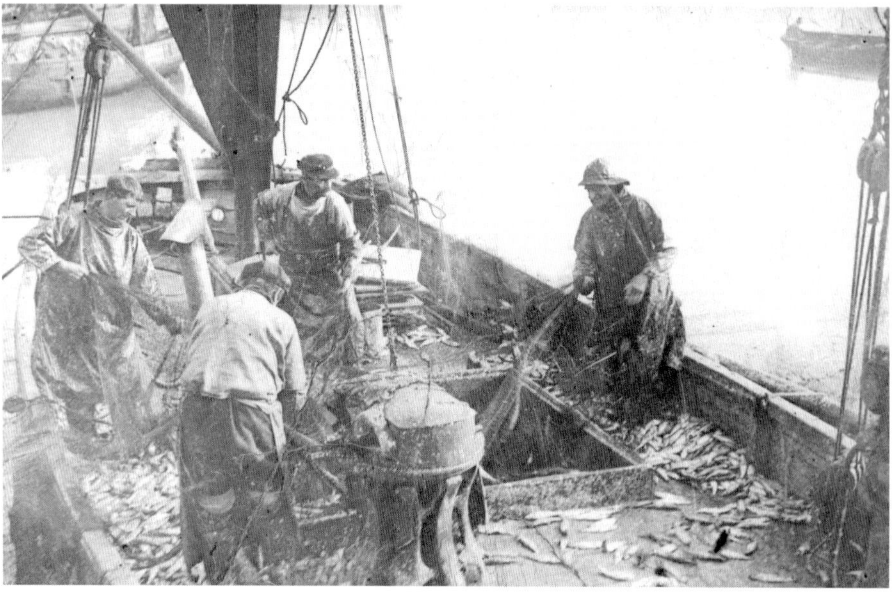

The fishermen are shaking their herring nets aboard the sailing lugger *Winifred* FE97, December 1913. The *Winifred* was owned by Mr William 'Muggy' Hall. Drifting for herrings is a trade which has long since passed.

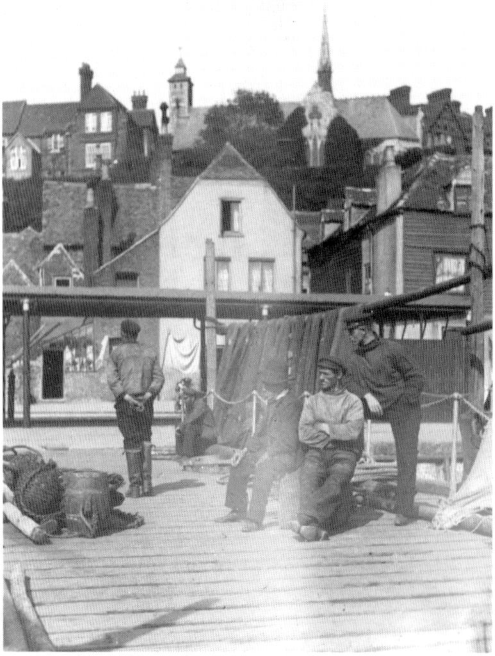

The fishermen's jetty in the outer harbour. Although these fishermen have taken time out for a rest, they are not concerned about the camera. The fisherman wearing the trilby hat is Mr 'Dicky' Penny.

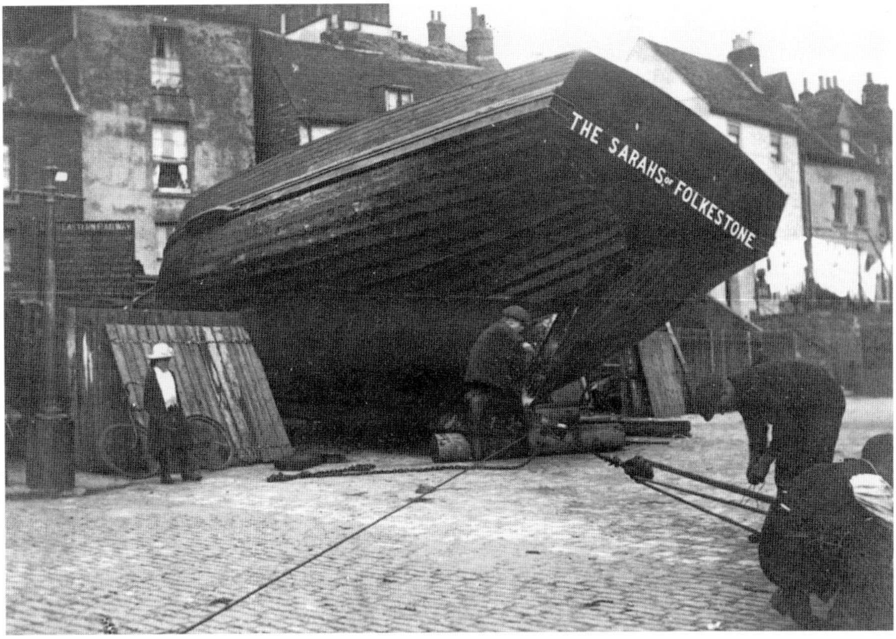

The Sarahs FE71, nicknamed 'Ugly Duckling', 1920. *The Sarahs* was built here on the Stade by Mr Tom Saunders. She is here being pulled out to the edge of the quay, where she was launched broadside.

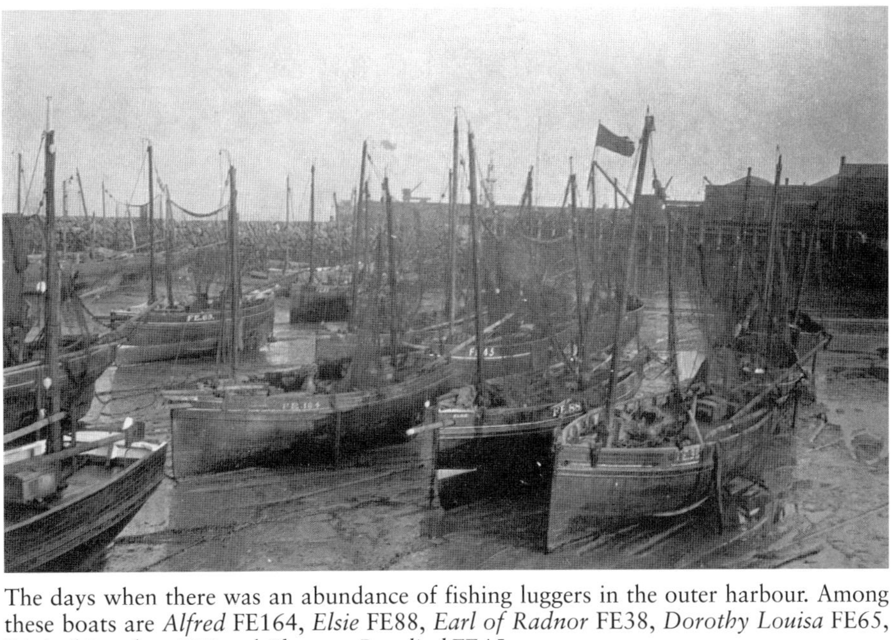

The days when there was an abundance of fishing luggers in the outer harbour. Among these boats are *Alfred* FE164, *Elsie* FE88, *Earl of Radnor* FE38, *Dorothy Louisa* FE65, *Bird of Freedom* FE9 and *Florence Roselind* FE45.

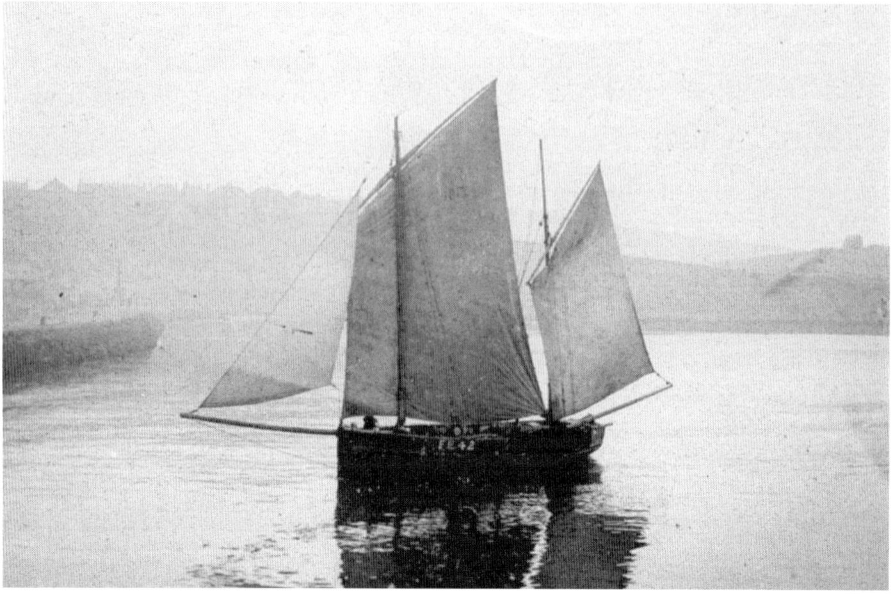

The fully-rigged sailing lugger *Jessica* FE42. On the foremast she is carrying a jib and dipping lugsail, while on the mizzen-mast she has a gaff-rigged mizzen-sail. Most of the sailing luggers had engines fitted in the early 1920s.

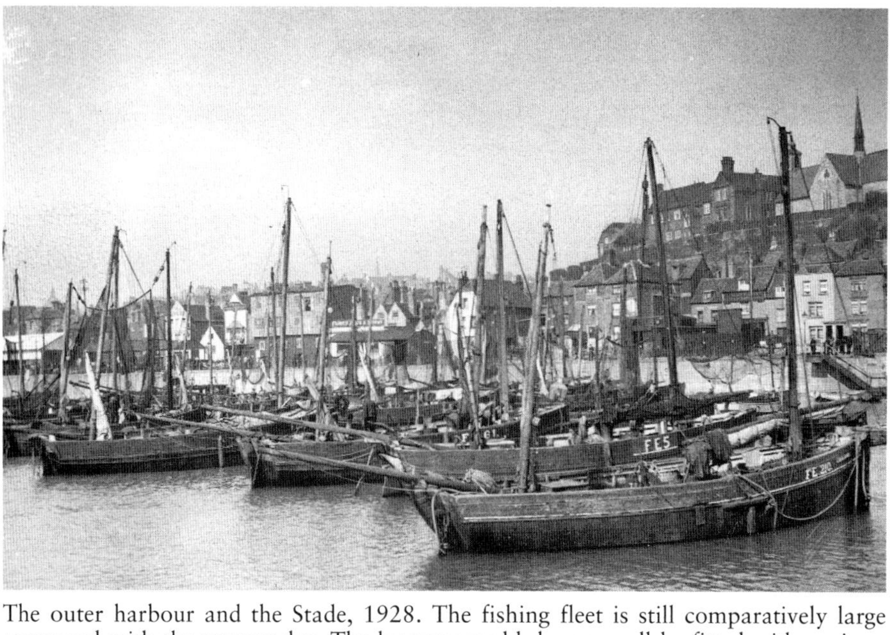

The outer harbour and the Stade, 1928. The fishing fleet is still comparatively large compared with the present day. The luggers would, by now, all be fitted with engines. Among these boats are: *Garland* FE210, *Happy Return* FE5, *Young Harry* FE61 and *Florence Nightingale* FE55.

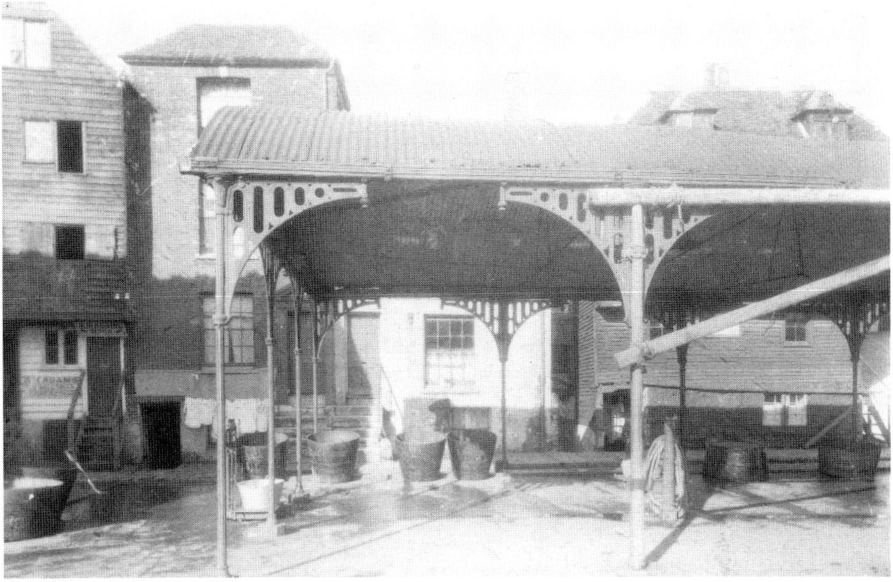

The old number one fish shed, November 1926. The old fish shed, built in 1860, is unsafe and due to be replaced: note the timber braces lashed to it. Behind it are the premises of fish salesmen Mr A.H. Adams, Mr H. May and Mr A. Goddard.

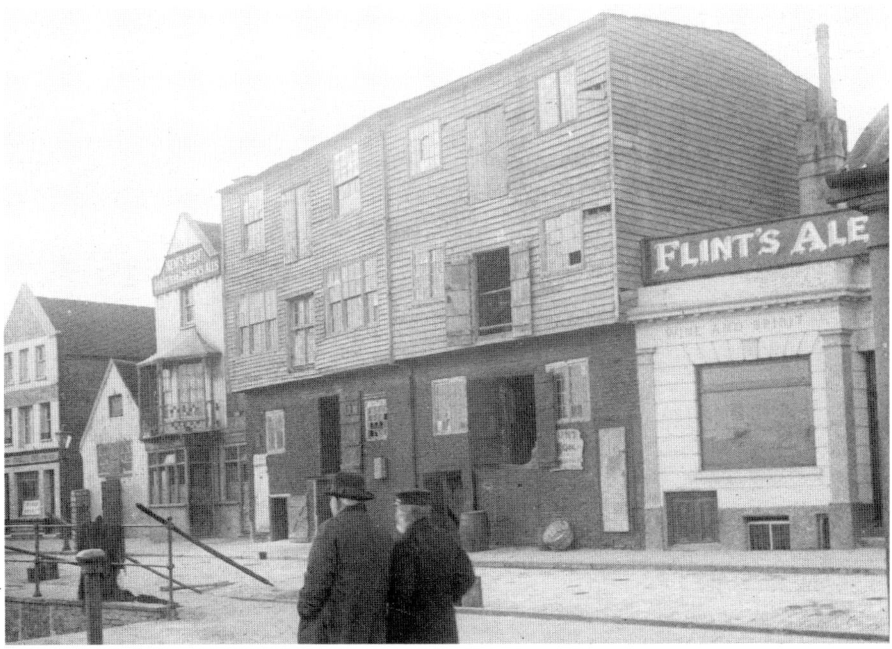

Further along the Stade, November 1926. From left to right is the Jubilee Inn, Oddfellows' Arms, Mr E. Nicholls, sailmaker, a shipping agent and the Ship Inn.

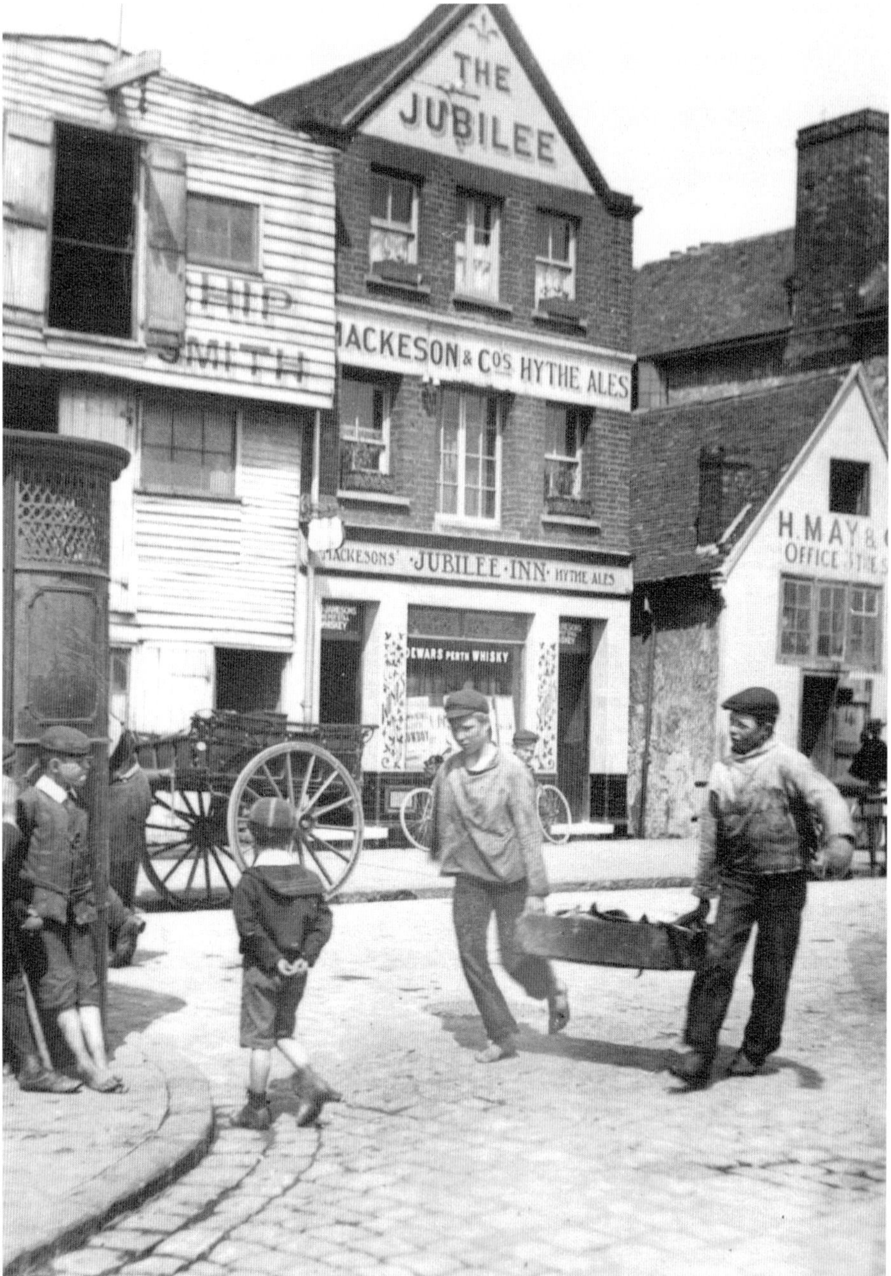

The Stade, *c.* 1910. Two fisherboys are carrying a box of dogfish while some small boys look on. Behind them are the premises of Mr W. Francis, general smith, the Jubilee Inn, and the office of Mr H. May and Co., fish salesmen.

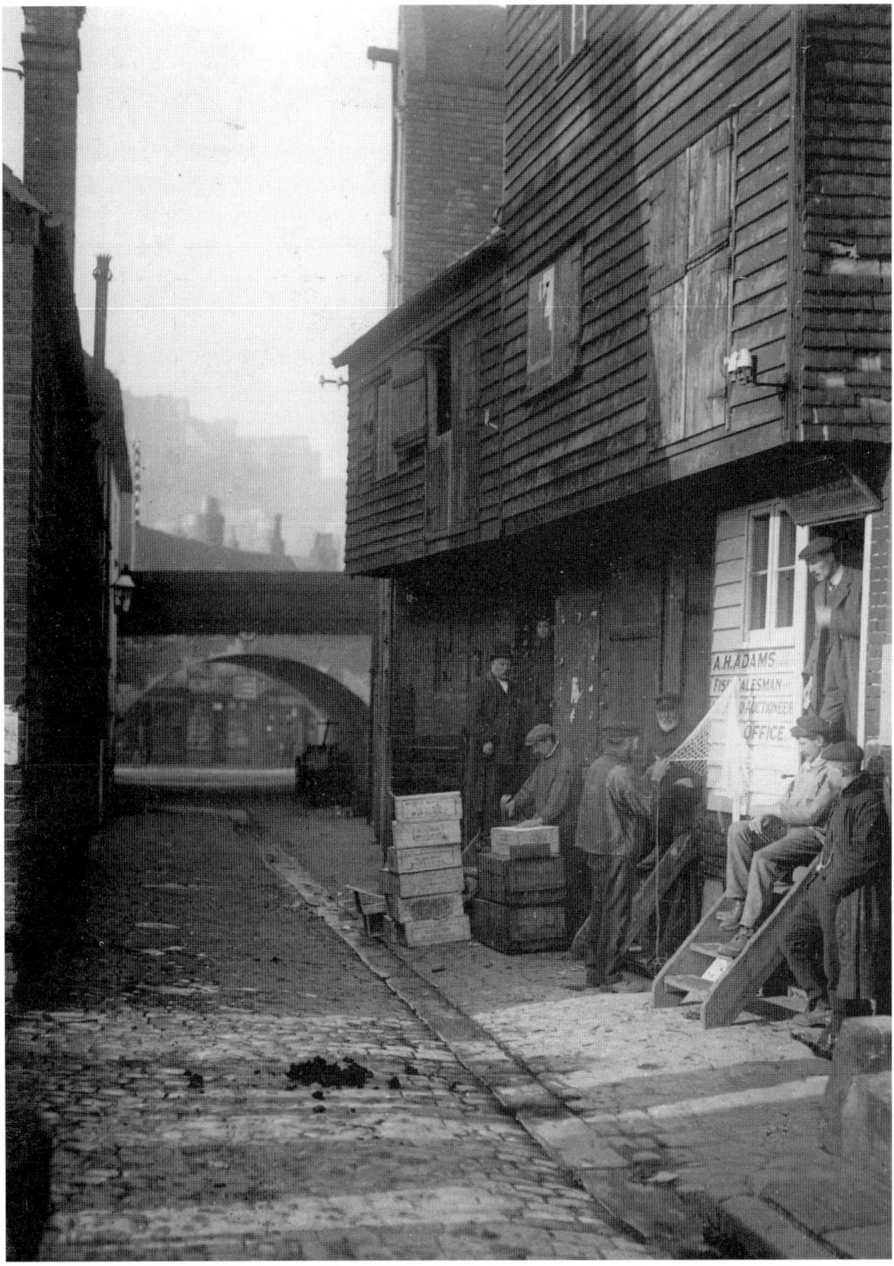

The Stade and weather-boarded buildings, 1920s. A number of people look on, including Mr Adams in his office doorway, while a fisherman makes a net and another man repairs fish boxes.

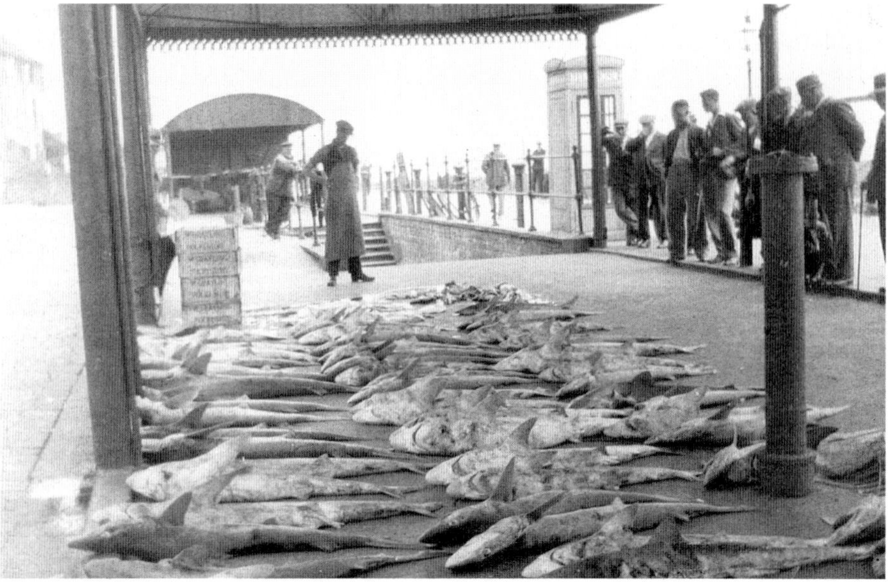

Fish sheds numbers two and three. Pairs of tope, locally known as rig, are laid out ready to sell. Beyond these are the market steps leading under an archway to a lower landing.

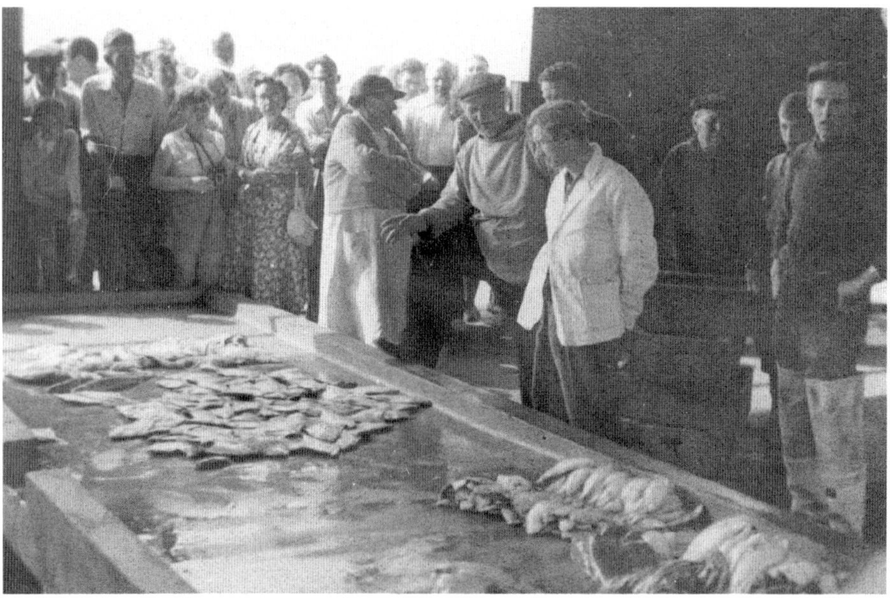

A fish auction being conducted in fish shed number one, *c.* 1956. Left to right: Mrs 'Lott' Waller (fish retailer), Mr 'Teddy' Fagg (selling the fish), Mr Ernie 'Skinny' Harris (fish retailer); behind him, Mr Henry Waller (fish retailer), Mr Joe 'Soldier Jack' Hopkins, Mr Bob Reed (boy) and Mr Val Noaks.

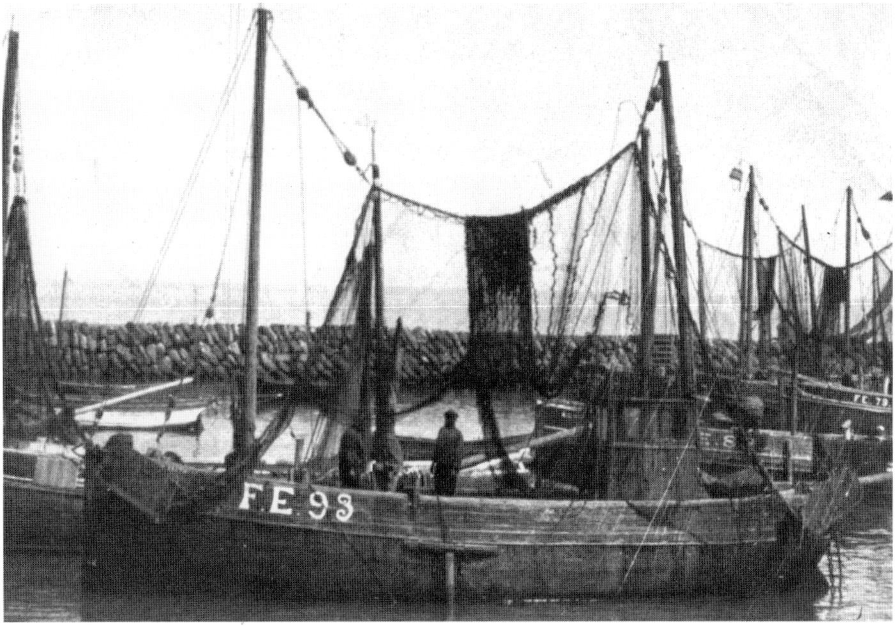

Three Brothers FE93 with her trawl-net hanging up to dry. The *Three Brothers* was built for Mr William Henry May at Mevagissey, Cornwall, in 1901. She is one of a very few sailing luggers that have survived and is now lying at Faversham after being restored to her original appearance.

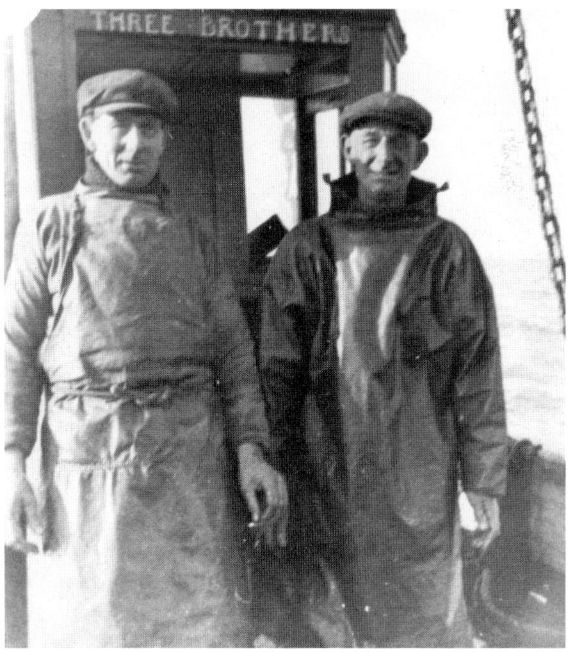

Mr Harry May (left) and Mr Bert May, sons of Mr William May, seen here in their oilskins aboard the *Three Brothers* just after the Second World War.

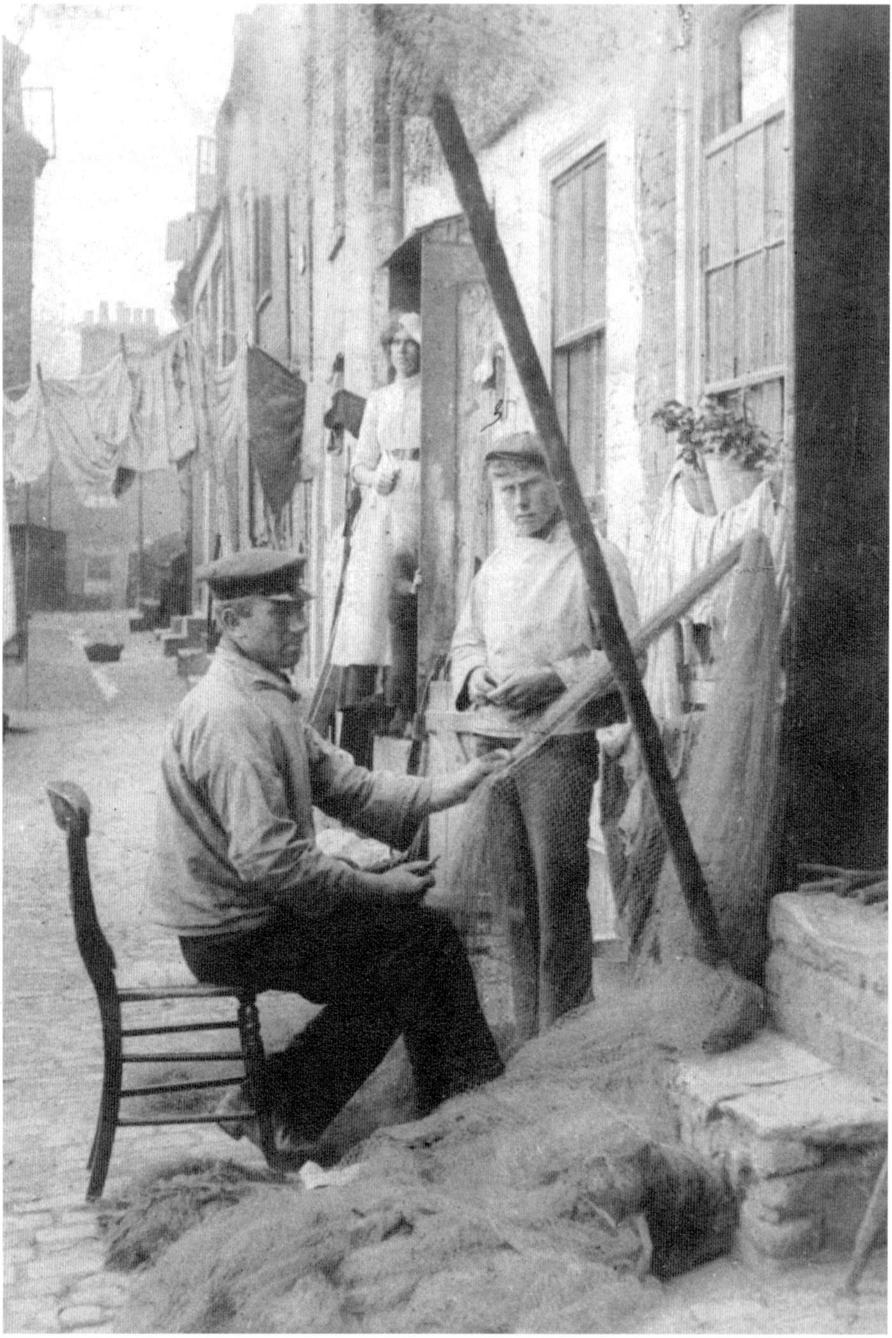

Old East Street, *c.* 1912. A fisherman is mending his herring or mackerel nets outside his house, while a fisherboy looks on.

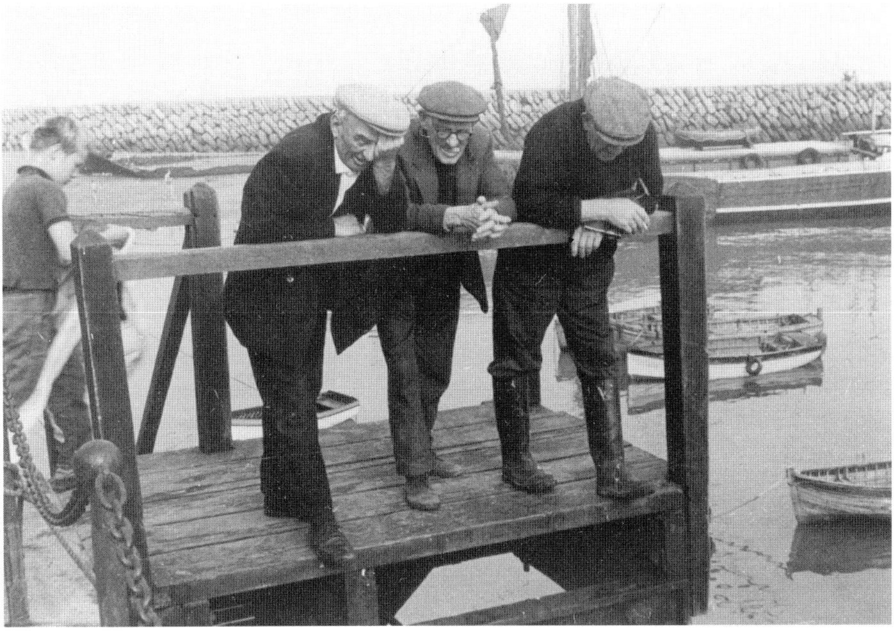

Three old fishermen leaning on the railing of the market steps, *c.* 1955. Left to right: Mr Jim Brickell, Mr Ernie 'Skinny' Harris and Mr Jim 'Bashie' Baker.

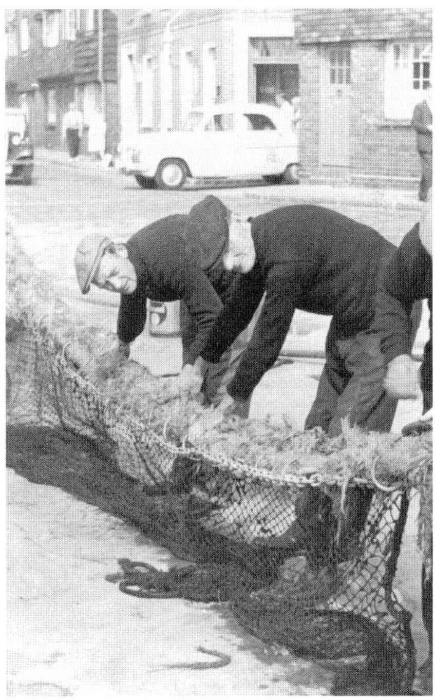

Many hours are spent ashore preparing fishing gear. Mr Charlie Petts (left) and Mr Frank Saunders, crew of FE93, are seen here tying a trawl-net into the ground rope in about 1956.

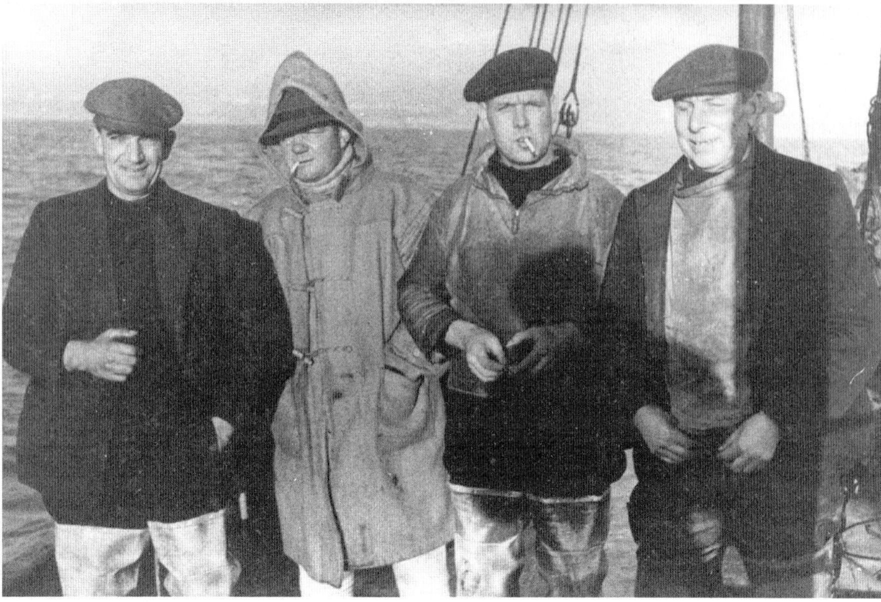

Some of the crew of the *Joan of Ark* FE15, seen here standing on her deck, mid-1950s. Left to right: Mr Jim 'Darky' Fagg (see p. 117), Mr Roland 'Fergy' Noble, Mr Stan 'Pommy' Heath, and Mr Joe 'Soldier Jack' Hopkins.

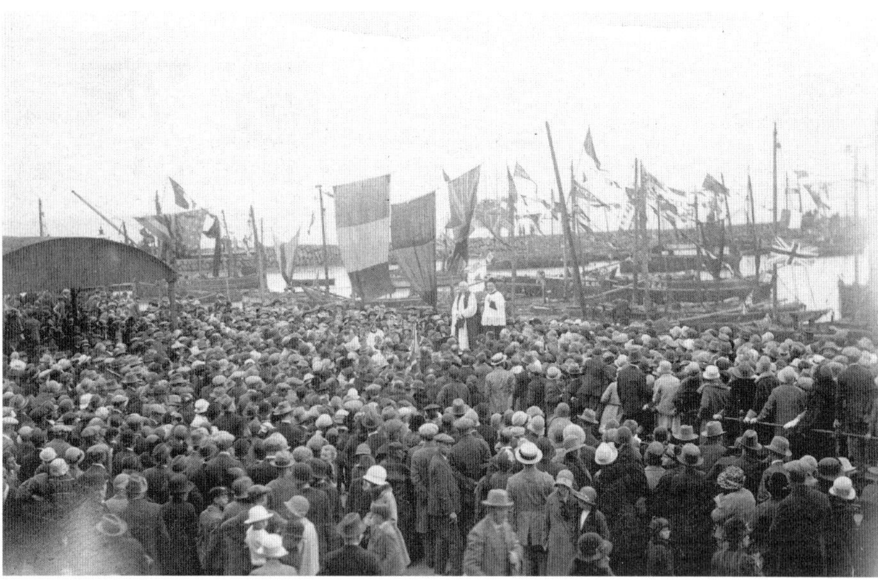

The annual event of the blessing of the fisheries, 1926. A large crowd is gathered on the Stade for the ceremony, conducted by the Bishop of Dover.

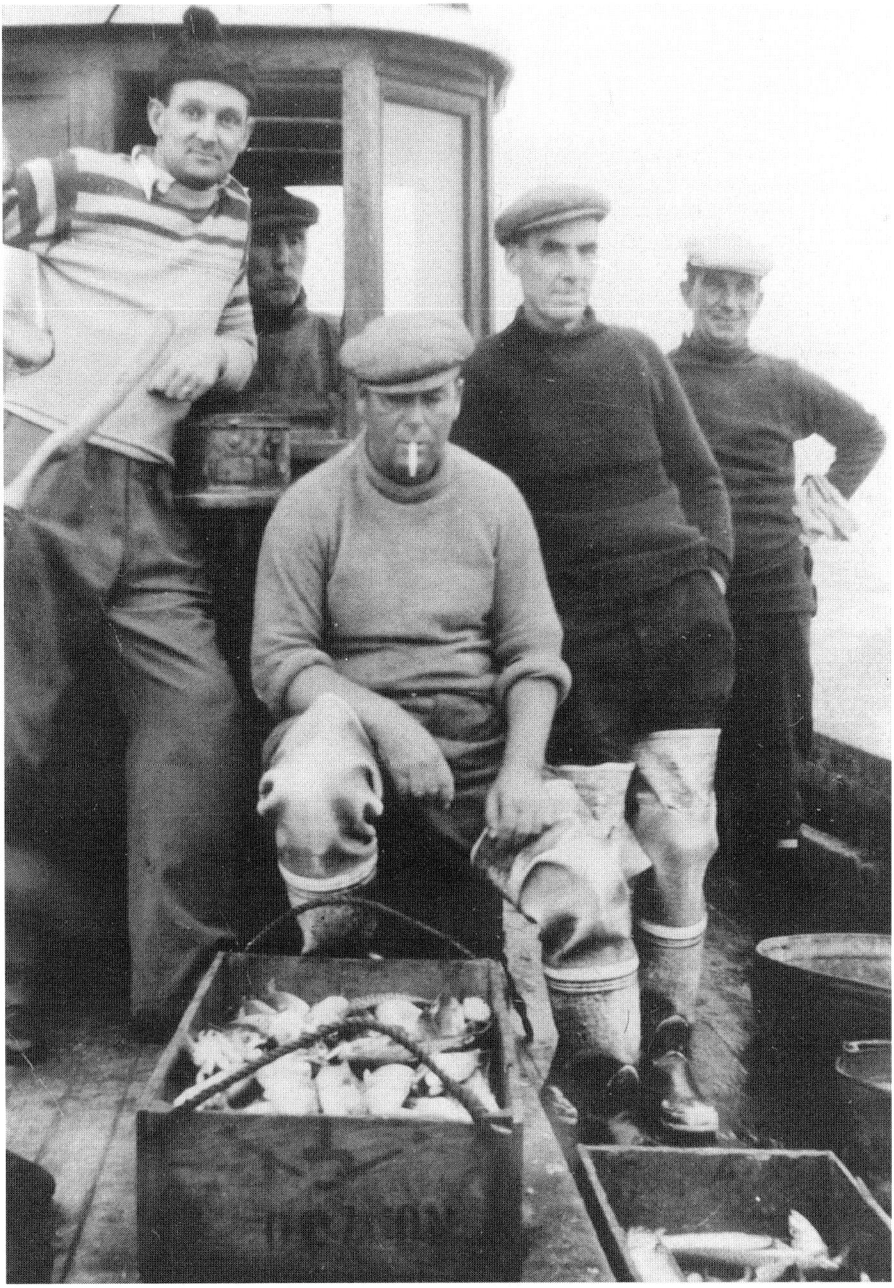

Some of the crew of the *Joan of Ark* FE15 with their catch of mackerel, 1958. Skipper Reg 'Knockout' Spicer is in the wheelhouse and outside are crew members Mr George Neal (sitting), Mr Dick Spearpoint and Mr Jim 'Darky' Fagg. The passenger on the left is Mr Harold Drury.

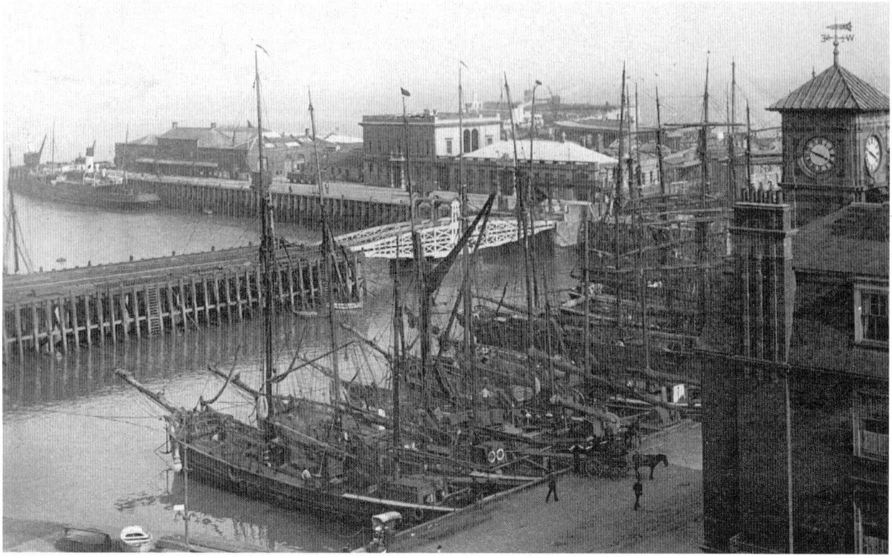

The inner and outer harbours, from the Bayle. The inner harbour is thronged with sailing ships unloading their cargoes. Most of these ships are moored stern to the quay, with a plank of wood from the ship to the shore used to walk on while carrying cargo ashore by hand.

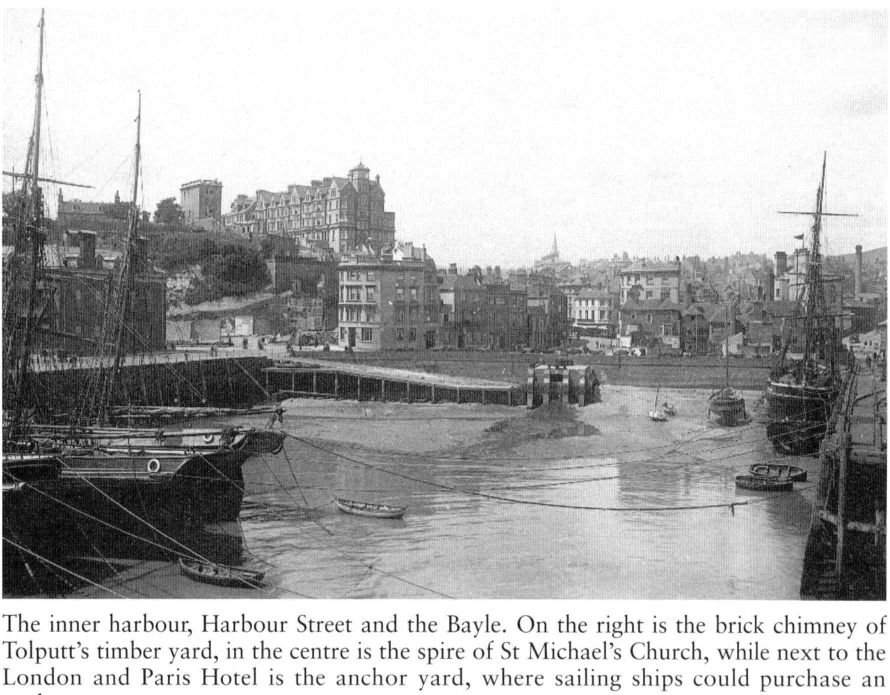

The inner harbour, Harbour Street and the Bayle. On the right is the brick chimney of Tolputt's timber yard, in the centre is the spire of St Michael's Church, while next to the London and Paris Hotel is the anchor yard, where sailing ships could purchase an anchor.

SECTION THREE

Seafront

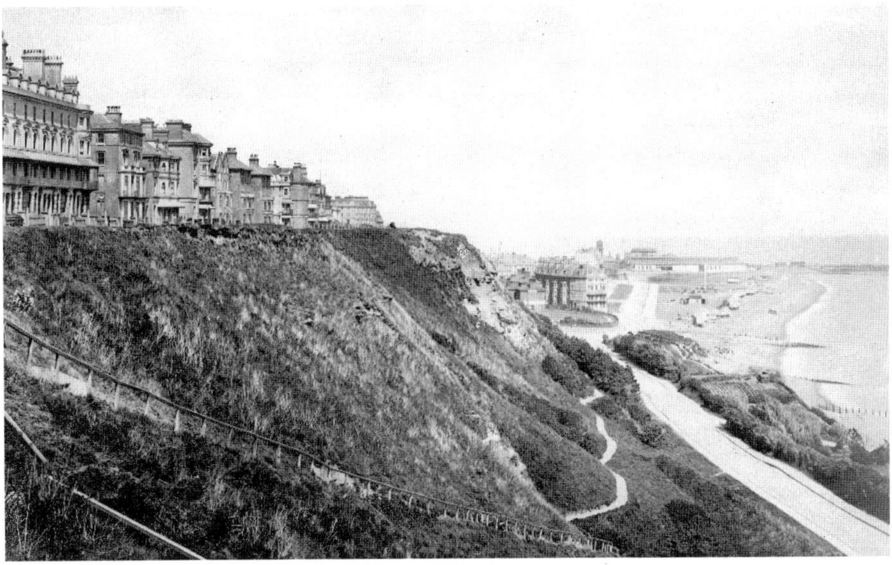

Lower Sandgate Road, the beach and harbour, 1882–3. The harbour station, built in 1850, and the first pier, or low-water landing as it was often called, built in 1860, are prominent features. Bathing wagons, too, are much in evidence.

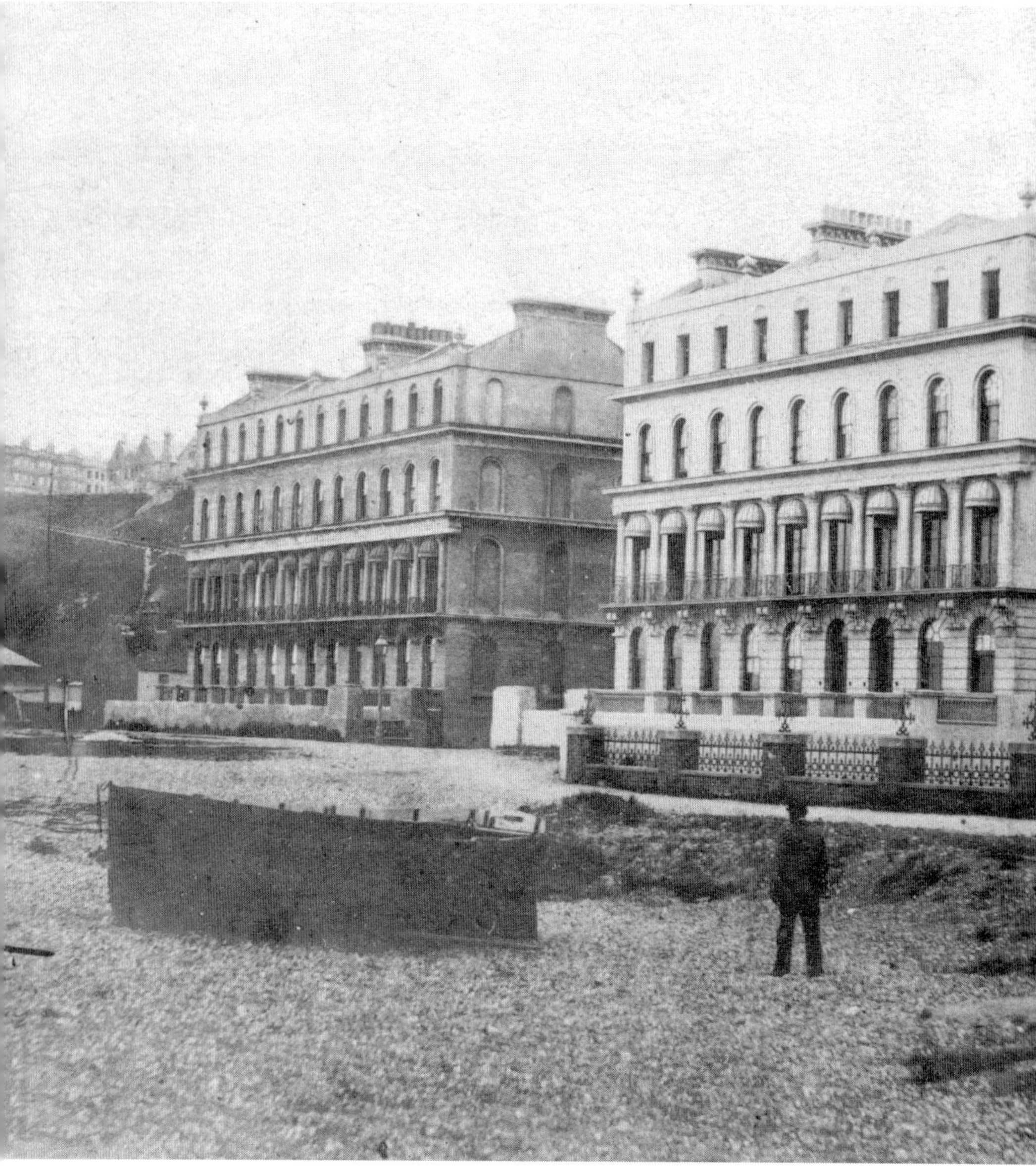

The foreshore and Marine Parade, taken from a stereograph, *c.* 1870. It is interesting to note that the area in front of Marine Parade has not been developed, the road has not been built and neither has the Marine Gardens, the latter being opened in June 1892.

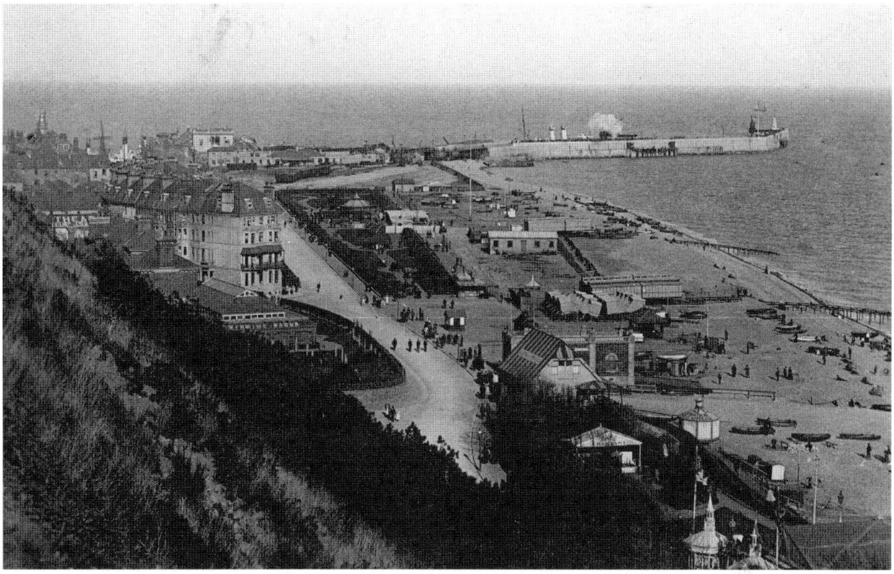

The beach, Marine Gardens and pier, *c.* 1909. In the middle foreground is the rowing clubhouse followed by the lifeboat house, some bathing wagons, Fagg's patent Bathing Machines, the Marine Gardens and the bandstand.

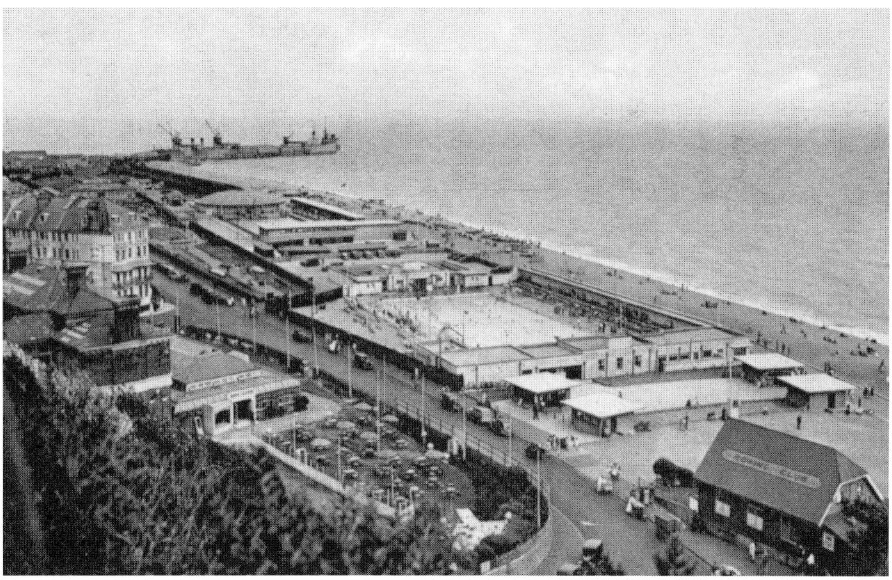

The beach, Marine Gardens and pier, *c.* 1947. Compare this with the above scene; it is taken after Lord Radnor's beach clean-up and development of 1936.

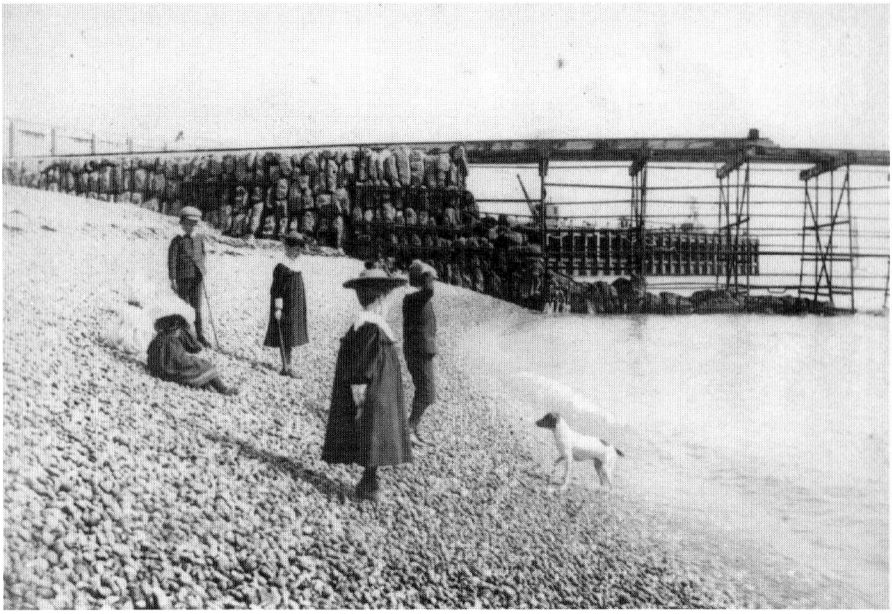

The pier before the extension of 1897–1904. In front of the pier is a rock groyne, built in 1844 from the south pier (outer harbour) straight out to sea. Its purpose was to stop the harbour mouth becoming blocked by shingle.

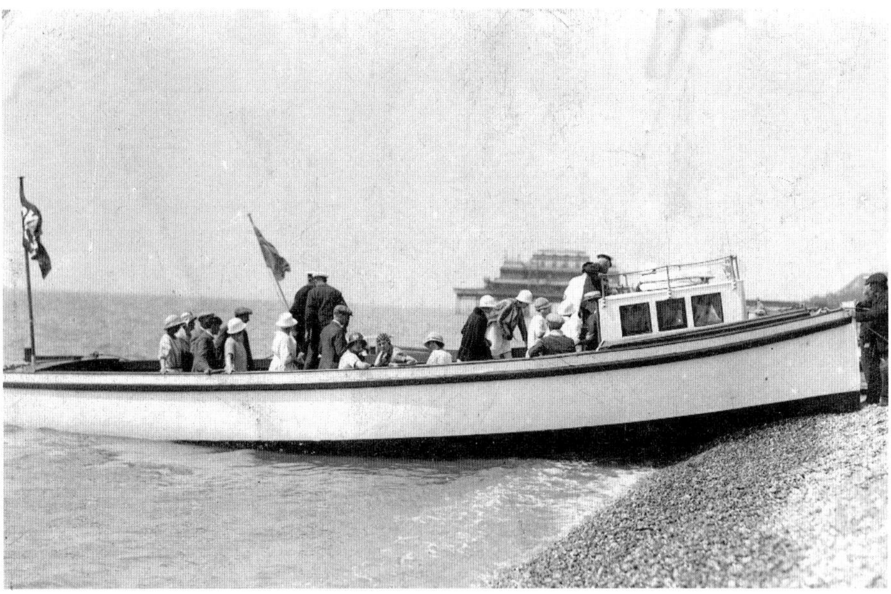

These were the days when one could take a boat trip around the bay. The *MV Josephine*, seen here discharging her passengers, is one of the many boats plying for hire in the 1930s.

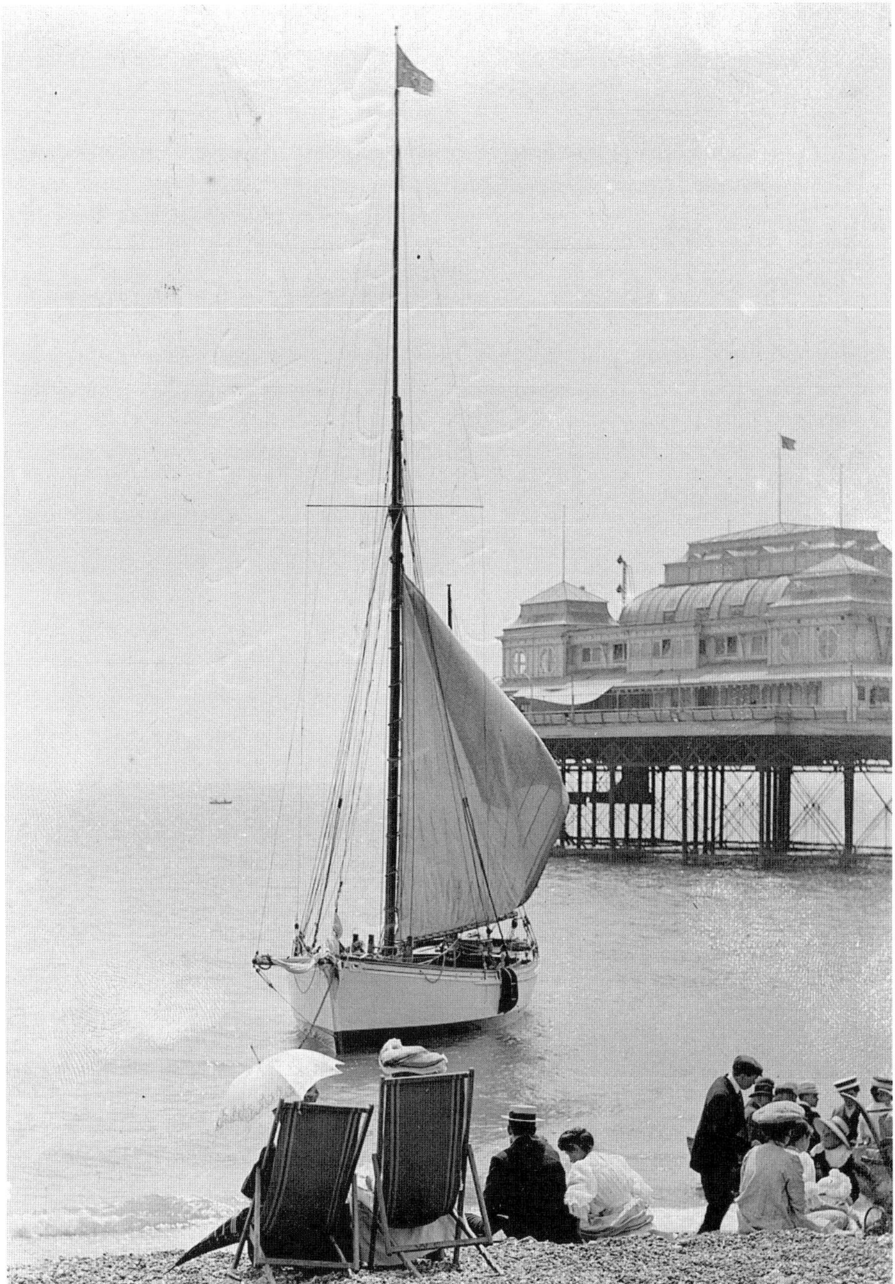

Before the advent of motor boats one could take a trip round the bay in one of two pleasure yachts, the *Maisie* or the *Gertie*. The latter is seen here anchored off the beach waiting for her passengers; they were ferried from the beach by rowing-boat.

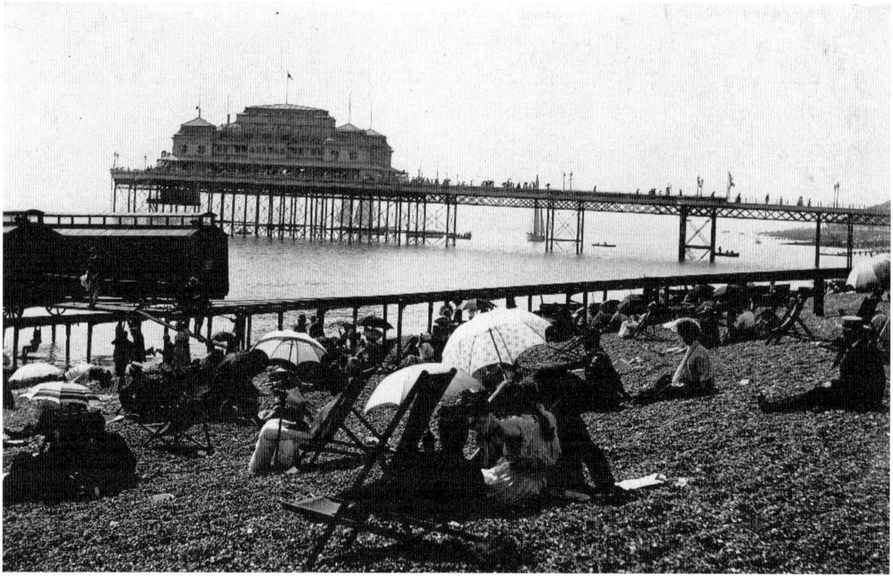

The Victoria Pier and Fagg's Patent Bathing Machines. In the days when changing on the beach was not allowed, people used changing tents, or, for those who were better off, these bathing machines.

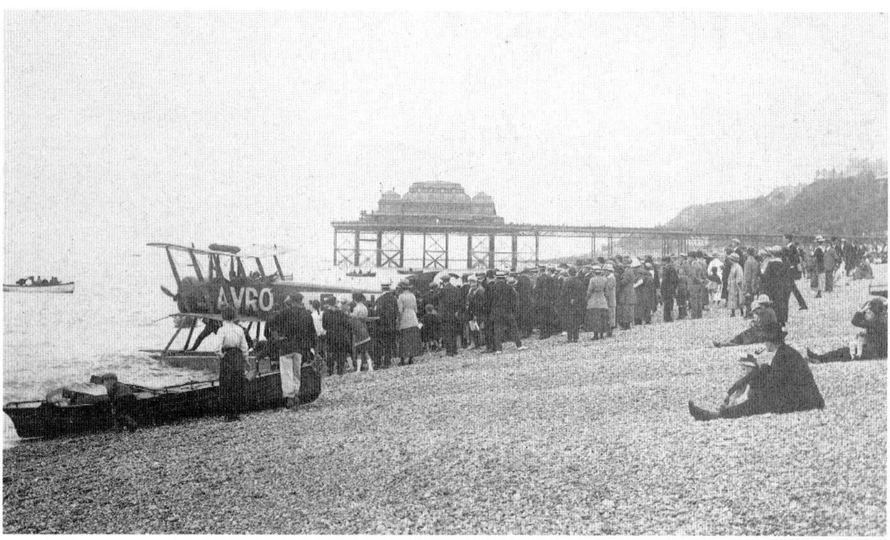

Crowds round a light aeroplane on the beach. The aeroplane gave sky trips from Lympne aerodrome.

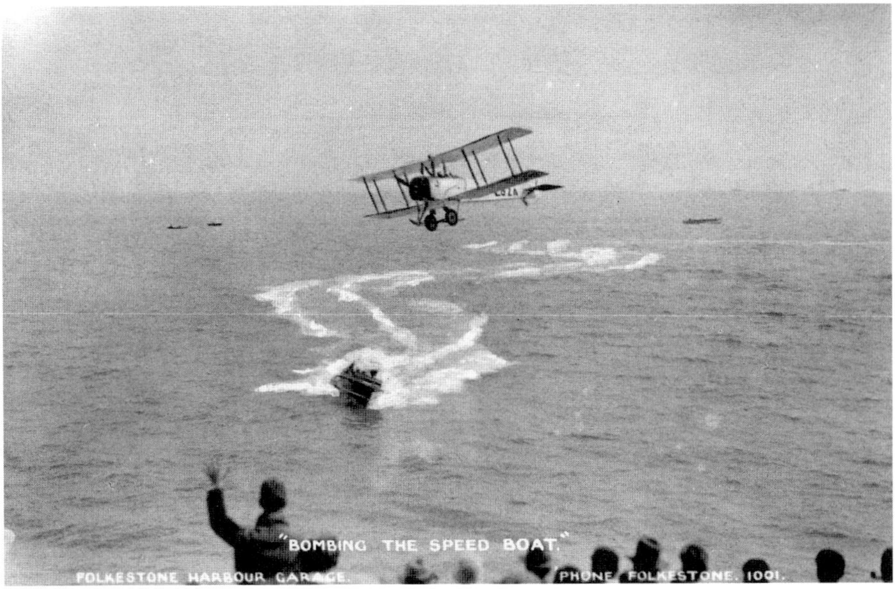

A display arranged at regular intervals during the summer by Mr Savery who owned the speedboat. The light aeroplane, in which sky trips were given, would try to bomb the speedboat with ½ lb bags of flour. Because of the manoeuvrability of the boat, direct hits were almost impossible, unless the skipper deliberately slowed down.

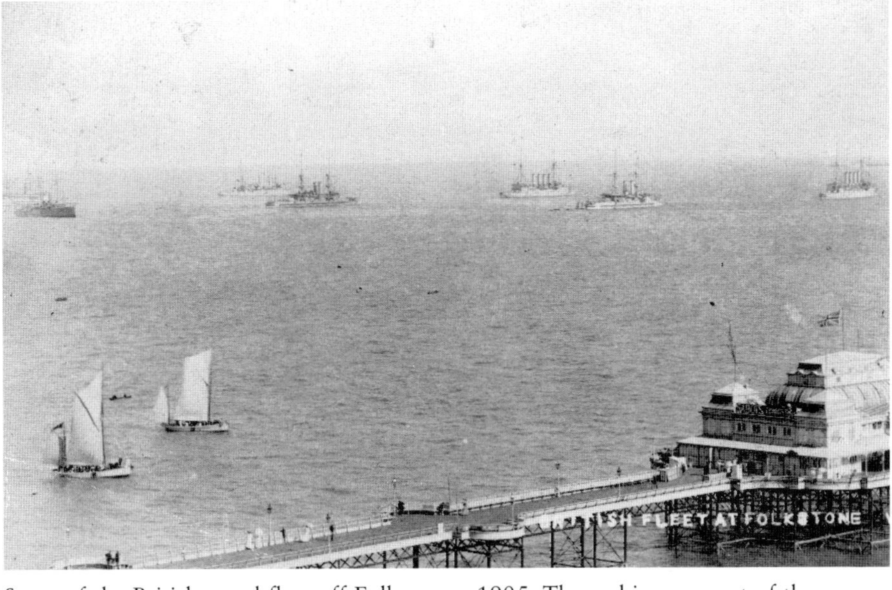

Some of the British naval fleet off Folkestone, 1905. These ships are part of the reserve squadron consisting of three battleships and six cruisers. The two with four funnels are the *Terrible* and the *Powerful*.

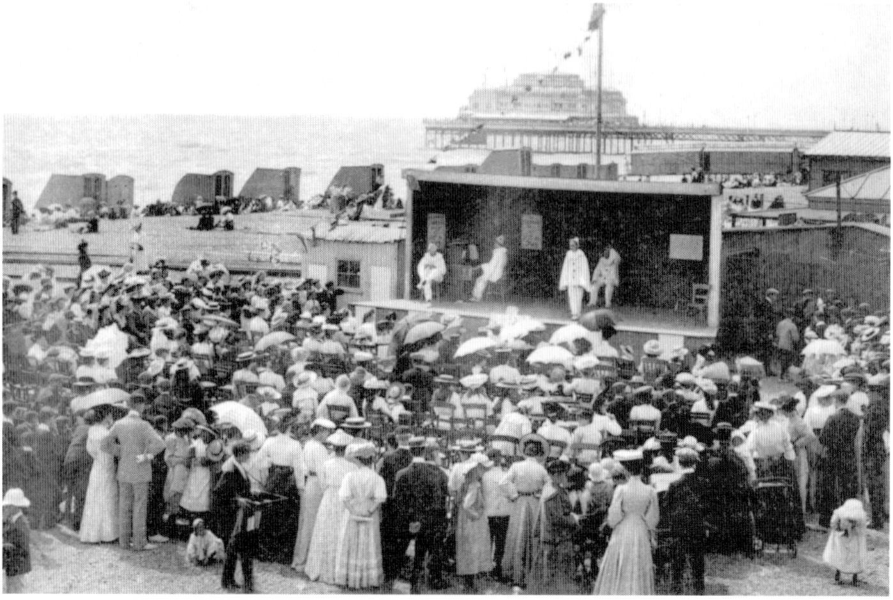

The days when most seaside towns had open-air concerts. A large crowd is on the beach watching the pierrots.

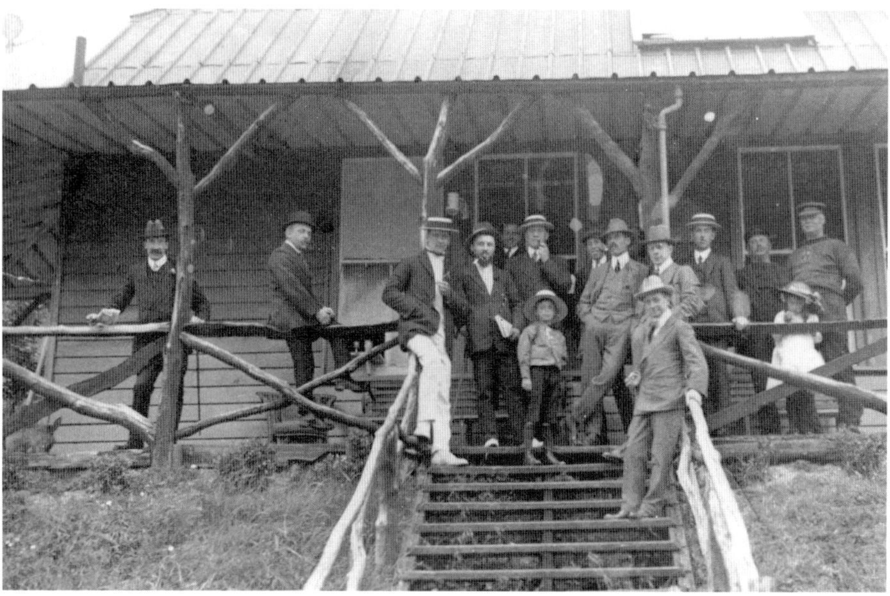

Club members and boatmen outside the Folkestone rowing club. The club was formed on 15 May 1874. This clubhouse was built in 1884, where the club remained until 1946 when it moved to Sandgate (see p. 73 for location of clubhouse).

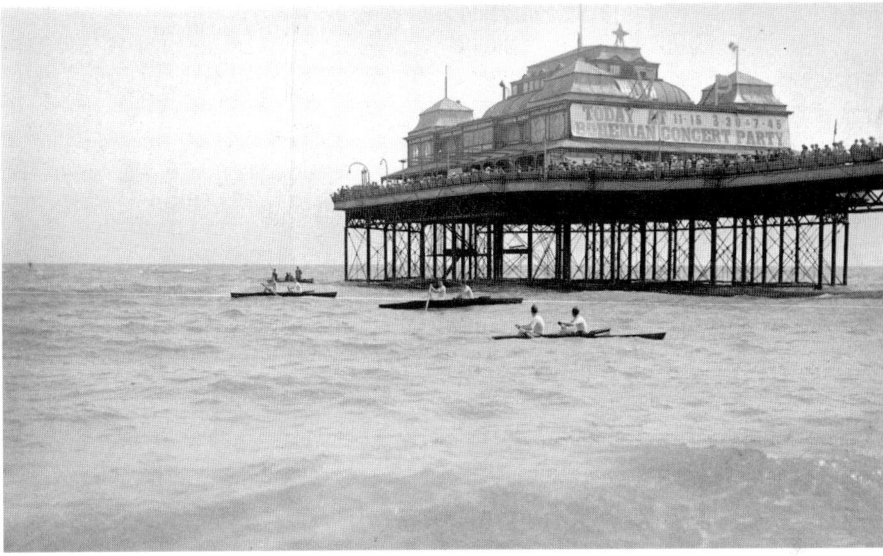

Regatta day, 1920s. The Victoria Pier is thronged with people watching the rowing. It would appear that the doubles are about to start their race.

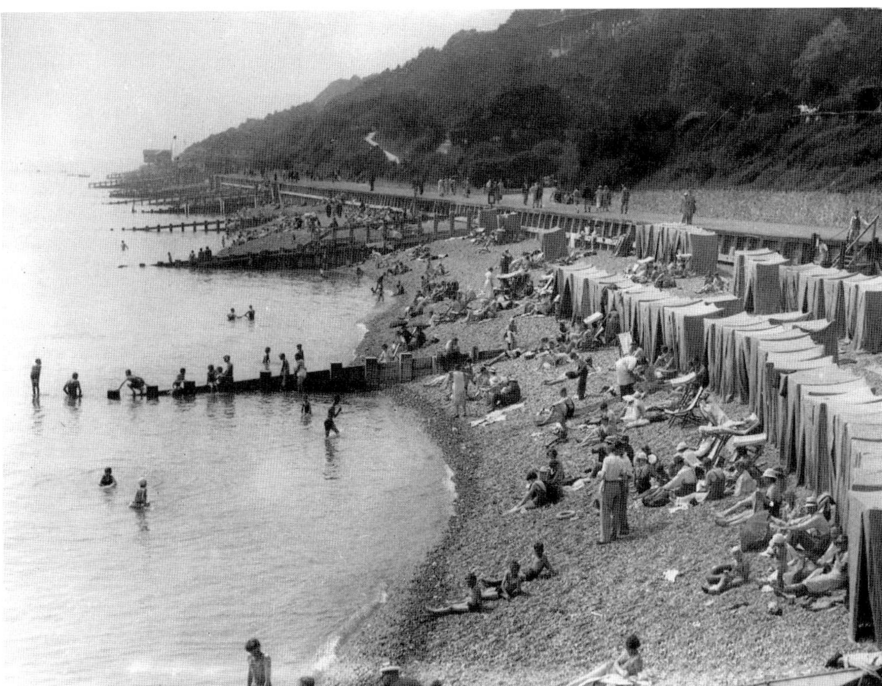

The Marine Walk and beach, 1930s. Before the Second World War changing on the beach was not permitted, so changing tents were provided, as seen here.

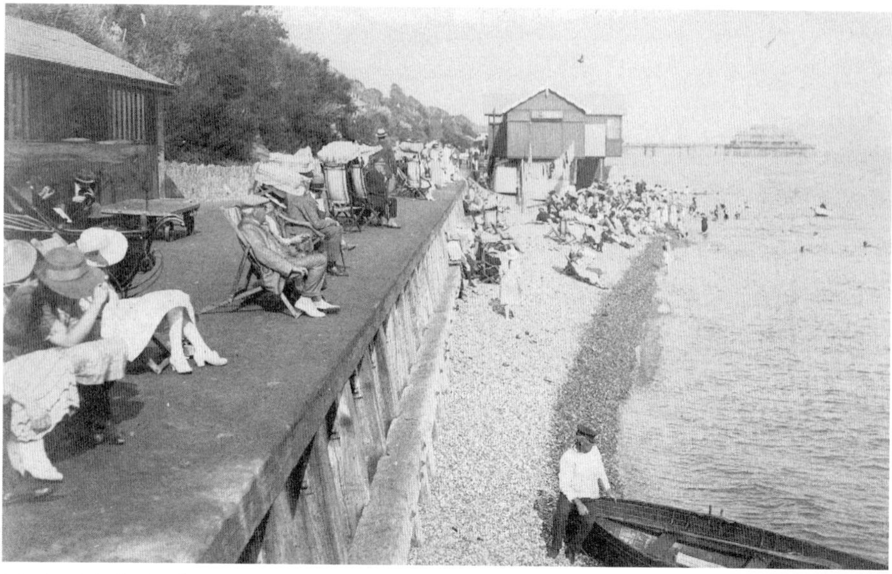

Marine Walk, looking towards the Victoria Pier. Some people are relaxing in their deckchairs while some are on the beach. The boatman in the foreground, who looks after the bathers, takes time out for his break.

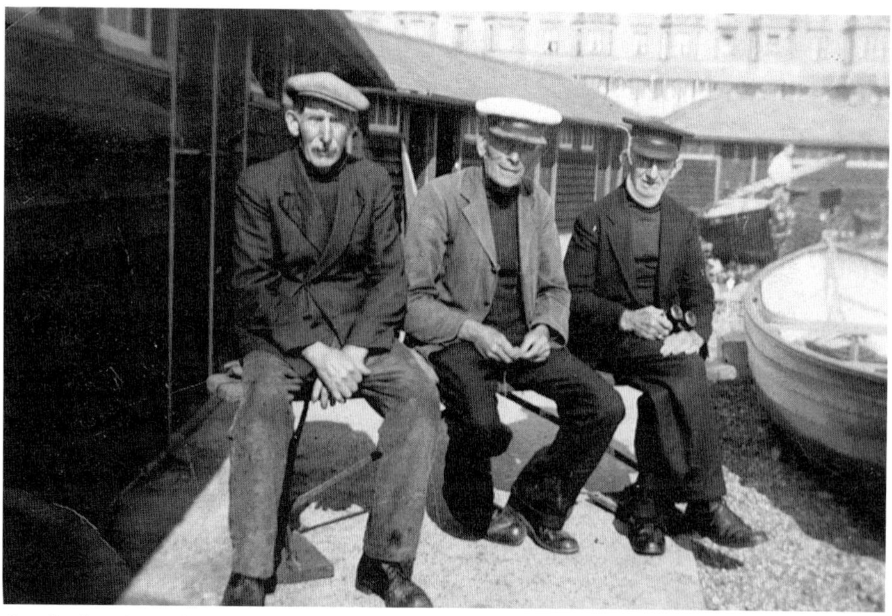

On the beach in the horseshoe of boatman's huts. The three boatmen are, from left to right: Mr 'Pin' Carter, Mr Steve 'Redun' Fagg (beach inspector) and Mr 'Jacko' Fagg.

SECTION FOUR

Lifeboats and Shipwrecks

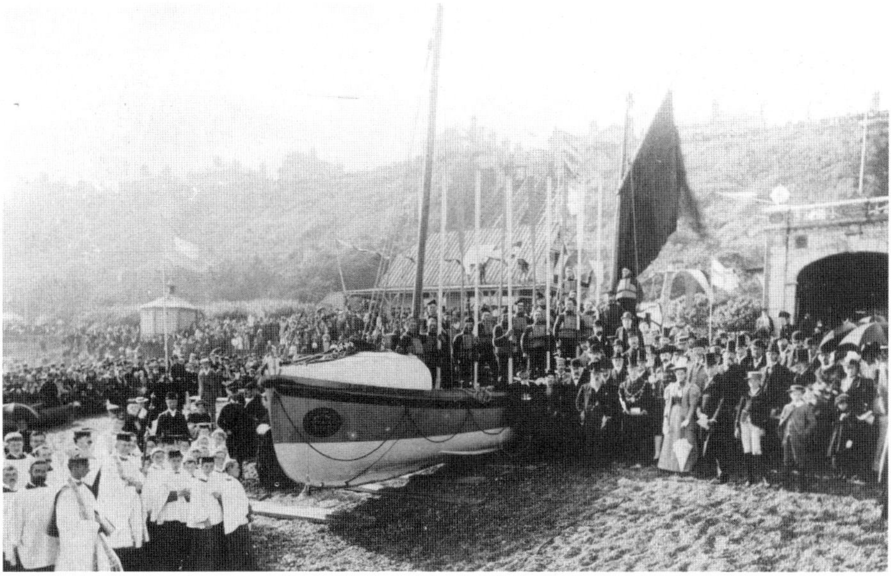

The inauguration of the lifeboat establishment on 25 July 1894. The mayor and invited guests are on the right of the lifeboat *J. McConnell Hussey*. The vicar of Folkestone with his curates, the organist and choir are stationed at the bow of the boat and the corporation and officials are gathered around her. After the speeches, at a given signal, the rope was loosened and the boat glided smoothly into the waves amid ringing cheers.

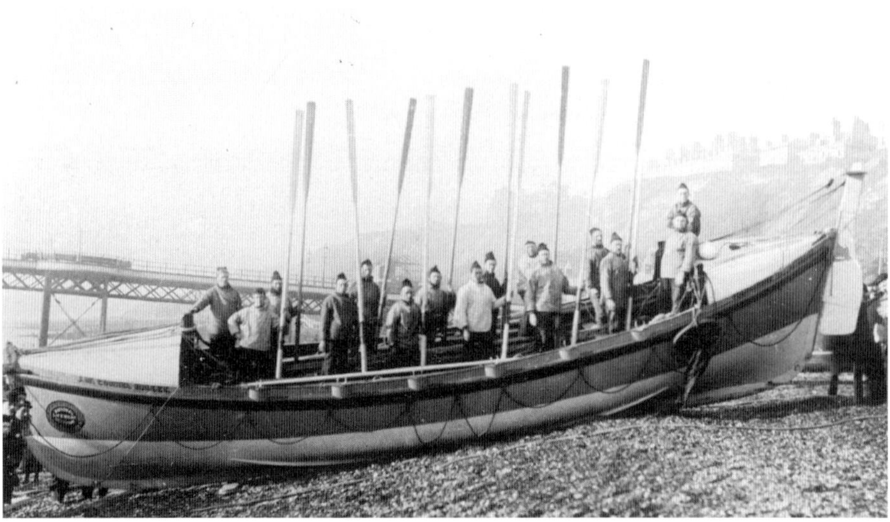

The lifeboat *J. McConnell Hussey* and crew with tossed oars. The boat was 38 ft long, 8 ft wide and rowed twelve oars double banked. The cost of the boat, carriage and equipment was £900 and was defrayed by Miss Curling of Denmark Hill, London. As desired by her the boat was named the *J. McConnell Hussey*. She was stationed at Folkestone from December 1893 to March 1903.

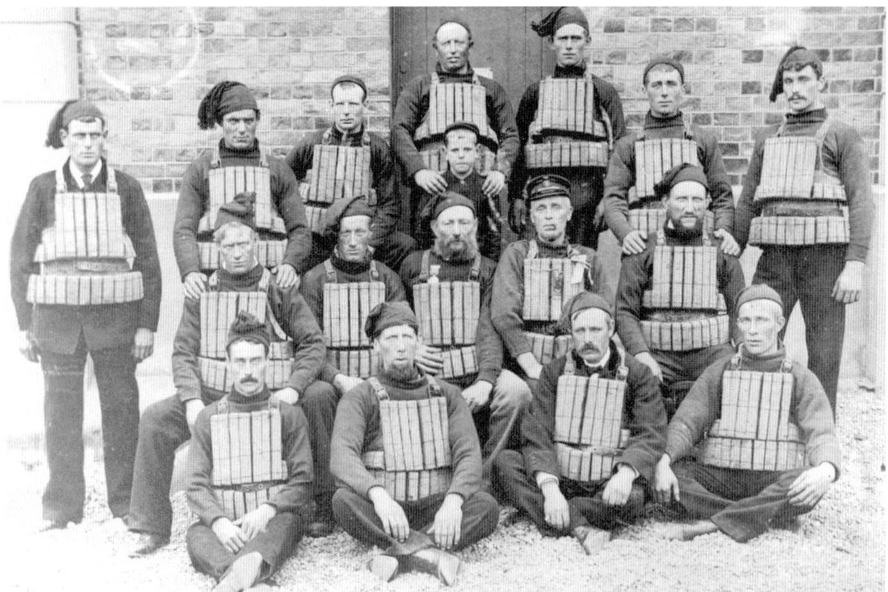

The Folkestone lifeboat crew, made up of volunteer fishermen. Note the early type of lifejackets made of cork. The crew's woollen hats are red. Front row, first on left: Mr Milton. Second row, fourth from left: Stephen Cook (coxswain from 1897 to 1919). Third row, second from left: Mr Fagg.

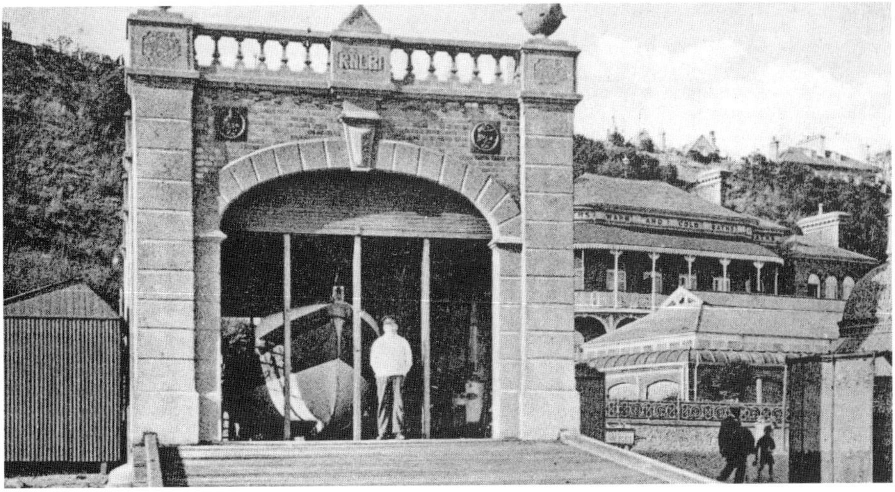

The lifeboat house. Tenders were received in July 1892 from eight local builders and the tender from Hayward & Paramor for £659 was accepted. The lifeboat-house keeper is Mr John Foad.

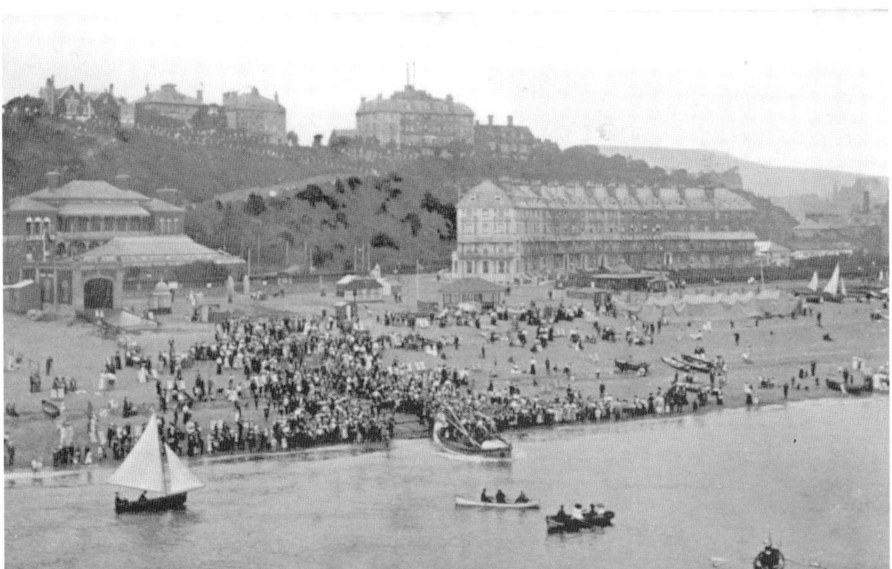

A lifeboat launch, 1912. Crowds look on as the lifeboat enters the water. A maroon was set off to alert the lifeboat crew; it also attracted many people in the locality.

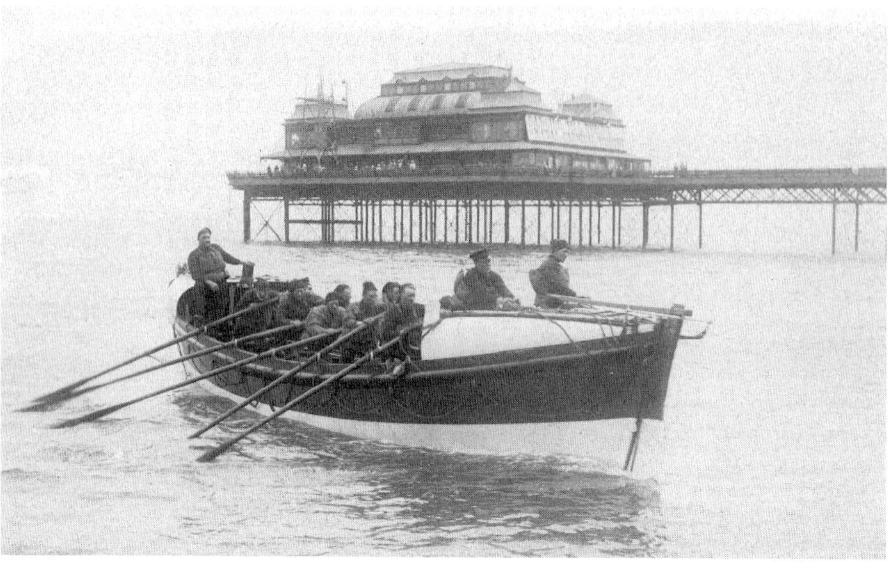

Folkestone's second lifeboat, the *Leslie.* The *Leslie* was in service at Folkestone from March 1903 to October 1930. She has just been launched and the crew have shipped their oars and started to row out to sea. The coxswain is Mr William Baker.

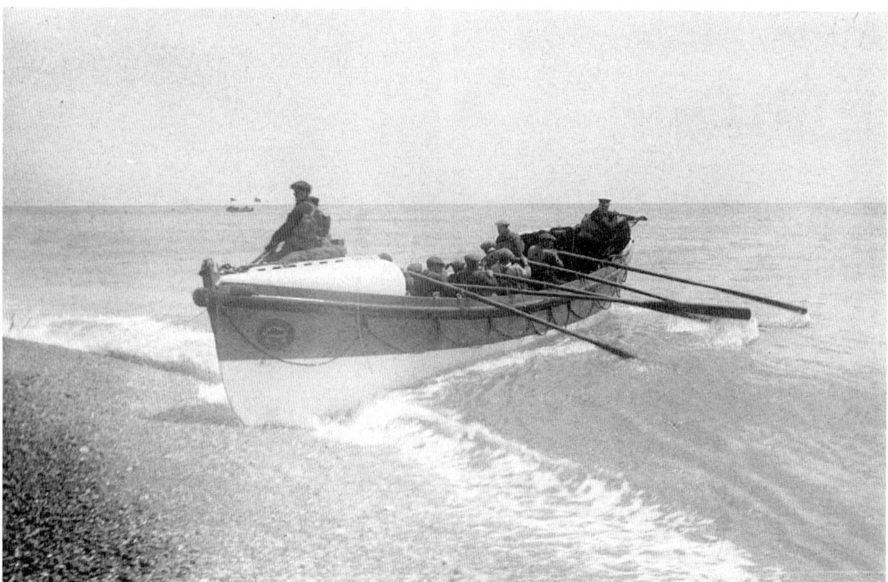

The lifeboat *Leslie* seen here coming ashore. The crew member at the front of the boat is the bowman. It is his job to get the rope ashore to haul the lifeboat up the beach.

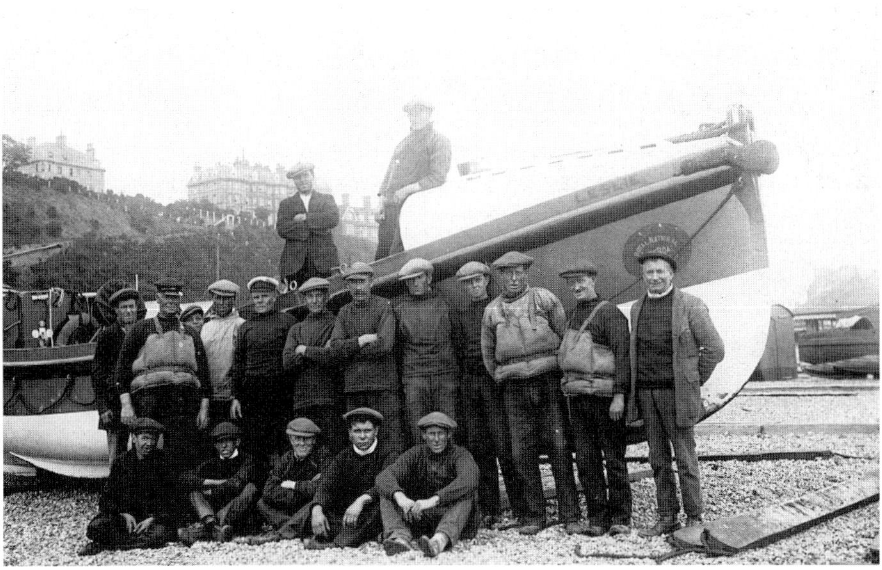

The lifeboat crew by the *Leslie*, 1925. Among the crew members are Mr Jack Tumber, Mr William Baker (coxswain), Mr Fred Pegden, Mr Bob Featherbee, and Mr Albert 'Nobby' Taylor.

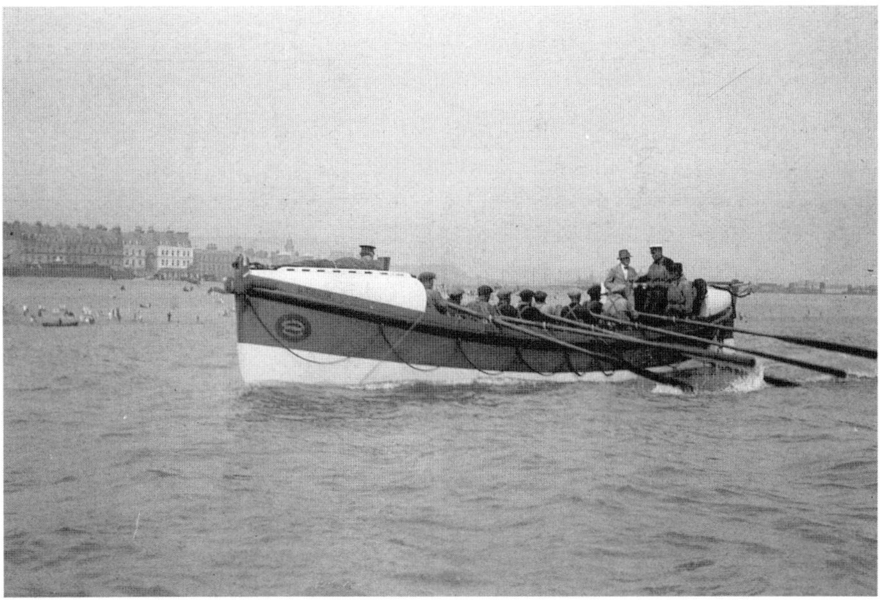

The lifeboat *Leslie* at sea. Each year the lifeboat had four practice launches. The gentleman in the stern, wearing a trilby hat, is the inspector from the RNLI.

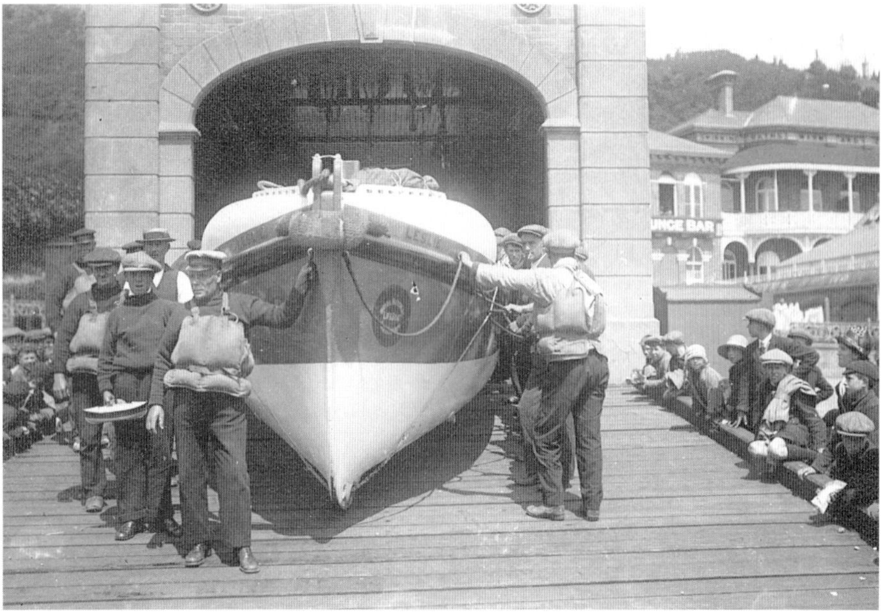

The lifeboat *Leslie* on the slipway outside the lifeboat house. In the left foreground is the coxswain, Mr William Baker. He was coxswain from 1919 until the station closed in October 1930.

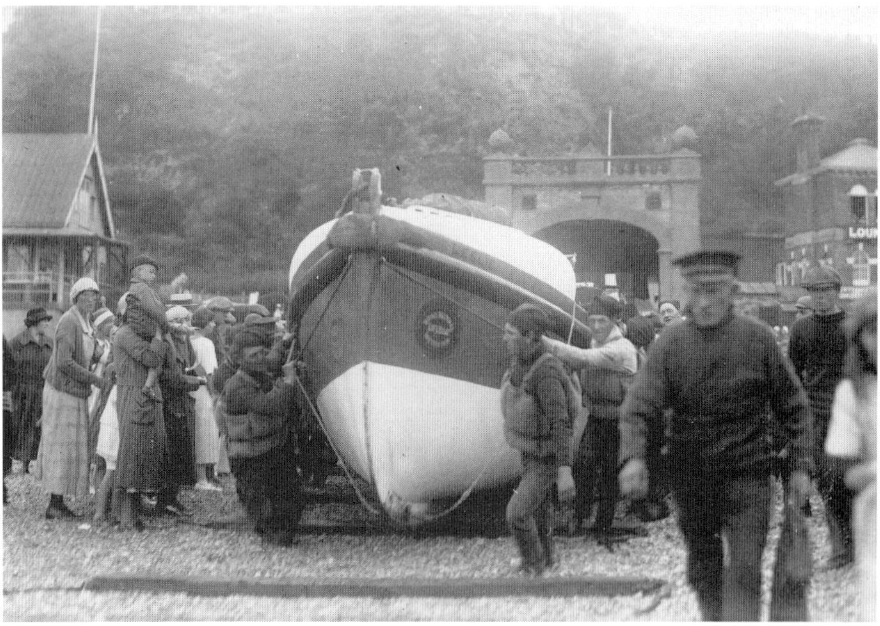

Preparing to launch the lifeboat *Leslie*. Launching the lifeboat was a hard and tiring job. It was pulled down the beach by hand on greased boards.

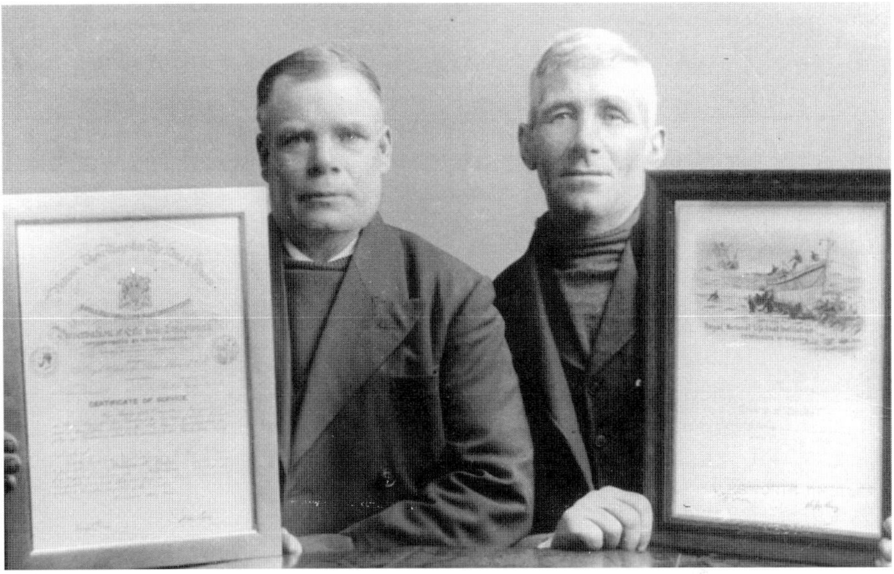

On 7 March 1931 the local committee of the RNLI gave a supper at the Clarendon Hotel for the crew of the Folkestone lifeboat. The chairman, Mr F. Scarborough, presented a certificate of service, the highest award of the RNLI, to Mr William Baker (left), retiring coxswain, for his eleven years service; he also gave a certificate to Mr Richard Cornish for his four years as second coxswain.

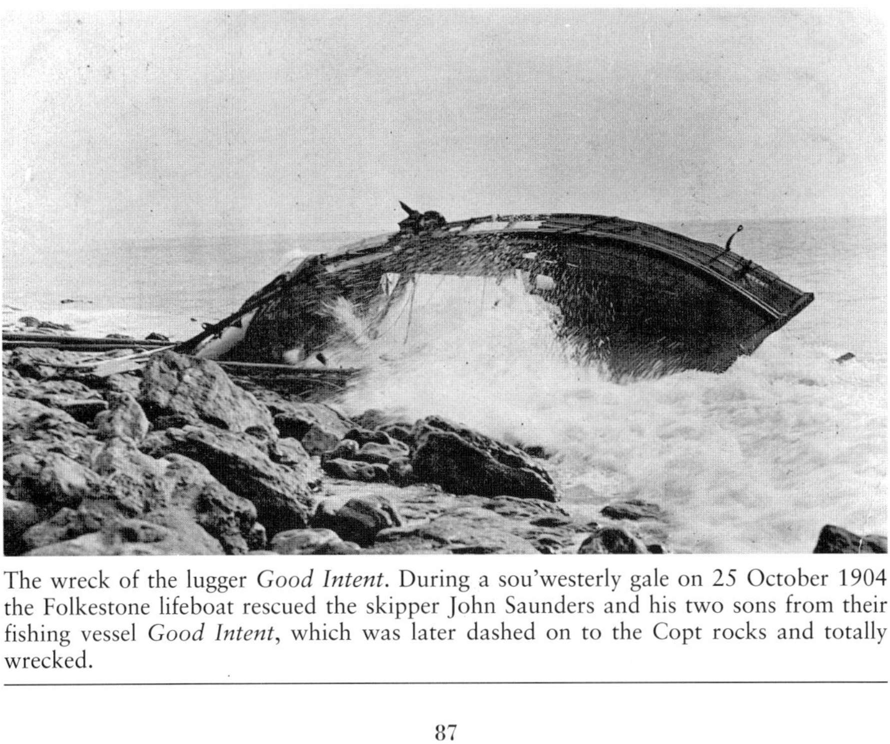

The wreck of the lugger *Good Intent*. During a sou'westerly gale on 25 October 1904 the Folkestone lifeboat rescued the skipper John Saunders and his two sons from their fishing vessel *Good Intent*, which was later dashed on to the Copt rocks and totally wrecked.

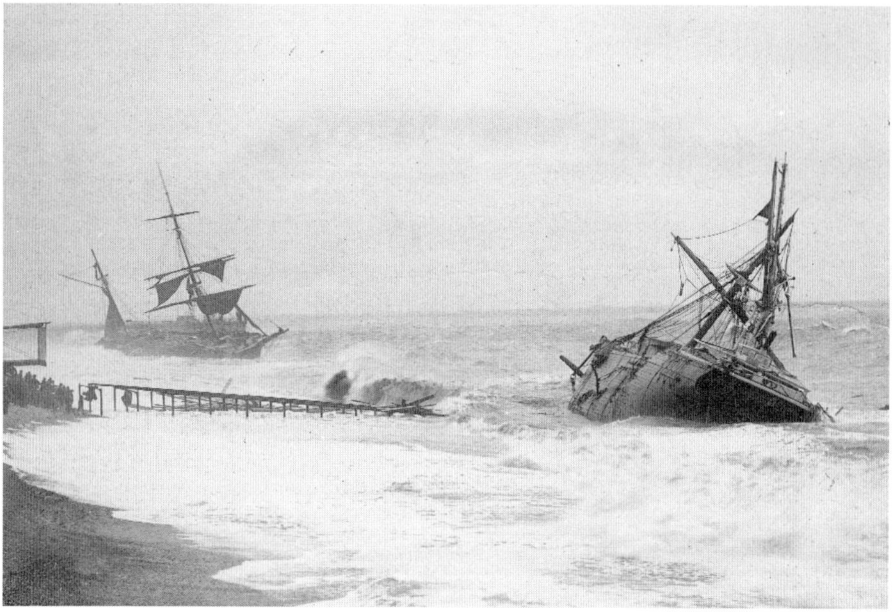

During a gale on 25 September 1896 the Norwegian barques *Baron Hoburg* and *Adger* were wrecked on Folkestone beach. Crew members from both vessels were rescued either by lifeline or by the Folkestone lifeboat.

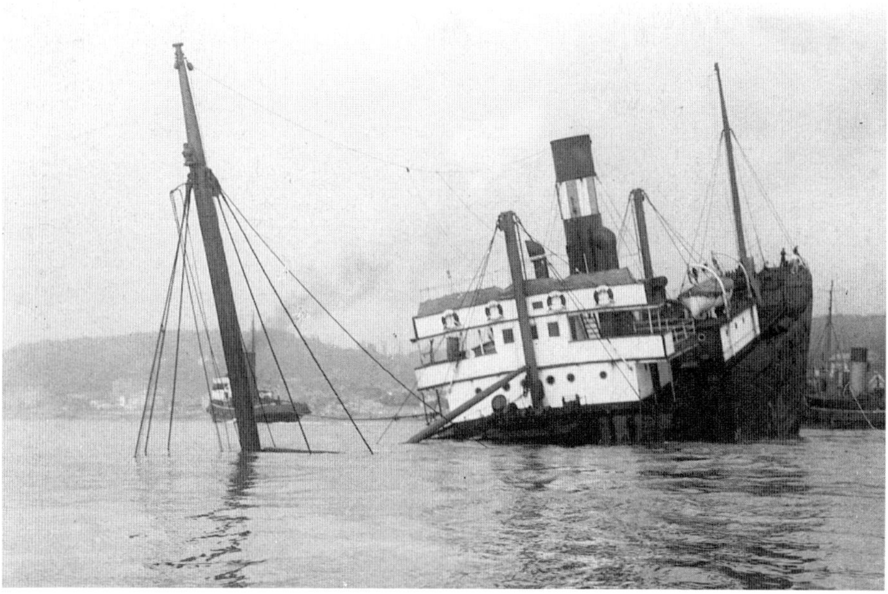

The French steamer *Cassard*. On 3 September 1926 the *Cassard* was in collision, in thick fog off Sandgate, with the steamship *Kurdistan*. The Dover tugs *Lady Brassey* and *Lady Duncannon* went to their assistance.

SECTION FIVE

The Leas

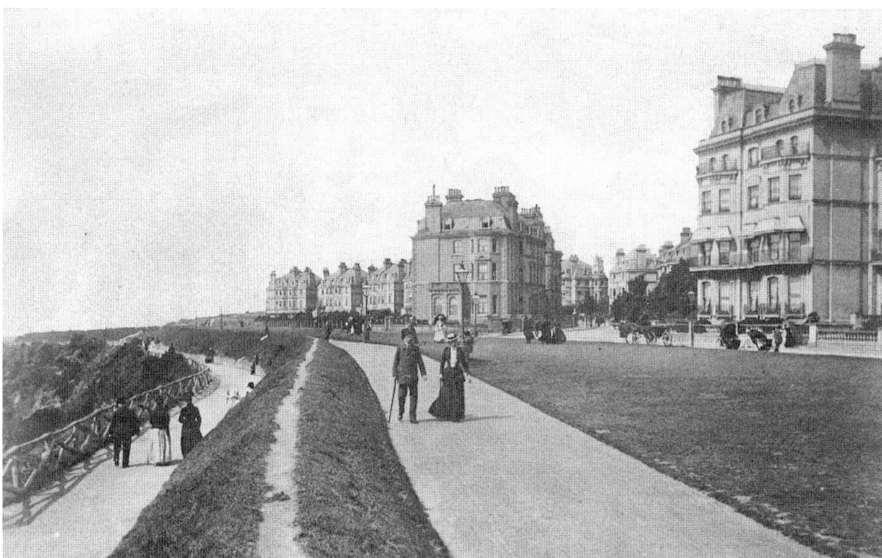

The west end of the Leas, Clifton Crescent and Madeira Walk, *c.* 1895. The building on the right is now the Salisbury Hotel, followed by Clifton Crescent. The lower path is Madeira Walk, originally a muddy footpath known as Cow Path, because Mr Clout's cows were daily driven along it. They went to and fro from his little farm, near the site of Trinity Church, to graze the undercliff.

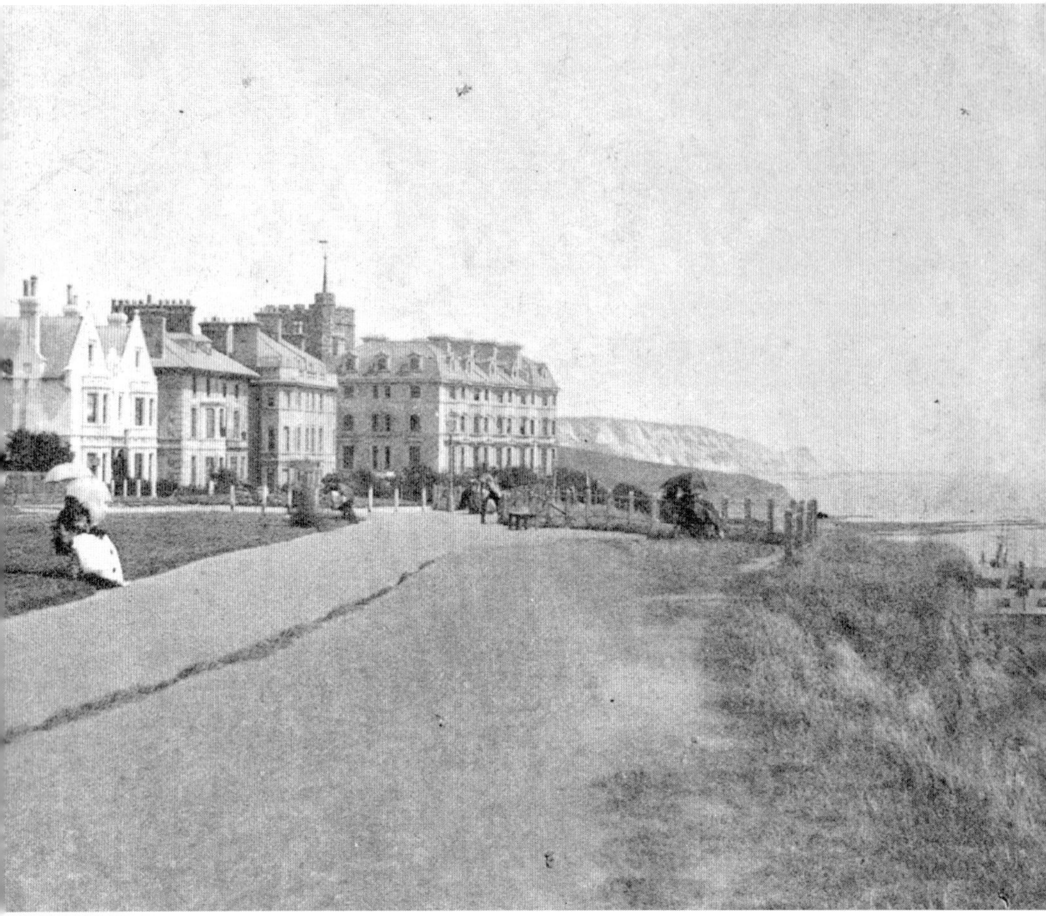

The east end of the Leas, taken from a stereograph, 1860s. 'Leas' is a Kentish dialect word meaning 'a common, or open space of pasture'. The buildings to the left are Albion Villas, followed by the Priory Gardens. The tower of the parish church of St Mary and St Eanswythe can be seen peeping over the rooftops. It is interesting to note that the edge of the Leas is not fenced off: this only occurs at the top of the Road of Remembrance, formerly the Slope Road.

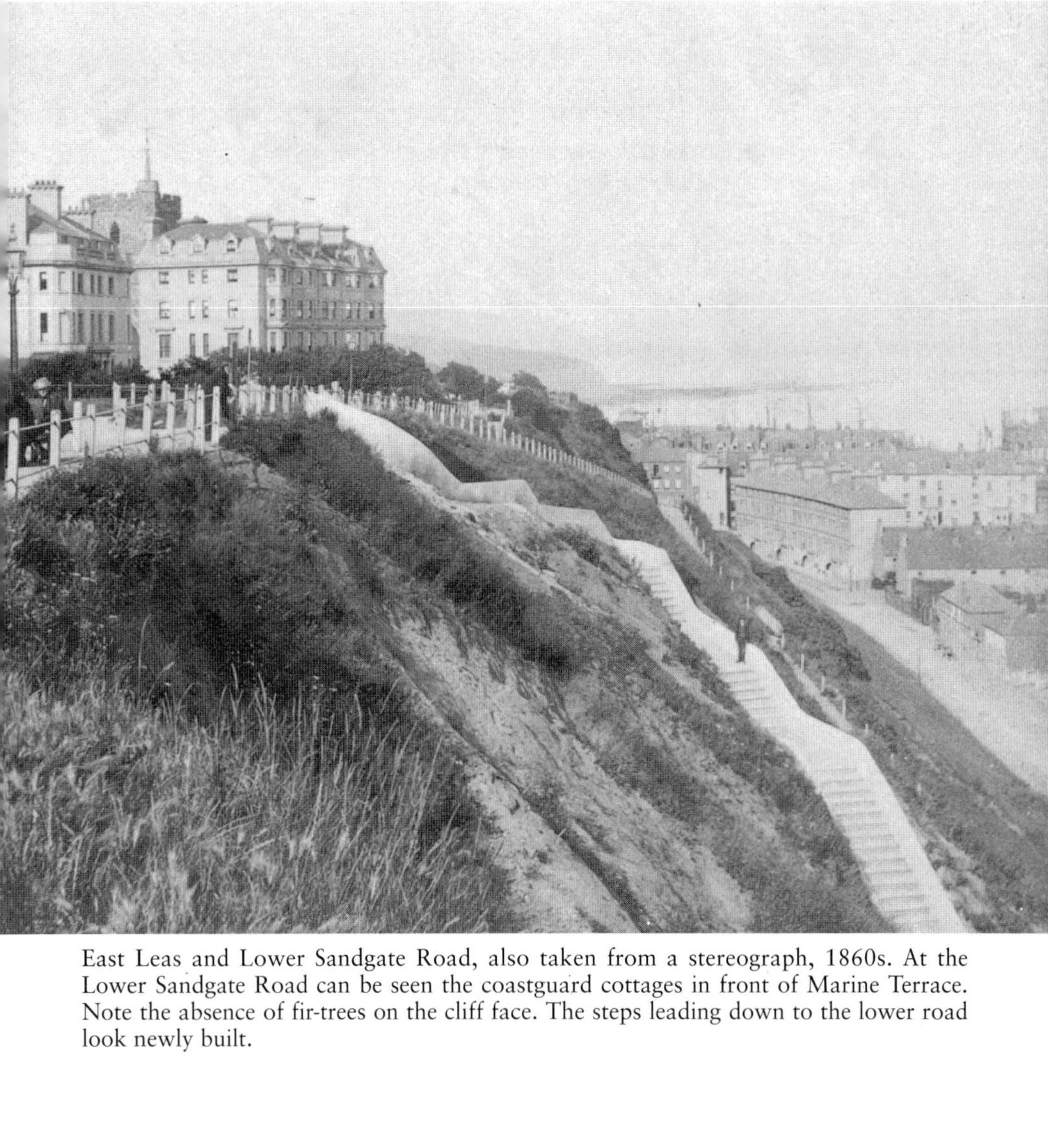

East Leas and Lower Sandgate Road, also taken from a stereograph, 1860s. At the Lower Sandgate Road can be seen the coastguard cottages in front of Marine Terrace. Note the absence of fir-trees on the cliff face. The steps leading down to the lower road look newly built.

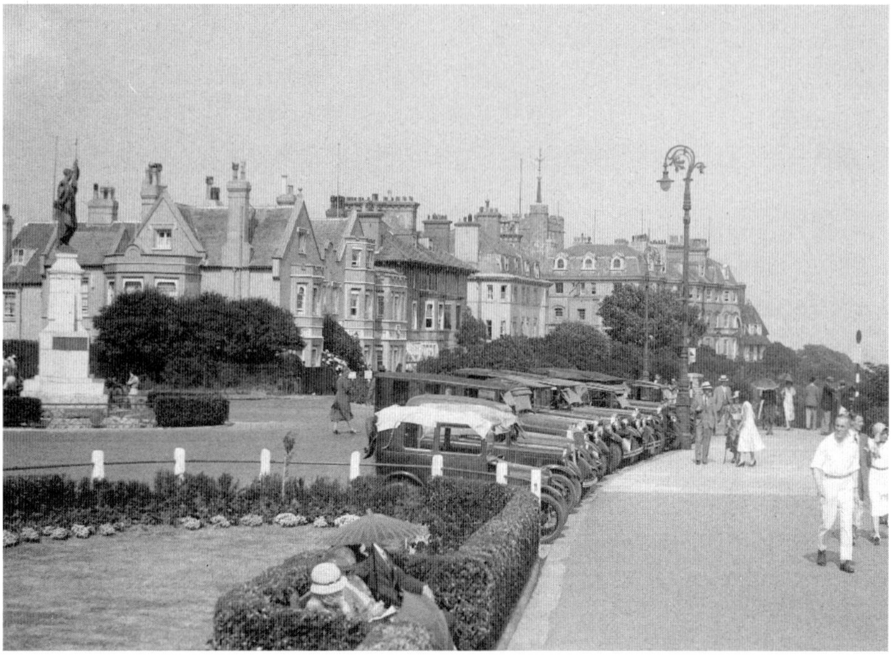

The War Memorial, Albion Villas and Priory Gardens, 1929. The War Memorial was unveiled on Saturday 2 December 1922. In front of the memorial are fine examples of cars from the period.

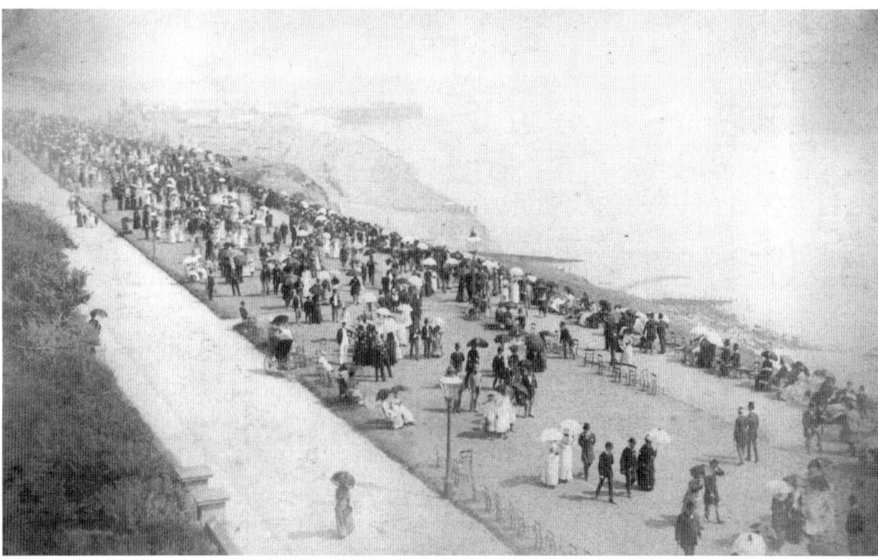

The Leas, early 1870s. The Leas was the place for elegant ladies to be seen promenading before and after church parade. It was also the place where mothers showed off their eligible daughters.

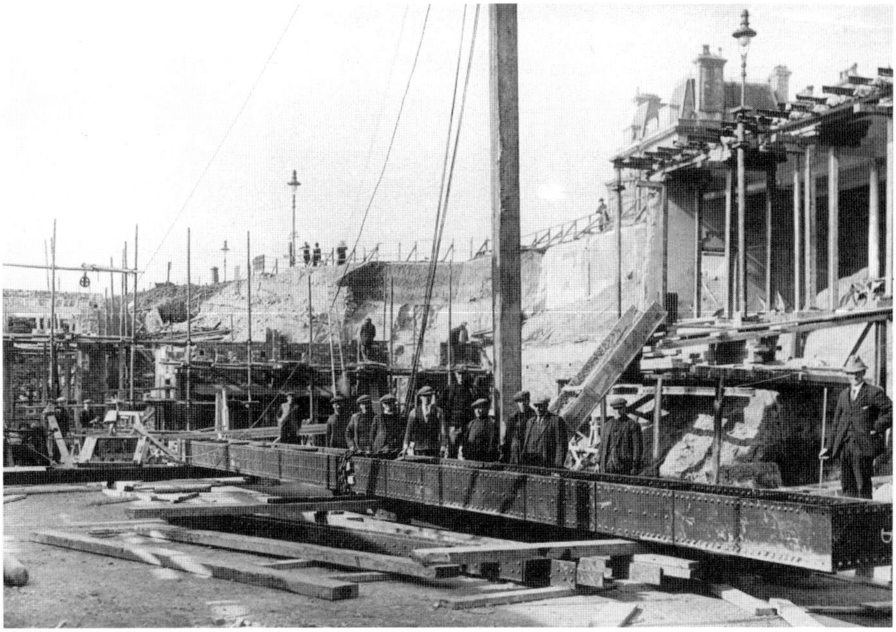

Building the Leas Cliff Hall. At the top right is part of the old Leas Shelter which was incorporated into the new building. The main building contractors were Mr D. Godden & Son, Ham Street, near Ashford.

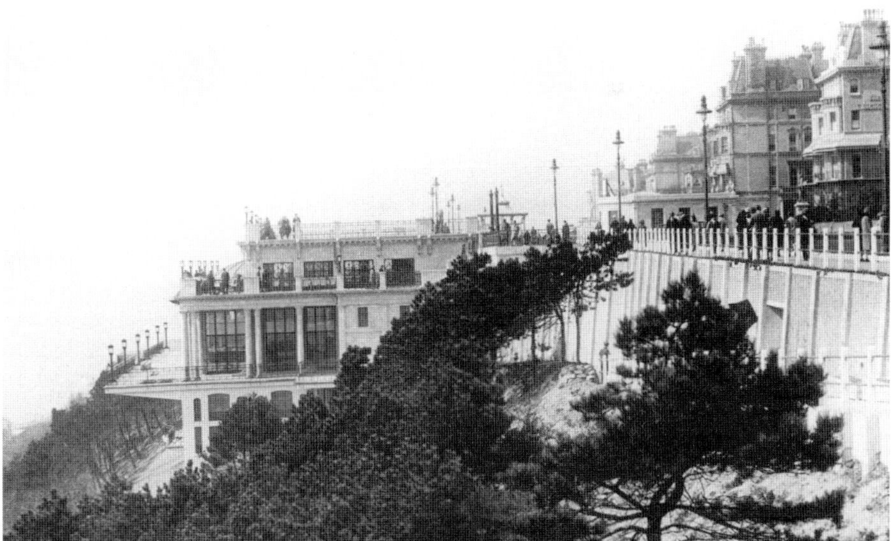

The east side of the Leas Cliff Hall, 1927. All the stone on the building was supplied and fixed by an Italian firm.

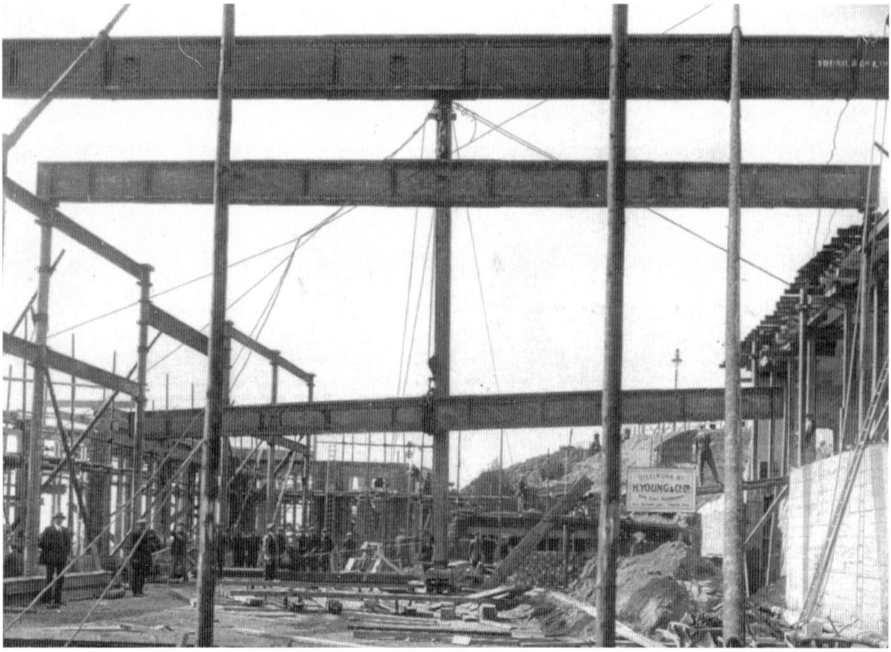

Erecting the steel work for the Leas Cliff Hall. The steel work was carried out by Mr H. Young & Co. Ltd of London. Crowds of people apparently went to see these iron girders being erected, mainly because they had never seen such large girders before.

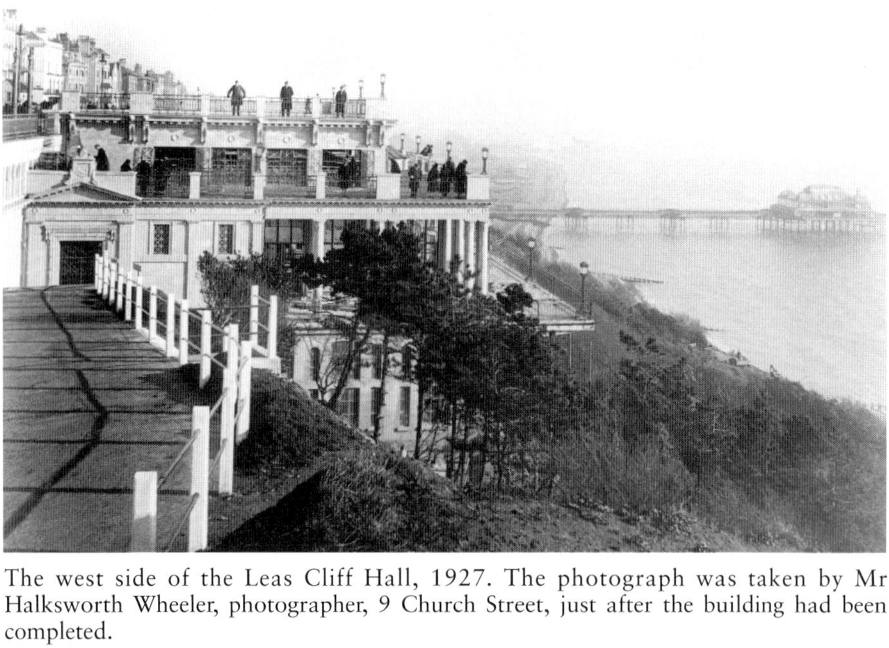

The west side of the Leas Cliff Hall, 1927. The photograph was taken by Mr Halksworth Wheeler, photographer, 9 Church Street, just after the building had been completed.

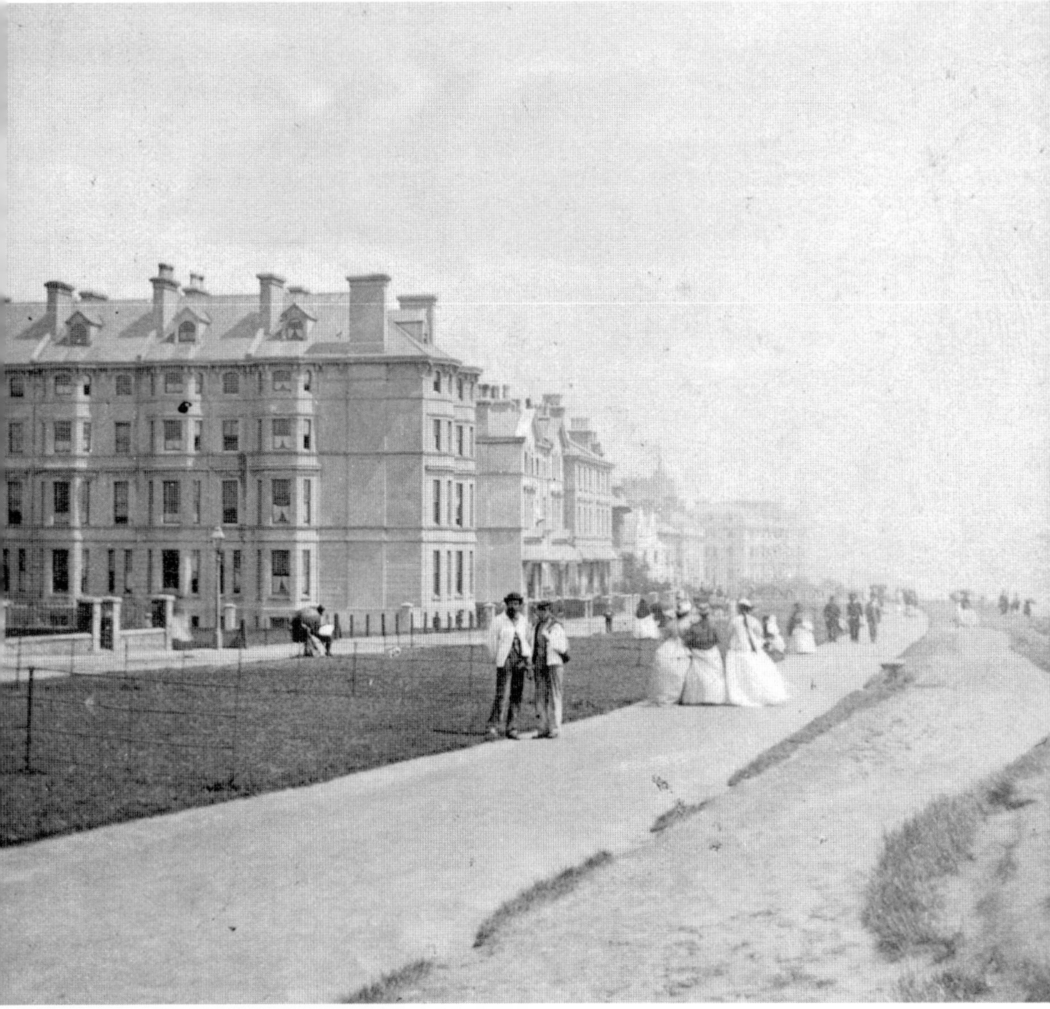

The Leas, 1860s, taken from a stereograph. The photographer was Mr Lambert Weston & Son, of Folkestone and Dover. The building nearest the camera is the Hotel de France, formerly the Longford Hotel, which was gutted by fire on 11 September 1993. These early photographs of the Leas recall the days, not too distantly passed, when corn grew where now is the Harvey statue and when town and country were not so sharply divorced as today.

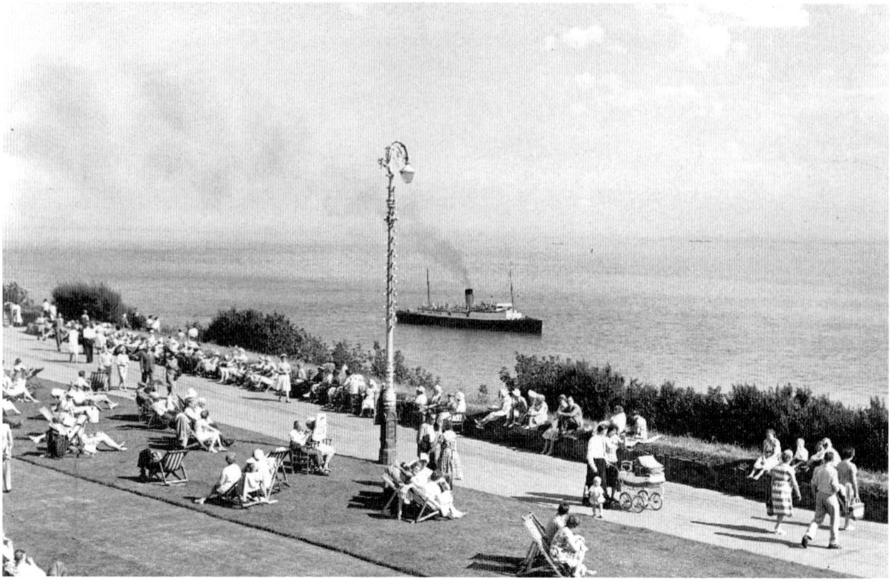

The Leas promenade, 1959. The ship at anchor is the cross-channel steamer *Isle of Thanet*. She was built in 1925 and scrapped in 1964.

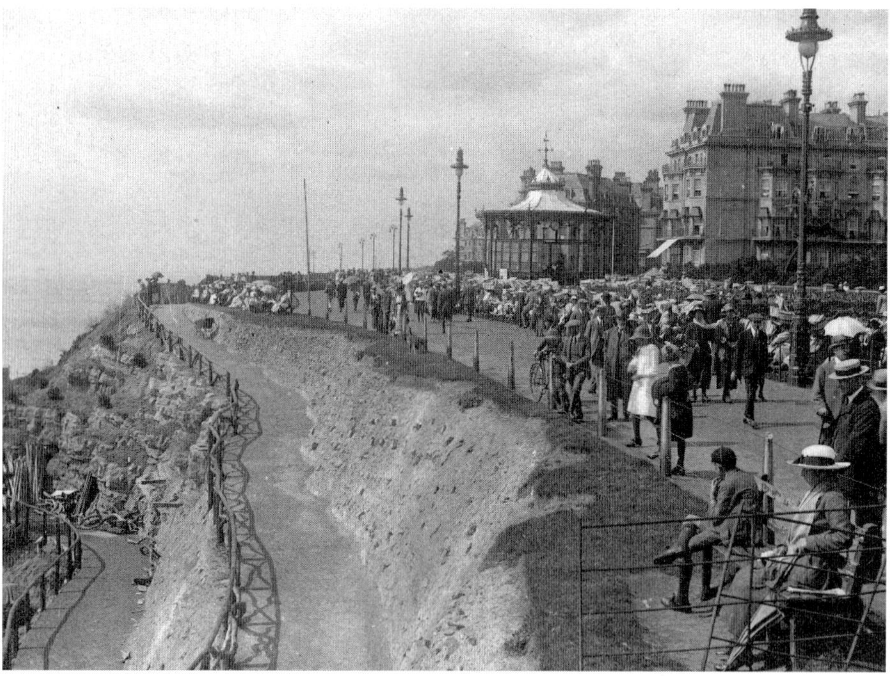

The Leas, lower bandstand and zigzag path, 1922. The building of the zigzag path is nearing completion. It was built with artificial rocks.

SECTION SIX

The First World War 1914–18

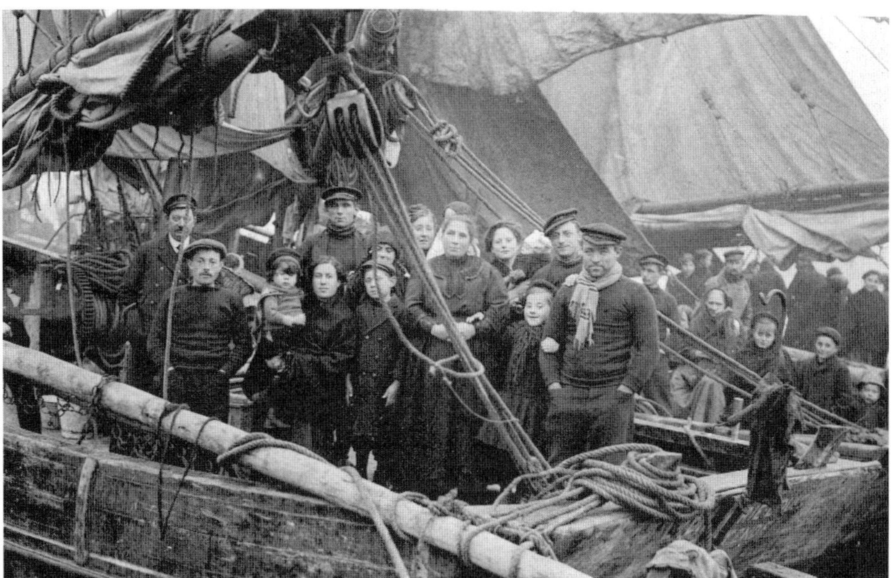

England's first contact with the grim horrors of war was in Folkestone, around 20 August 1914, when boats came into the harbour crowded with Belgian refugees. The earliest arrivals came in fishing boats, as seen here. The visitors were terror stricken, and many of them absolutely refused to leave the boats.

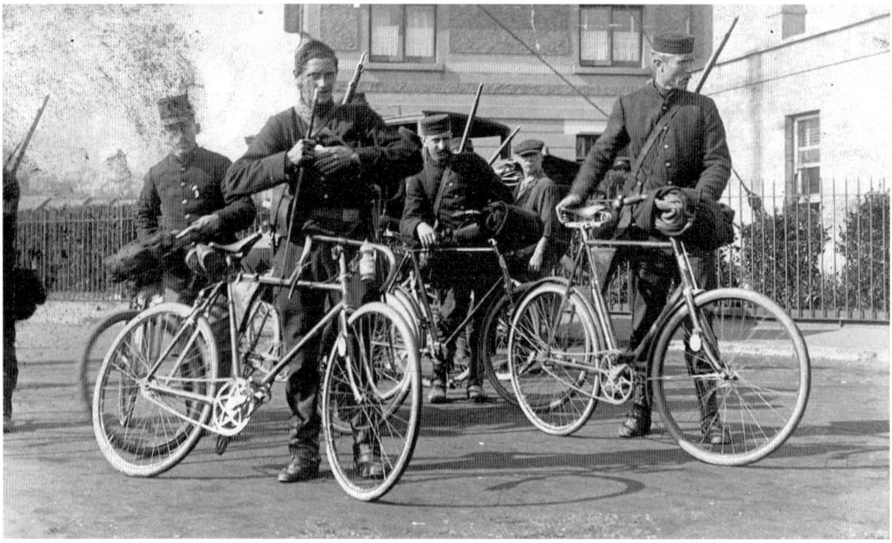

Belgian soldiers from the cycle corps. They had to evacuate from Dieppe to Folkestone after fighting the Germans at Namurbut. They are seen here at Folkestone Harbour station, on their way back to the front.

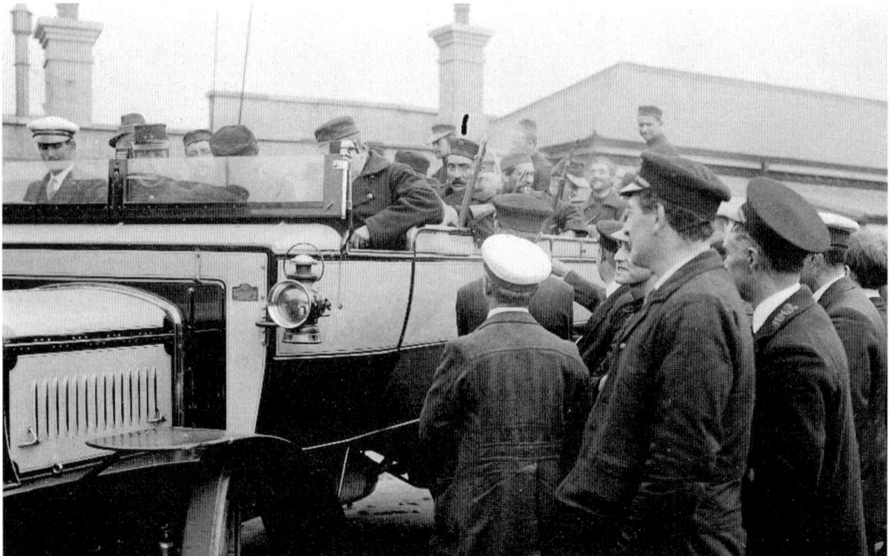

Belgian soldiers arrive at Folkestone harbour, 14 October 1914. They have just boarded a charabanc outside Folkestone Harbour station. One of these soldiers saw his four brothers and father killed.

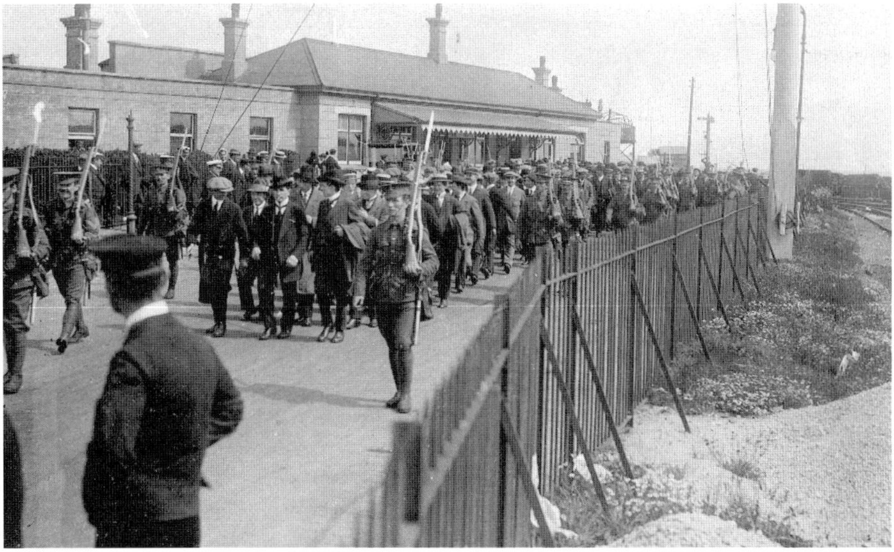

Germans under arrest at Folkestone Harbour station, 1914. These were on their way to join the Kaiser's army when they were arrested at Folkestone harbour and imprisoned at Shorncliffe Camp.

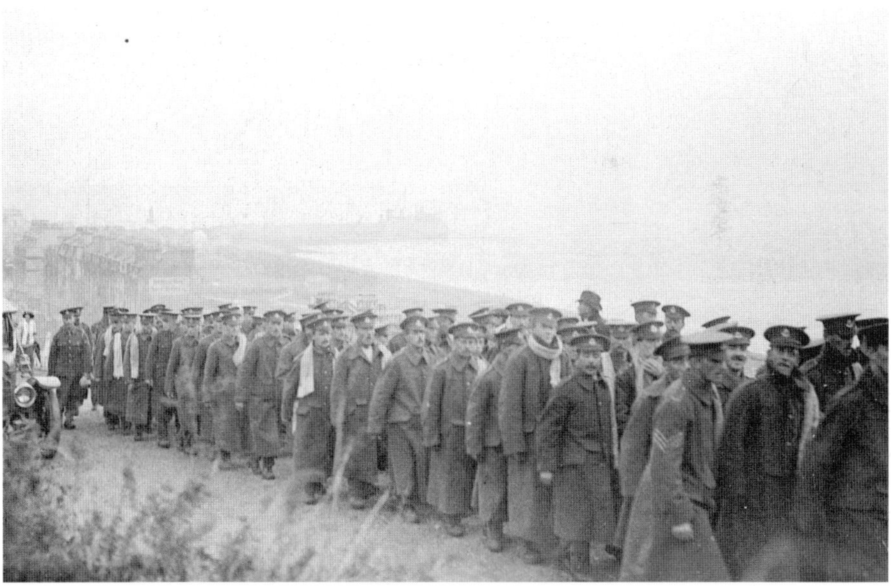

British soldiers coming up the Slope Road, 1914. They are returning from a bathing parade. The Slope Road had its name changed to the Road of Remembrance, after the First World War, in memory of the tens of thousands of British soldiers who passed along the road on their way to and from the battlefields of Europe.

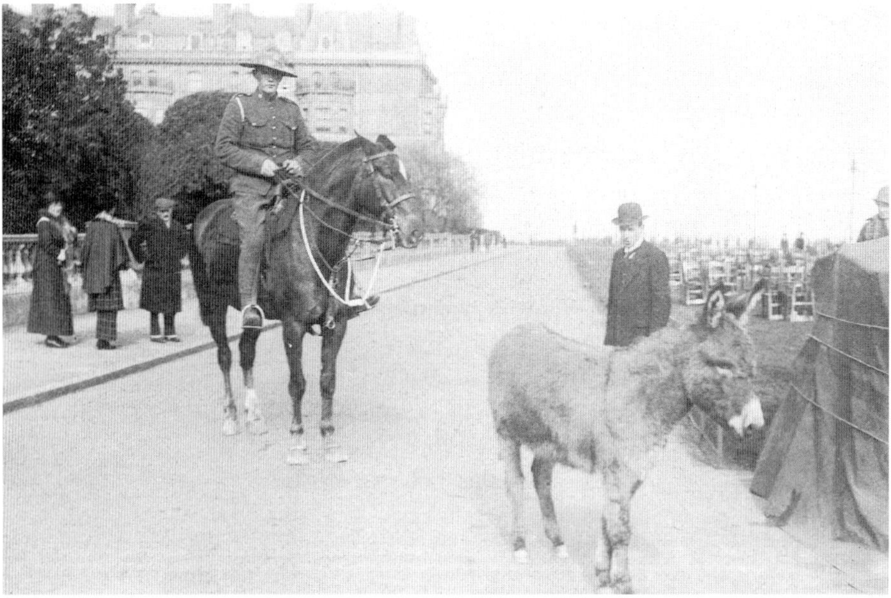

There was a large contingent of Canadian soldiers stationed at Shorncliffe camp in the First World War. On this occasion a lone mounted Canadian soldier and his donkey mascot make their way along the Leas.

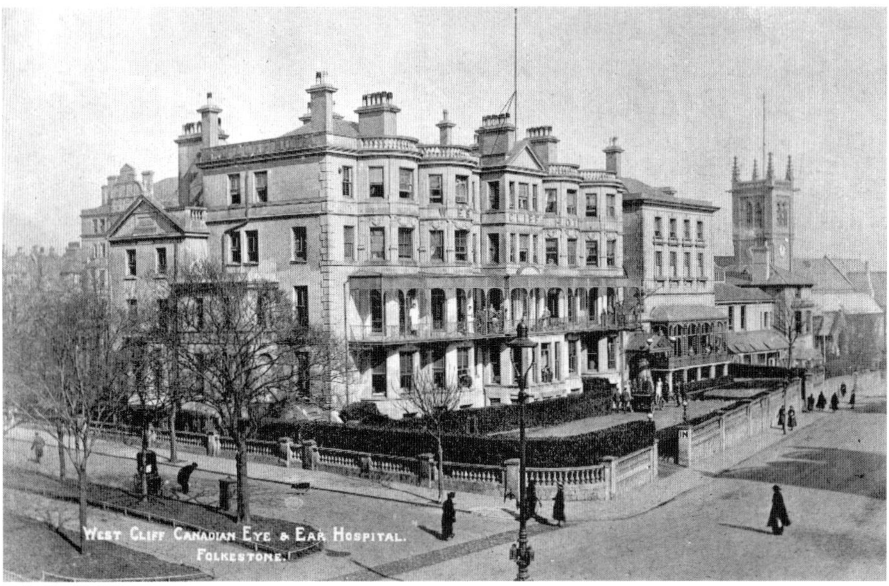

The West Cliff Hotel, corner of Sandgate Road and Castle Hill Avenue. The hotel was used as a Canadian-run eye and ear hospital during the First World War. Majestic Parade now occupies part of the site.

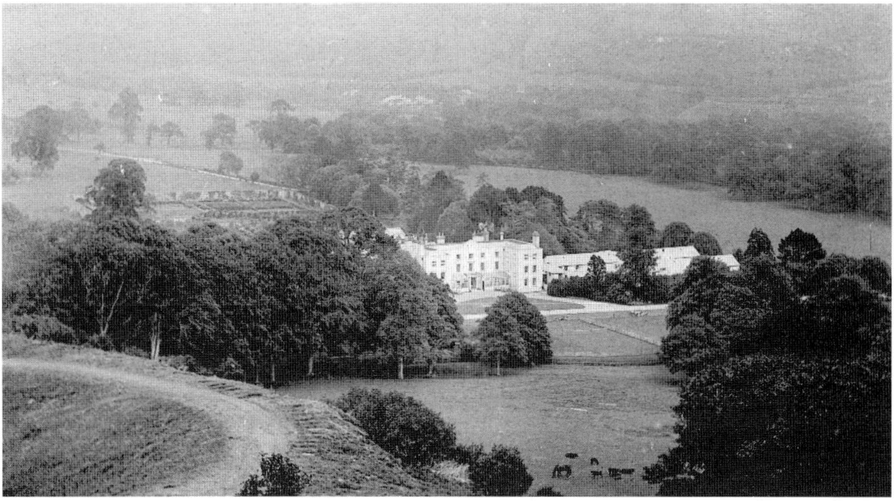

Beachborough House, home of Sir Arthur Markham, MP. It was used as a Canadian hospital from October 1914 until it closed early in 1919. During this time 3,000 soldiers passed through the wards; only thirty died.

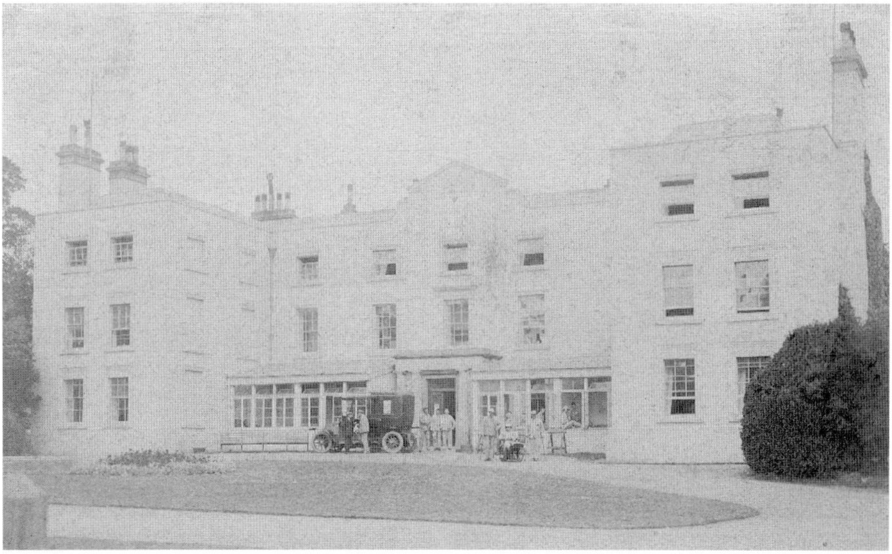

Beachborough House during the First World War. At this time it was being used as the Queen's Canadian military hospital.

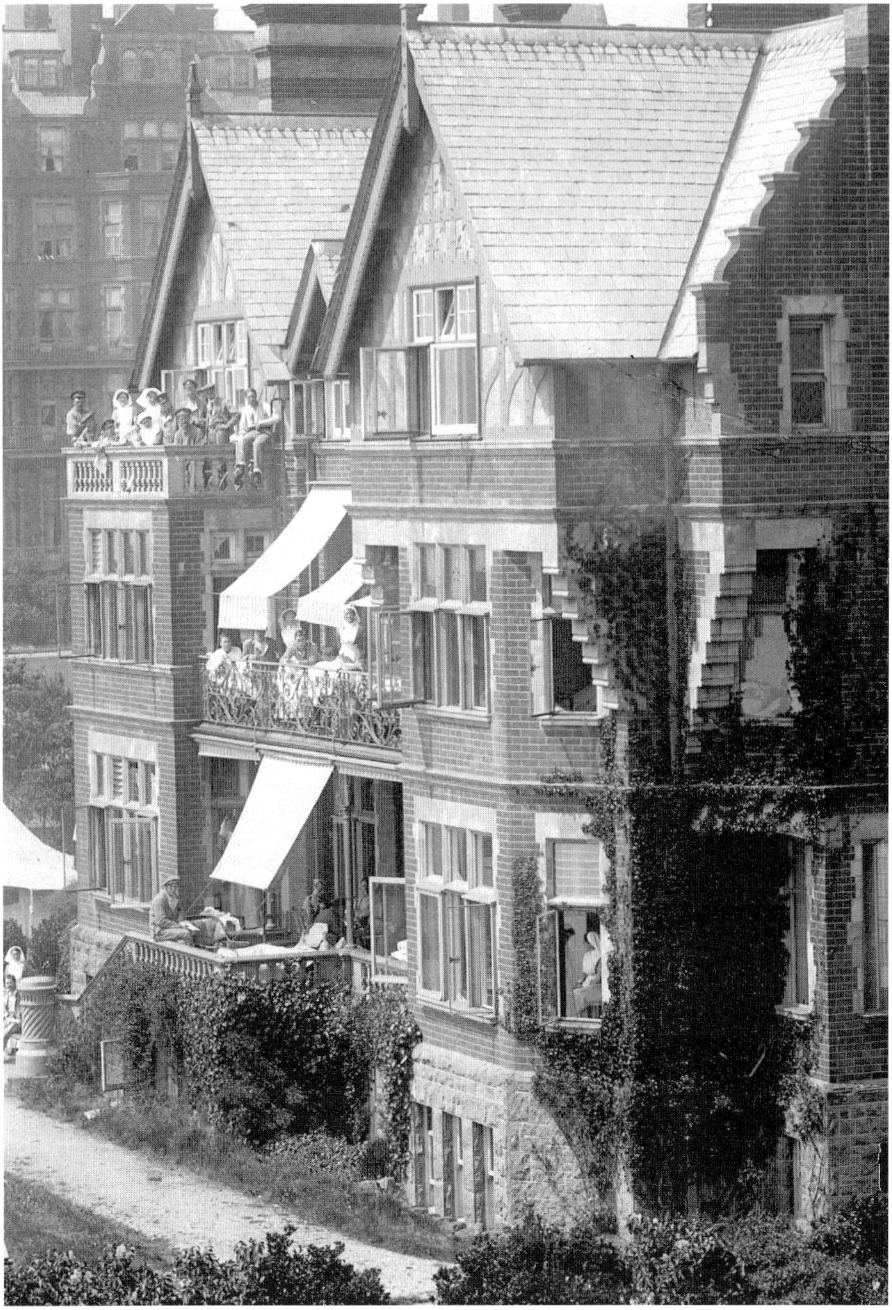

The Manor House on the Leas, May 1917. This belonged to the Earl of Radnor and was, like many other large houses and hotels in Folkestone, used as a military hospital during the First World War.

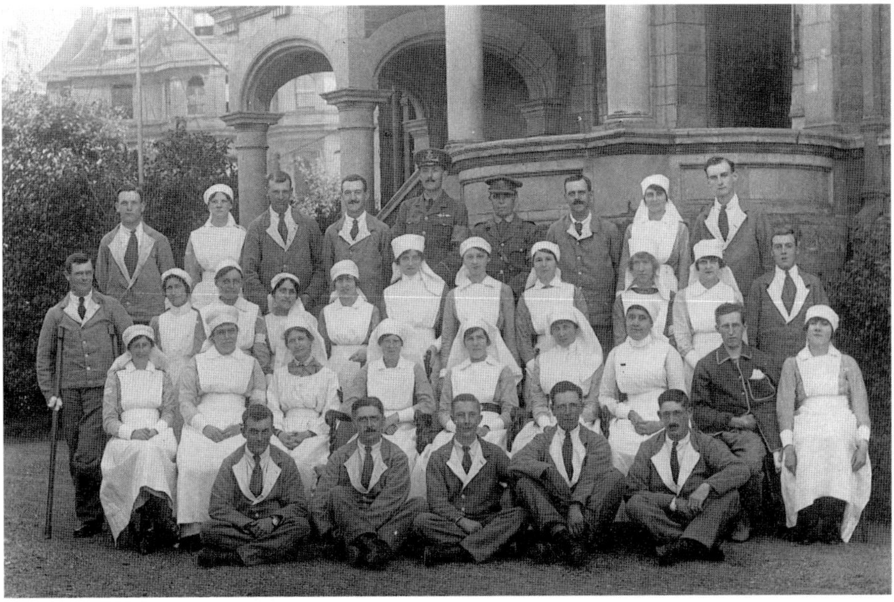

Staff of the Manor House military hospital during the First World War. The Honourable Florence Daly was Commandant.

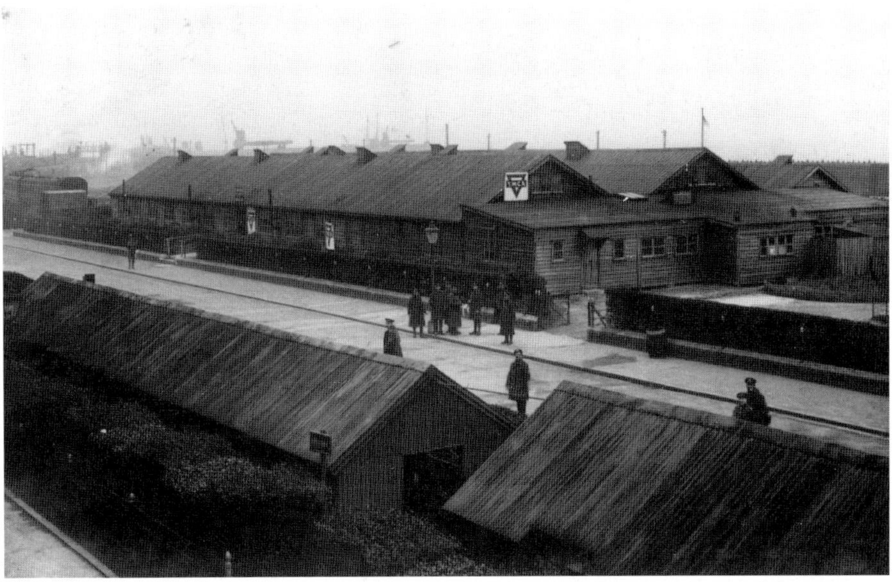

In August 1915 Colonel R. Burns-Begg was sent from the War Office to Folkestone to organize a system of rest camps. In 1915 blocks of houses in Marine Parade, Marine Crescent and Marine Terrace were acquired, and, in January 1916, number one rest camp was opened, with Lieutenant-Colonel H.F. Sparrow as Commandant. The huts seen here are on Marine Parade and on the site of the present Parisienne nightclub.

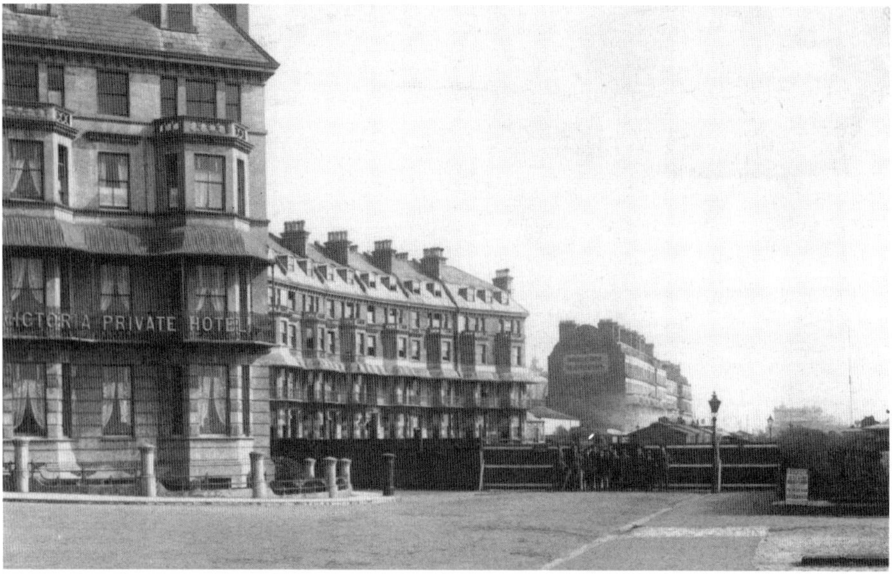

Number one rest camp, showing the entrance at Marine Crescent. There were four rest camps set up in Folkestone during the First World War. They provided accommodation for the troops to rest in while on their way to and from the battlefields in Europe.

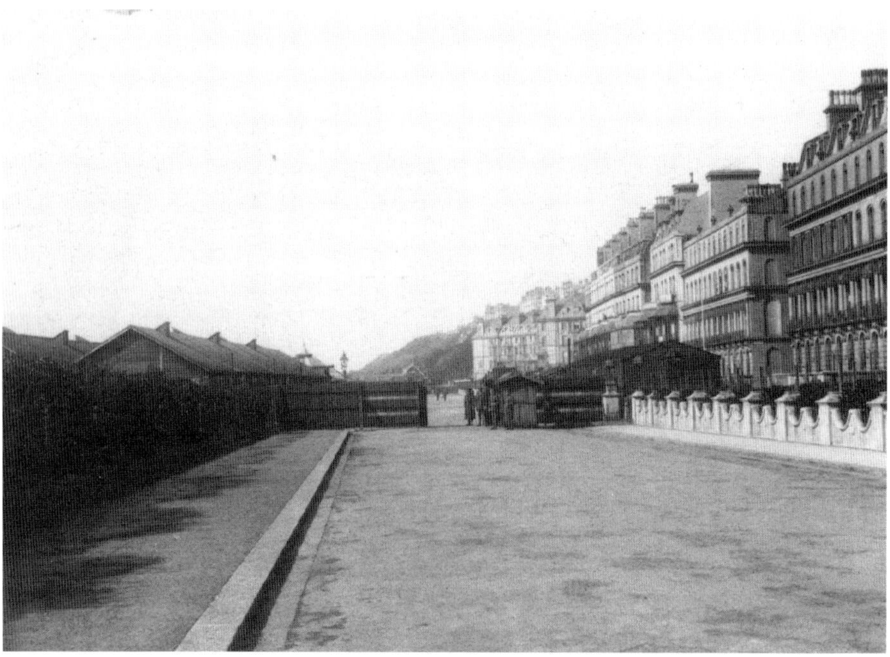

The entrance to number one rest camp at the Marine Parade end. The British YMCA was involved with the running and the cooking at these rest camps.

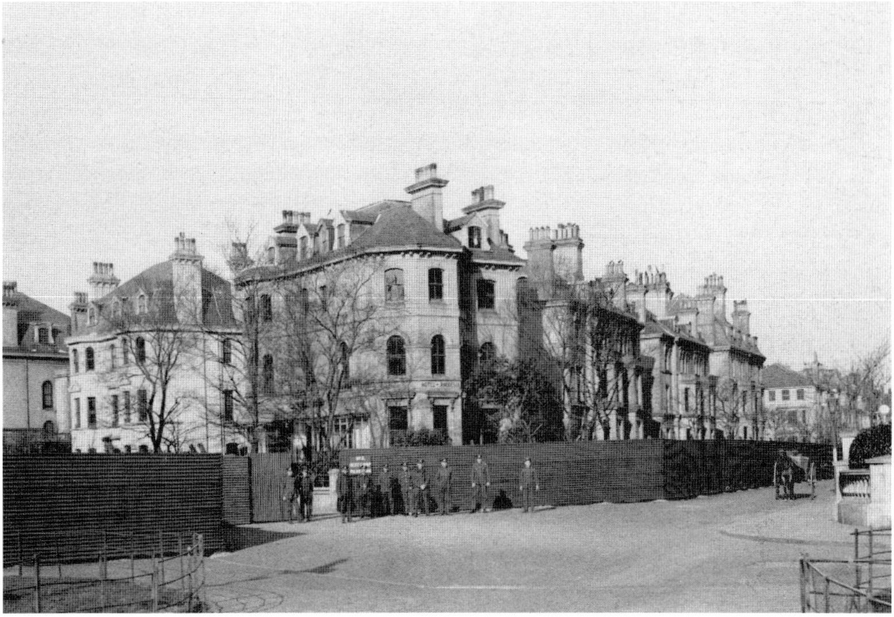

Number three rest camp at the junction with the Leas Clifton Road and Clifton Crescent. In November 1916 blocks of houses were acquired on the Leas, Clifton Crescent, on the east side of Earl's Avenue, on the south side of Sandgate Road and on the west side of Clifton Road; the camp opened early in 1917.

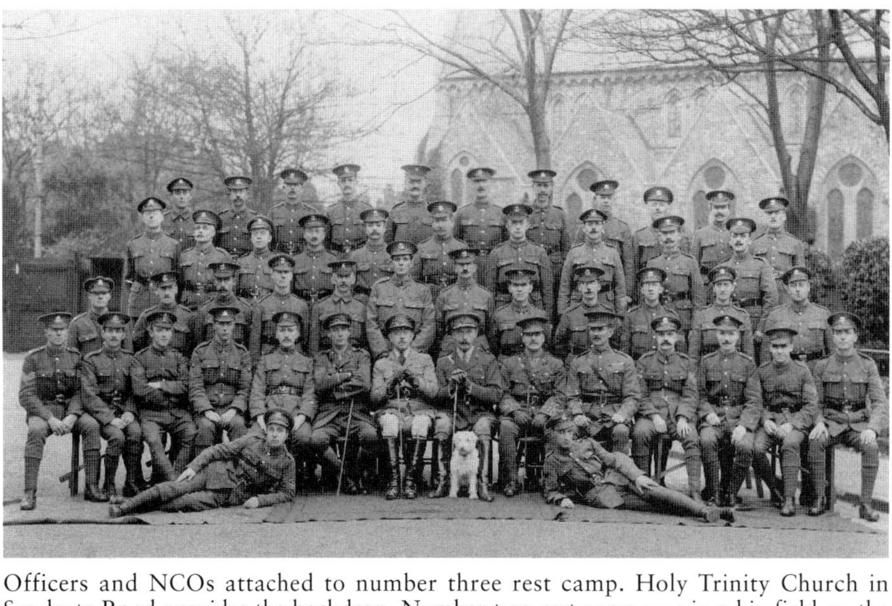

Officers and NCOs attached to number three rest camp. Holy Trinity Church in Sandgate Road provides the backdrop. Number two rest camp was in a big field on the West Cliff Estate, off Bathhurst Road, and number four was at the drill hall.

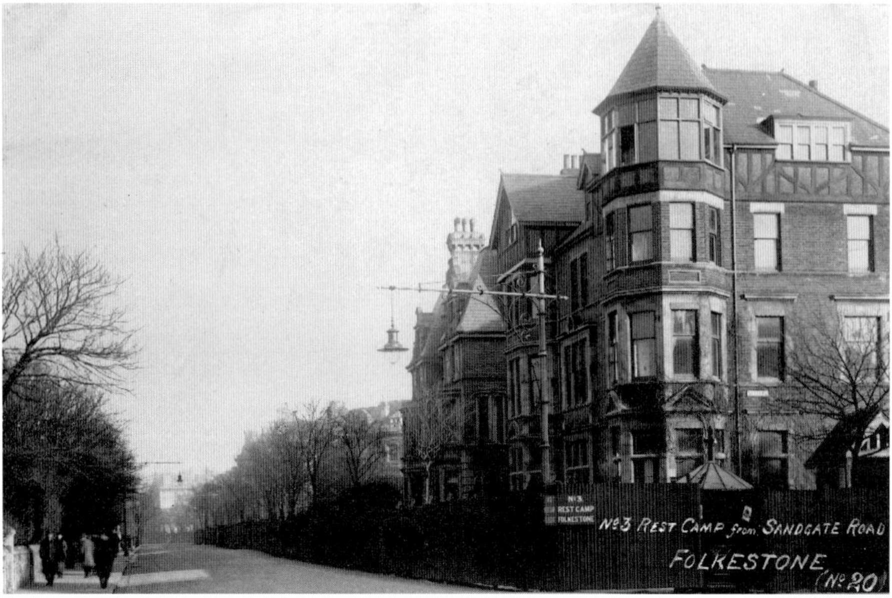

Number three rest camp at the junction with Earl's Avenue and Sandgate Road. The accommodation at number three rest camp held 5,000 men. The average number of men passing through the camps daily during 1917 and 1918 was between 8,000 and 9,000. During March and April 1918, the numbers rose to 12,000 daily.

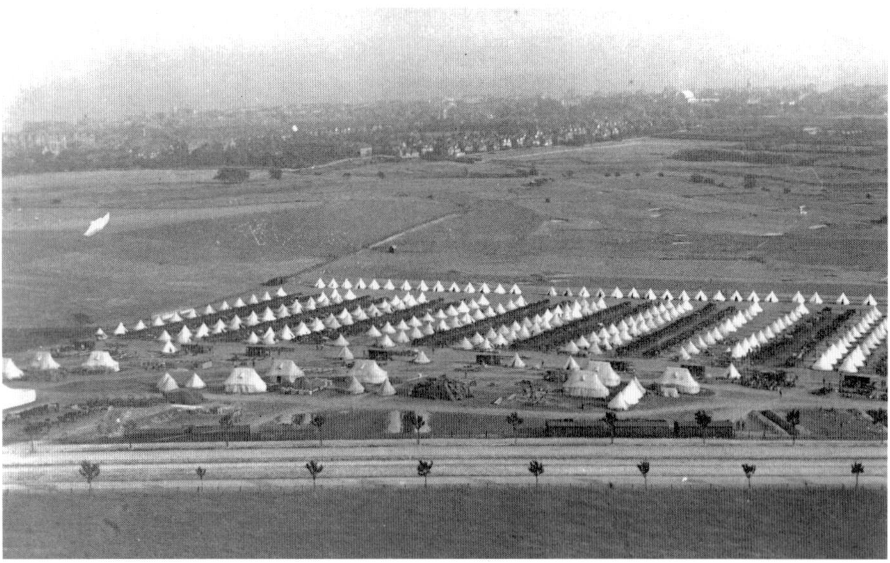

Tented camp pitched on Park Farm, April 1917. This camp was designed to accommodate 2,000 Chinese or Kaffirs and was designated the labour concentration camp, under the command of Lieutenant-Colonel F. Hopley. The site is now occupied by Texas Homecare.

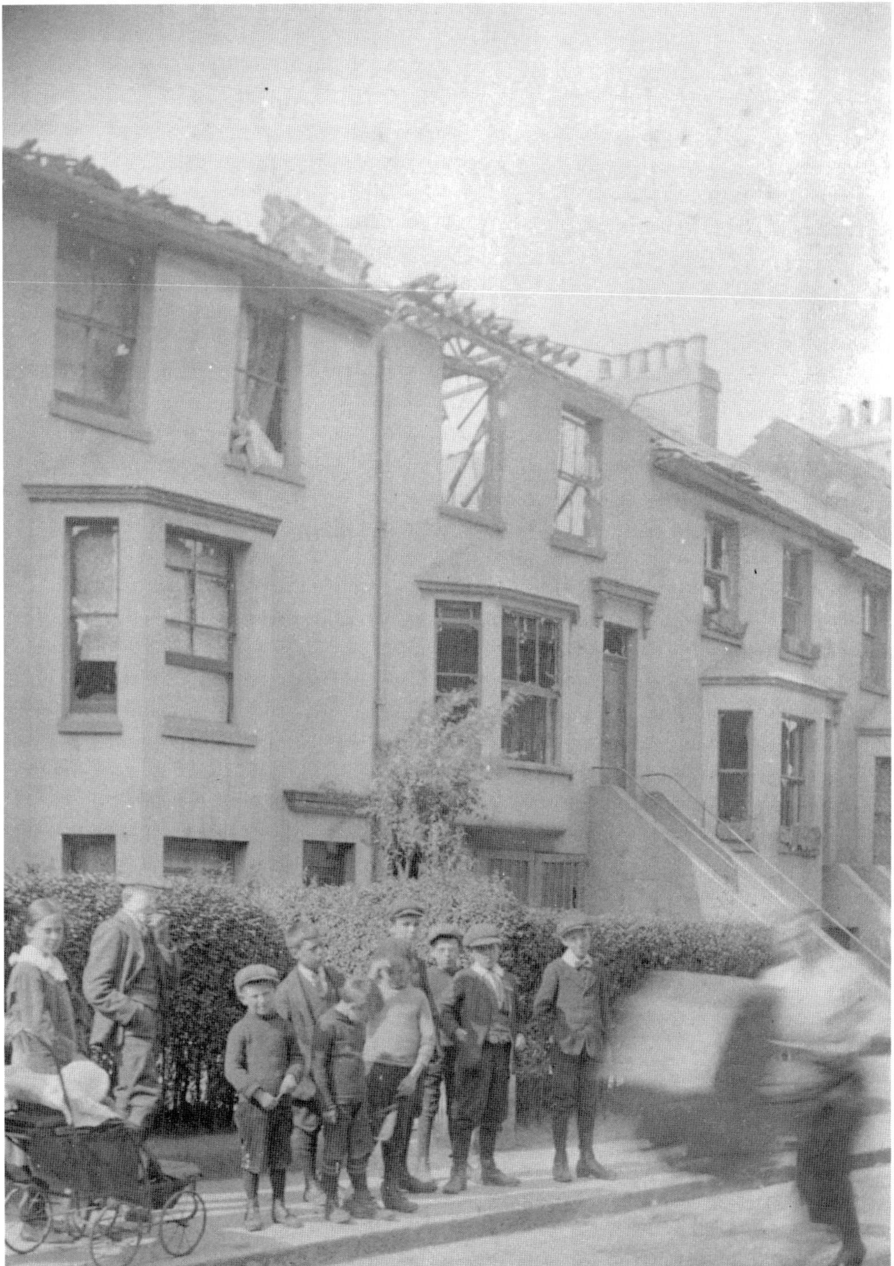

On 27 May 1917 three bombs narrowly missed the south side of the railway embankment, between the viaduct and Junction station. One bomb partly demolished this house, 28 St John's Street, with resulting loss of life.

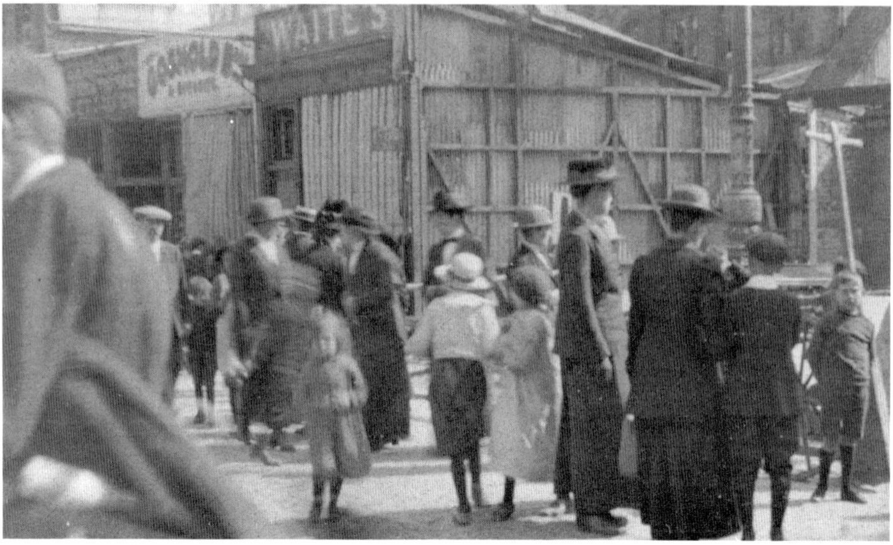

The site of Messrs Stokes' greengrocery stores, Tontine Street. A score of German Gotha bombers returning from London on 25 May 1917 unloaded their remaining bombs on Folkestone, killing seventy-one people, among them many women and children.

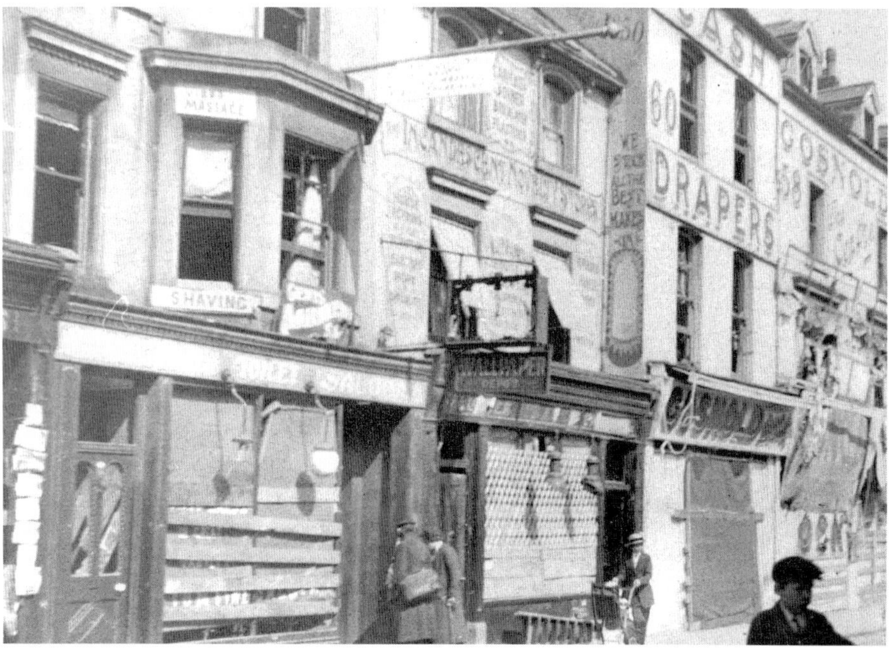

Damage to the shops opposite Messrs Stokes from the same air raid. The drapery emporium of Messrs Gosnold Bros, at 56, 58 and 60 Tontine Street, took the brunt of the damage. The area damaged extended from the Congregational church (now Tontine House) to no. 35, Mr Henry Warren's fruit shop.

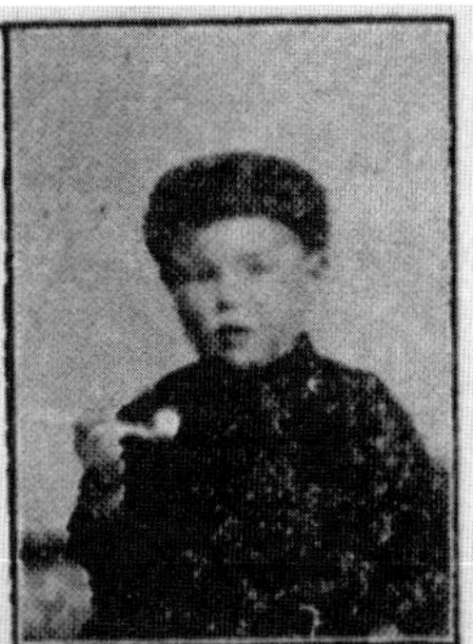

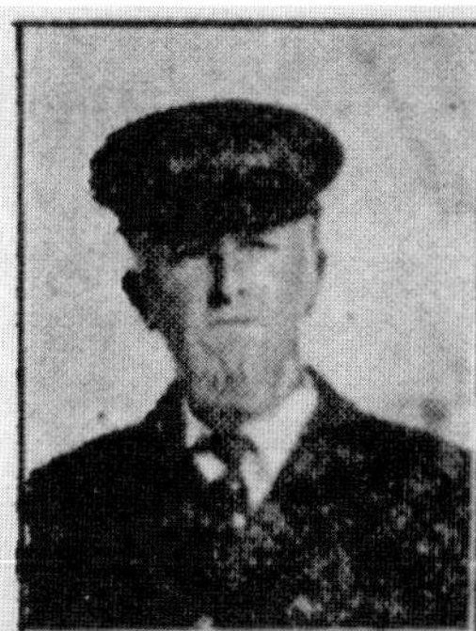

Will anyone fill daddy's pipe?

Tune—' Has anyone seen my cat."

My daddy to the war is gone to fight the Ger man,
And all our brave British soldiers are doing all they can,
But when the battle's o'er they lay tired on the field,
They need a smoke to cheer them so to you I make an
appeal.

CHORUS.

Will anyone fill daddy's pipe?
Will anyone fill daddy's pipe?
Smoke, smoke smoke, bacca, bacca, bacca,
Will anyone fill daddy's pipe?

Now Tommy Atkins loves a smoke as everyone does know,
He gets plenty of shot and shell but tobacco comes in slow.
So let us do our level best to cheer him on the field,
So once more to you again I make an appeal.

CHORUS.

Now all you that stay at home and enjoy your evening pipe,
Think of your brother Tommy on the battlefield to-night,
The rain comes down, he's cold and wet through,
He needs a smoke to cheer him, so once again I appeal to
you.

God save the King

Composed by the Folkestone Town Crier,
Aged 65,
and his little grandson, aged 3.

Mr John 'Chopper' Anderson, town crier from 1912 to 1931, composed a number of patriotic verses during the First World War. These were published in postcard form.

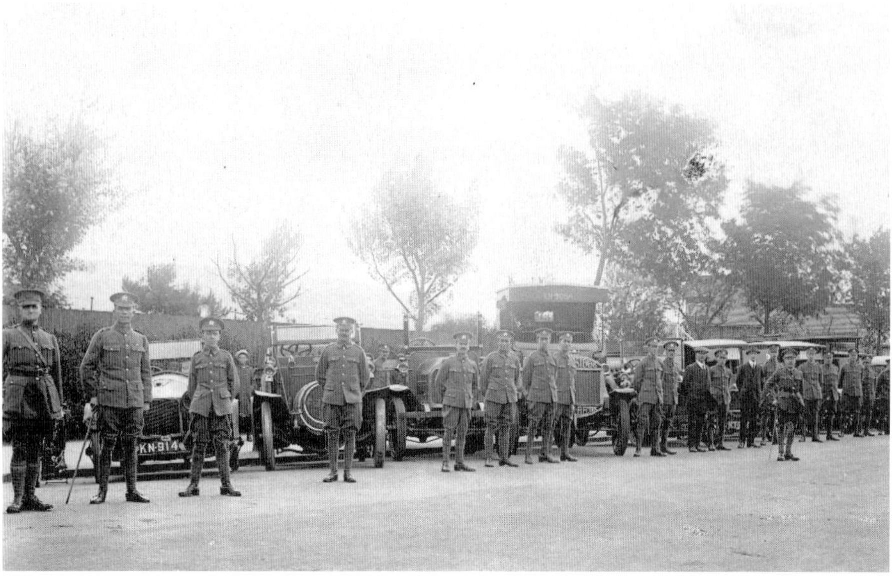

A duty test and inspection of the Kent Army Service Corps Mechanical Transport (Volunteers), Sunday 13 October 1918. This was carried out in Cheriton Road by the Officer Commanding Lieutenant-Colonel Upton, ASC Dover.

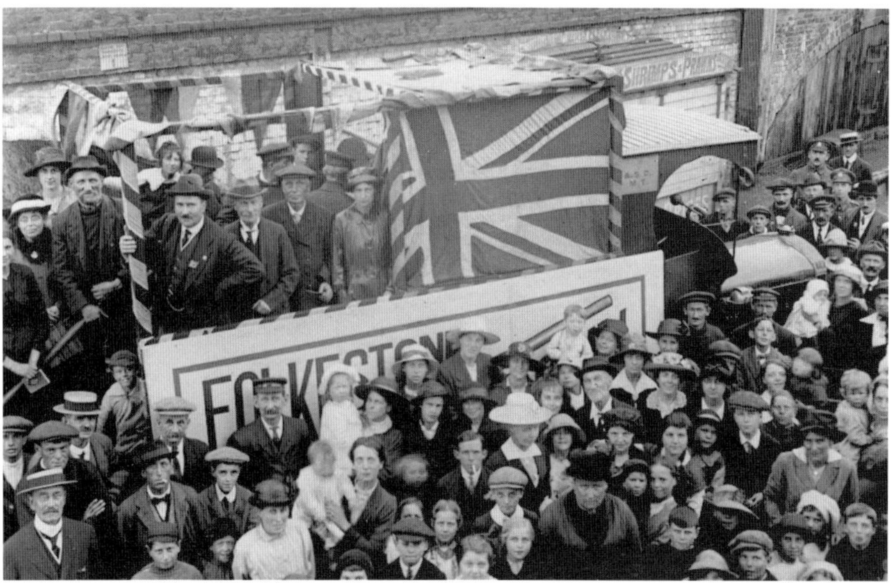

Big gun week, 14–20 July 1918. Big gun week was a campaign to raise money for war loans. The campaigners are in Beach Street, by the railway arches.

SECTION SEVEN

More Glimpses of Bygone Folkestone

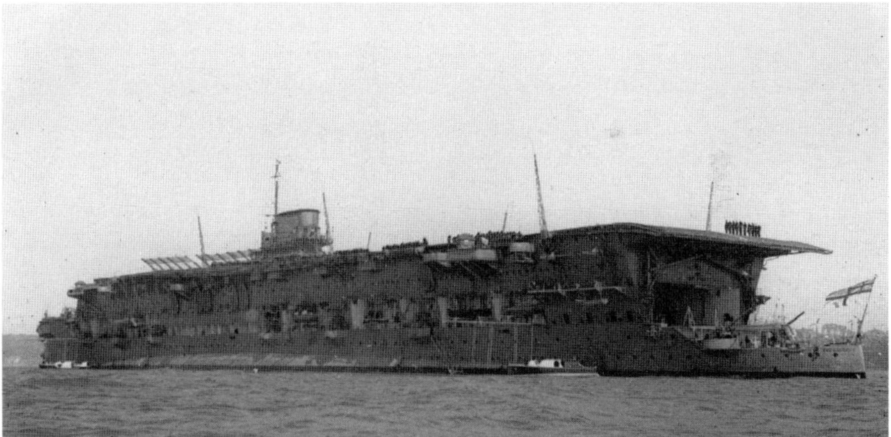

HMS Courageous lying off the beach, July 1934. The *Courageous* was built in 1915 as a light battle-cruiser. She was converted to an aircraft-carrier around 1925 and was sunk in September 1939.

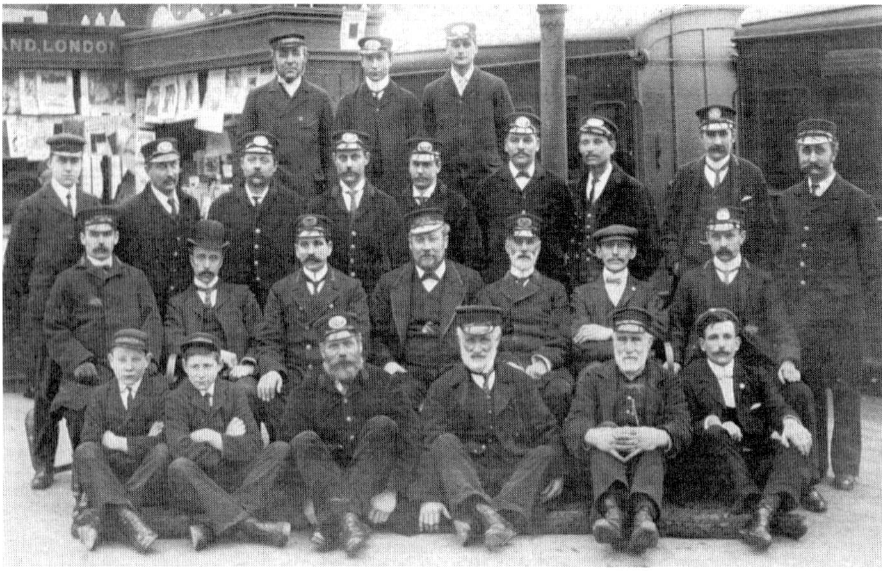

Staff of the South Eastern and Chatham Railway at the Central station between 1901 and 1909. In the front row on the left the two boys have W.H. Smith on their caps. Second row, third from left: Mr Youden. Second row, centre: Stationmaster, Mr Henry J. Bridges. Back row, centre: Mr Ernest Bridges, son of Henry.

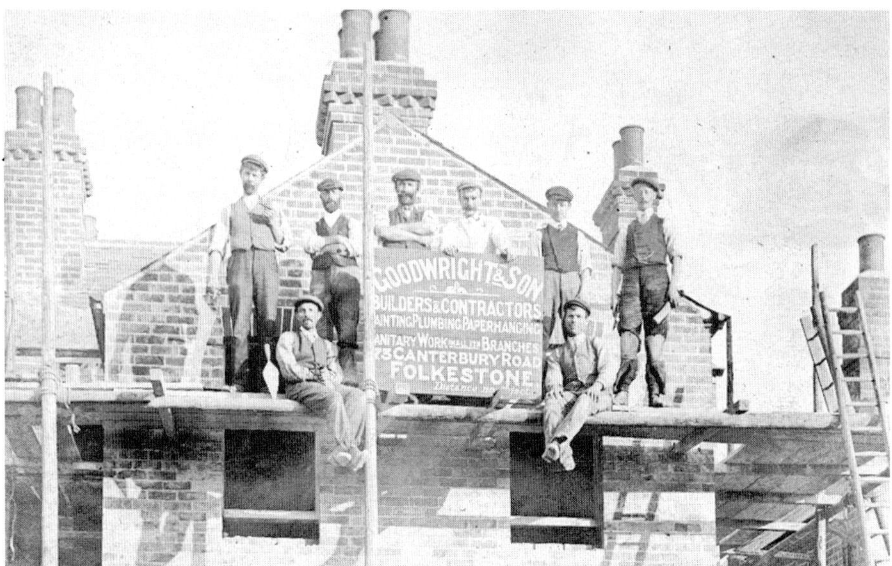

The staff of Goodwright & Son, builders and contractors. Goodwright & Son were in business from 1906 to 1930. Note the wooden scaffolding, which is lashed together with rope.

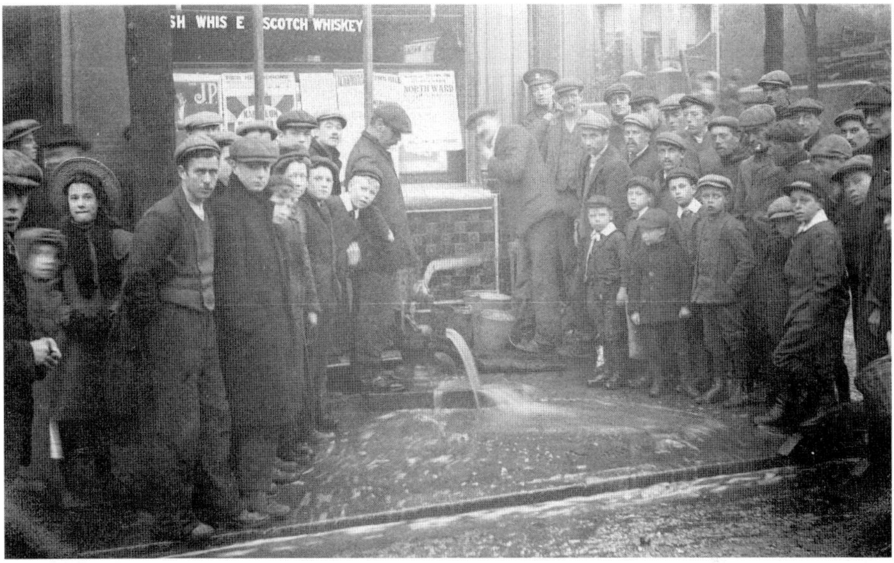

Much damage was done by the great floods of 29 October 1909. The men are pumping out the cellar of the Imperial Hotel, Black Bull Road, while a crowd of people look on.

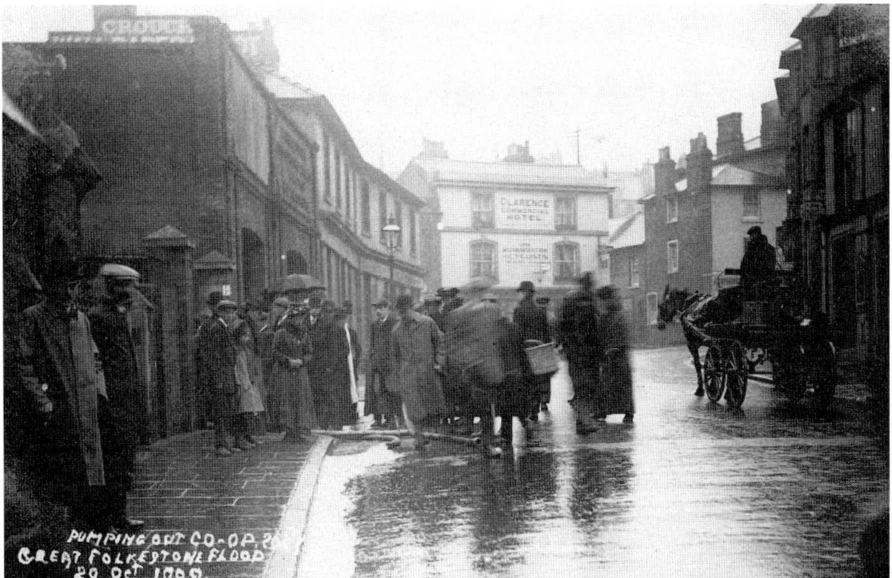

Another casualty of the floods on 29 October 1909 was the Co-operative. The men are pumping out the shop from the back in Tontine Street. Note the Clarence Hotel in Dover Road; this closed in 1918.

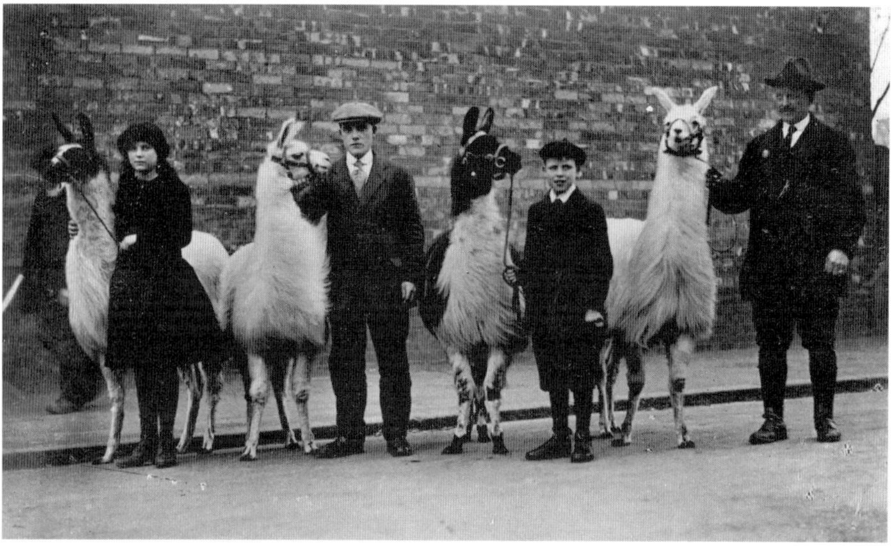

Llamas, Folly Road, *c.* 1930. This curious domesticated animal is the South American equivalent of the camel. Seen here is Mr Rodwell and his family, who operated llama rides.

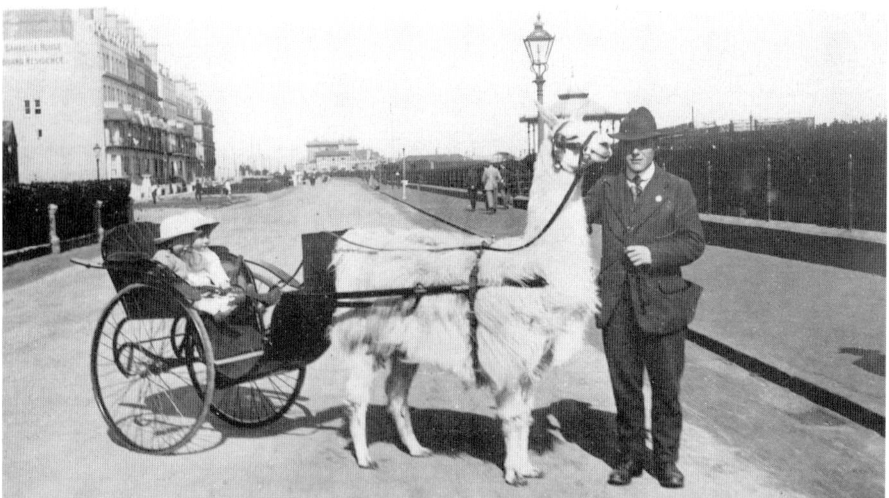

Mr Rodwell with his llama and cart, Lower Sandgate Road, *c.* 1930. The cart has two young children sitting in it. If they were paying customers, a ride cost 1*s*.

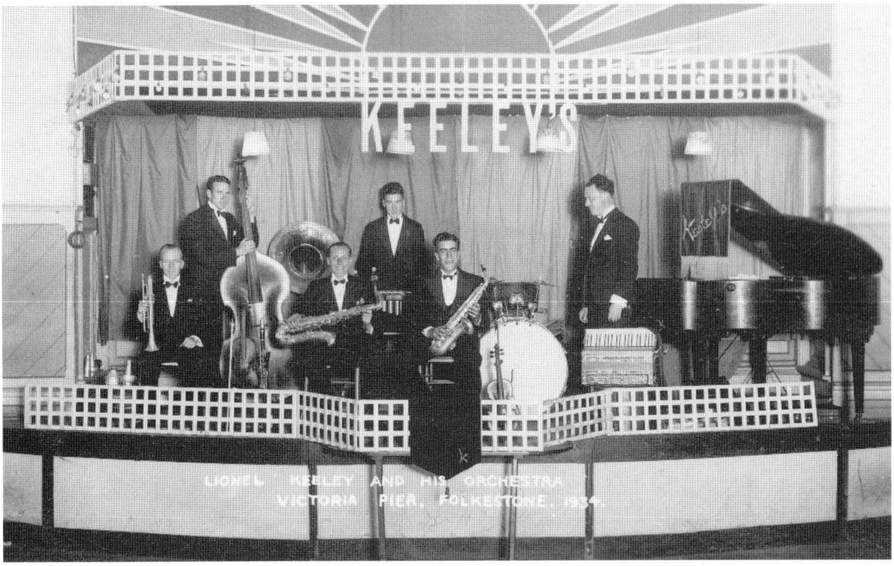

The Keeley's, Victoria Pier, 1934. One of the well-known popular dance bands in the 1930s, the Keeley's was run by Lionel Keeley.

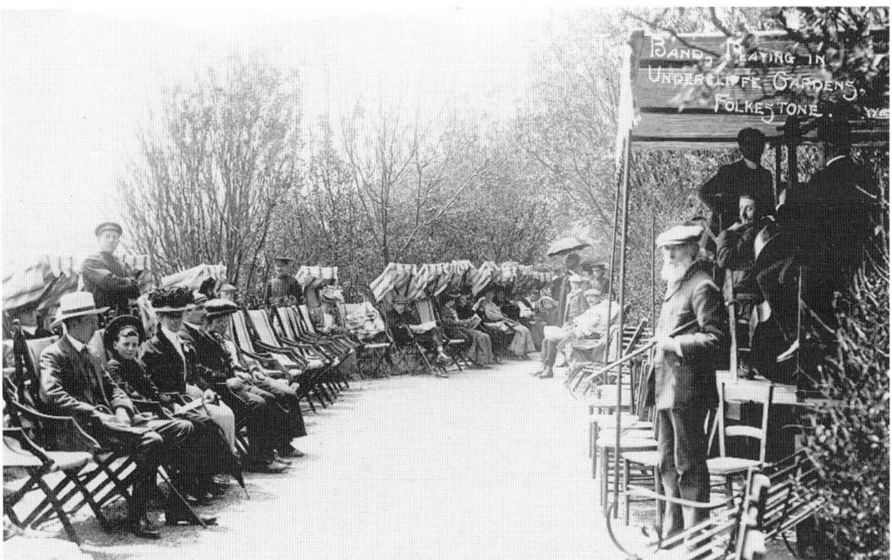

The Undercliffe Gardens, Lower Sandgate Road, 1908. This seems rather an unusual place for a band to play, and with its make-shift bandstand is obviously only a summer venue.

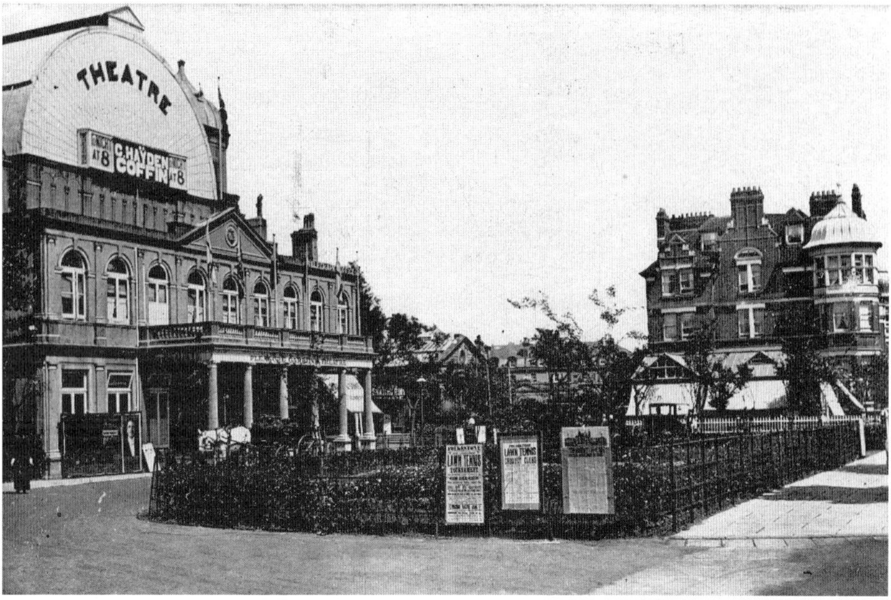

The Pleasure Gardens Theatre, Bouverie Road West. The Pleasure Gardens Theatre opened in 1888 and closed in 1960. The site is now occupied by the Orion Insurance Companies offices. The building on the right is the Princes Hotel, formerly Hundert's Hotel. It was demolished in 1975 and the site is now part of the Orion's gardens.

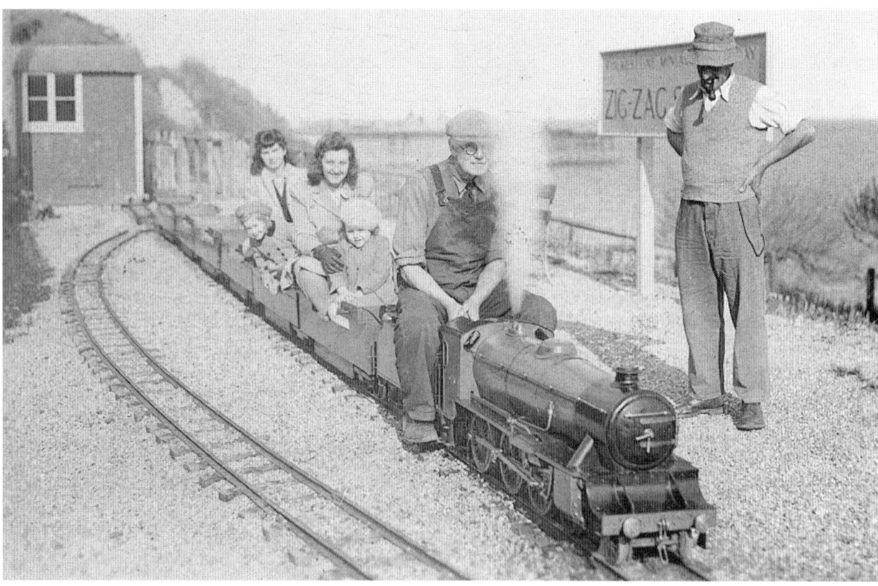

Minature railway, Lower Sandgate Road, *c.* 1948. The railway started just past the Leas Cliff Hall and ran almost to Toll Gate Cottage. The proprietor, Mr F. Strange, is standing to the right of the engine.

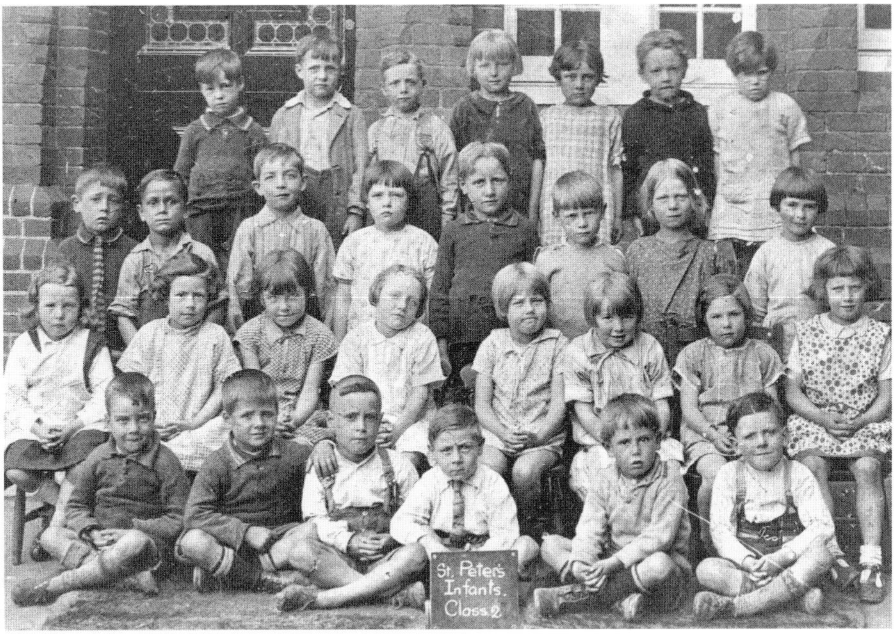

St Peter's School, Class 2 infants, *c.* 1930. Front row, left to right: Alfie King, 'La-La' Taylor, Percy Lee, -?-, Jack Stockley, Gerald Wigg. Second row: Hilda Sharp, ? Chapman, Pat Curry, ? Flood, -?-, Winnie Philpott, -?-, -?-. Third row: Jimmy Symonds, 'Chas' Featherbee, Percy Kitchen, ? Frodshom, Harry Hall, -?-, ? Hughes, -?-. Back row: Ronnie Heath, Ron Prior, -?-, -?-, -?-, Albert Holliday, ? Godden.

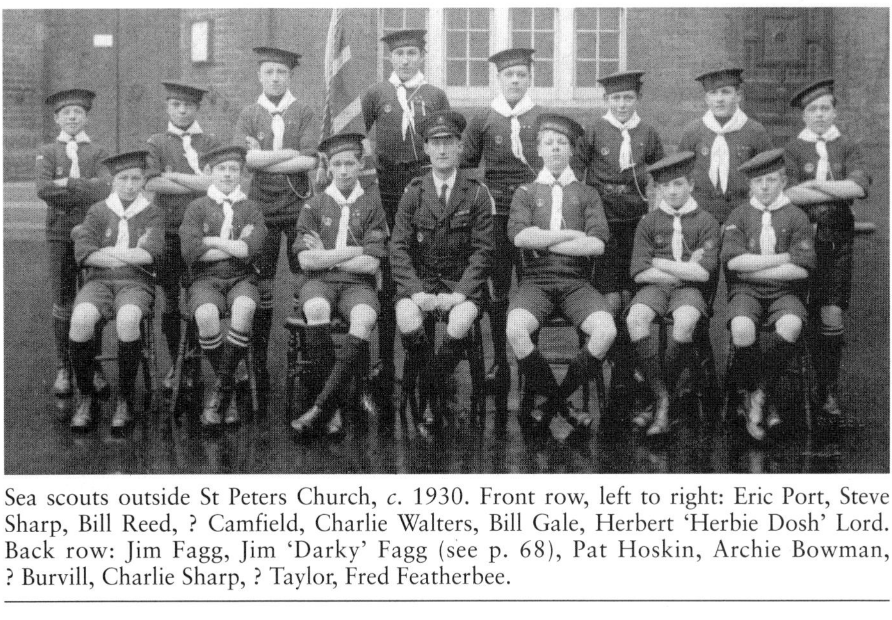

Sea scouts outside St Peters Church, *c.* 1930. Front row, left to right: Eric Port, Steve Sharp, Bill Reed, ? Camfield, Charlie Walters, Bill Gale, Herbert 'Herbie Dosh' Lord. Back row: Jim Fagg, Jim 'Darky' Fagg (see p. 68), Pat Hoskin, Archie Bowman, ? Burvill, Charlie Sharp, ? Taylor, Fred Featherbee.

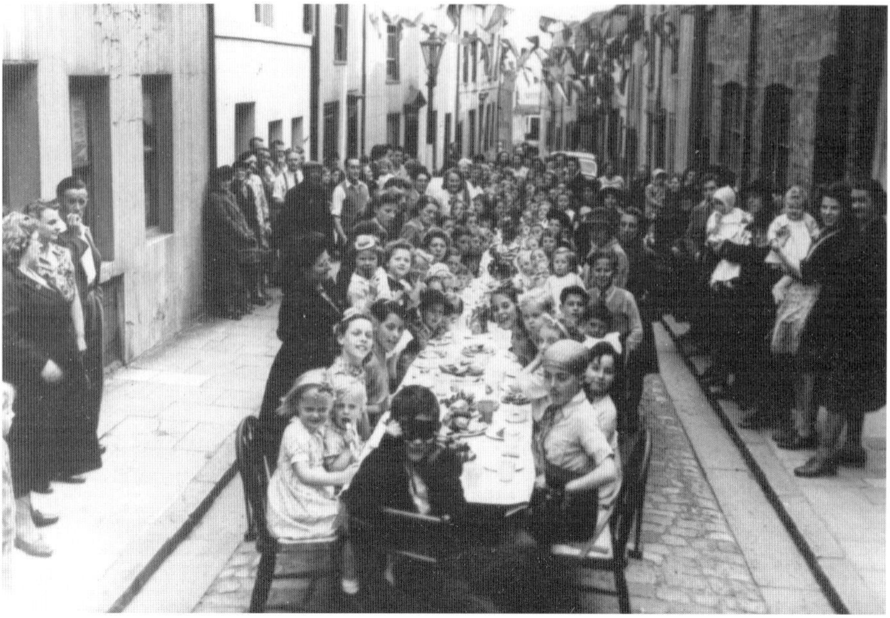

North Street victory party, 1945. The first boy on the right-hand side is Kerry Ryan, who is dressed as a pirate. Most of these houses, some of which date from the seventeenth century, were demolished in 1953.

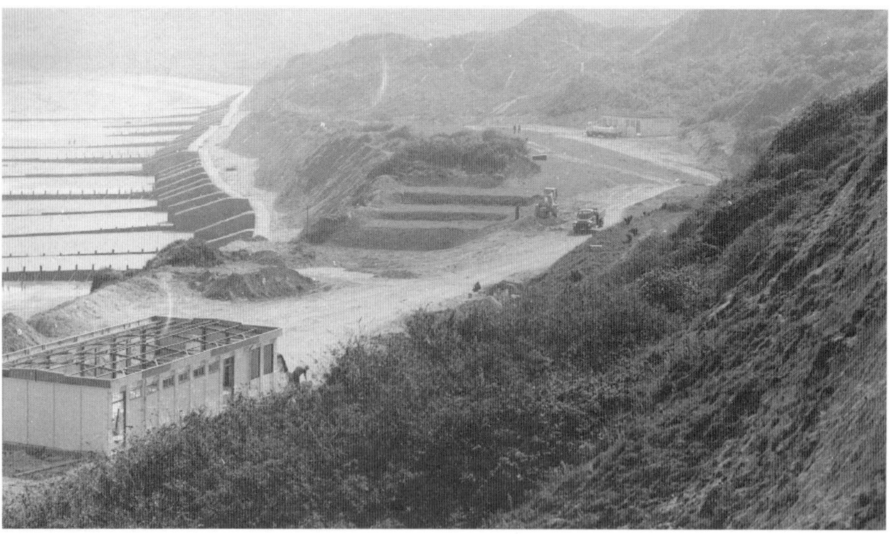

The Warren camp-site during construction, 12 May 1965. The site is owned by the Shepway District Council and run by the Camping Club of Great Britain. It holds between 75 and 80 campers and cost £20,000 to build. In the left foreground is the shop, under construction, while the building further away is to house the toilets and washing facilities.

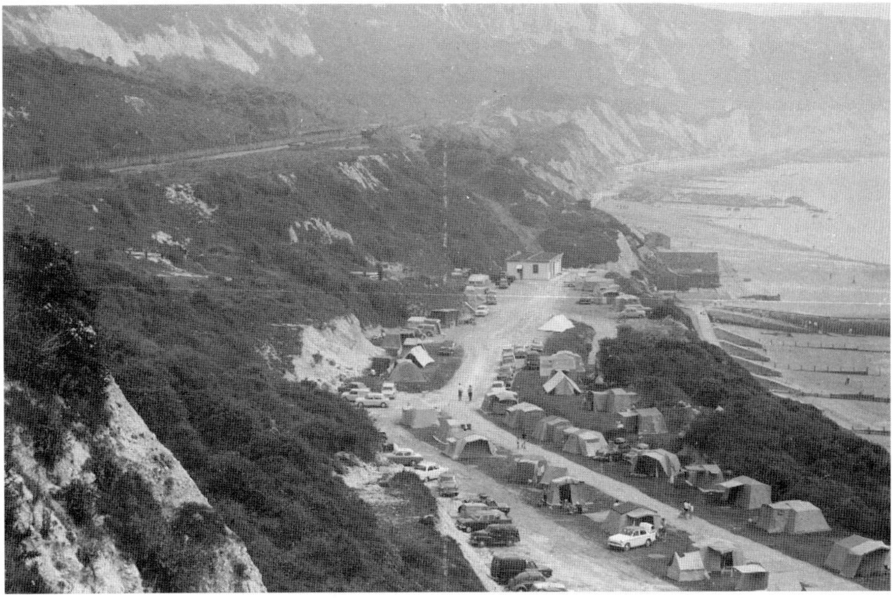

The Warren camp-site, 7 June 1965. The site is completed and occupied, covering four acres of land. The cars are now dated, but the tents are still much the same style as today.

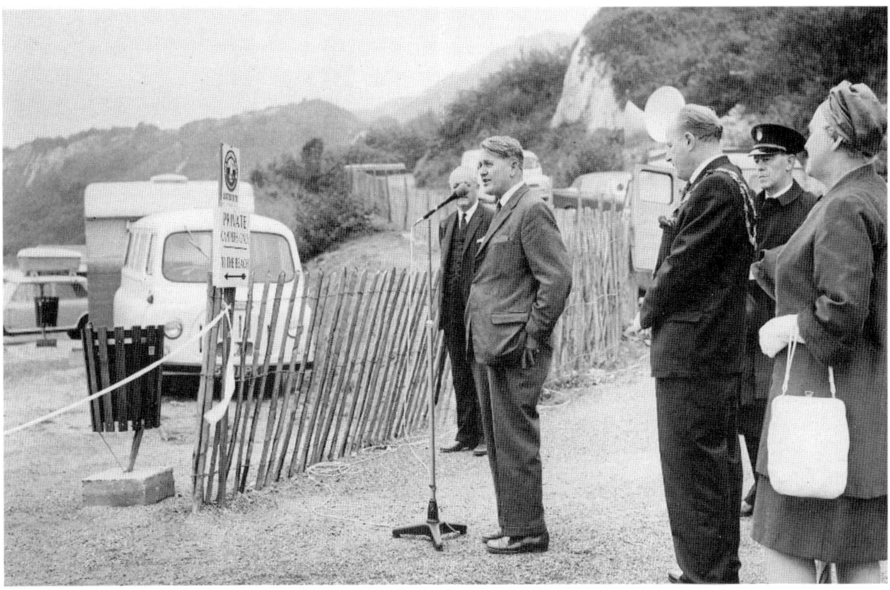

The official opening of the Warren camp-site, Wednesday 27 July 1965. It was opened by Mr Cyril Bence, MP, deputizing for the Minister for Sport, Mr Denis Howell. Mr Bence is at the microphone and behind him is the Mayor of Folkestone, Alderman Wilf M. Harris, JP.

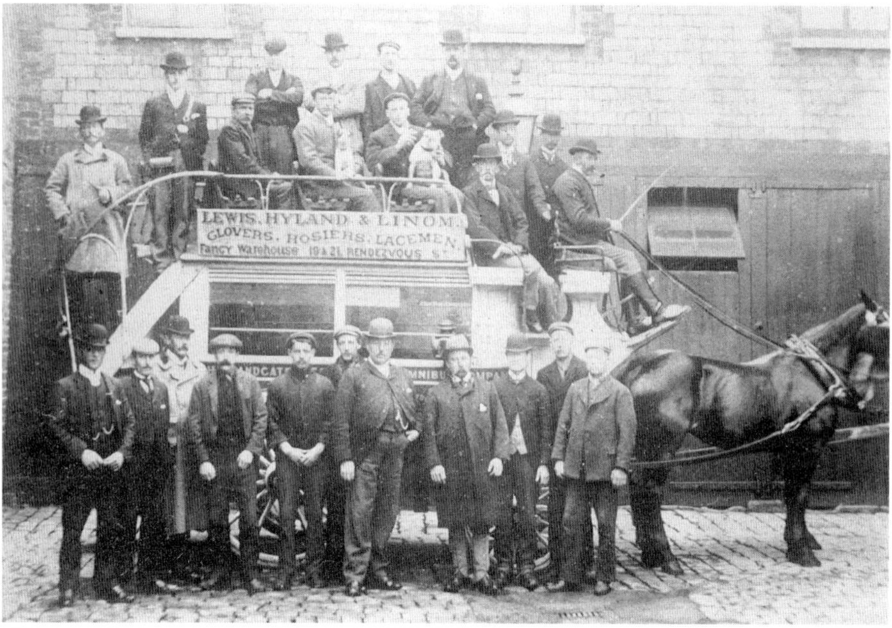

The Hythe, Sandgate & Folkestone Omnibus Co. Ltd, 10 East Street, Hythe, 1900. These are possibly the staff as the venue appears to be the company's mews. Note the advertisement for Lewis, Hyland & Linom, glovers, hosiers, lacemen and fancy warehouse, 19 and 21 Rendezvous Street (see p. 25).

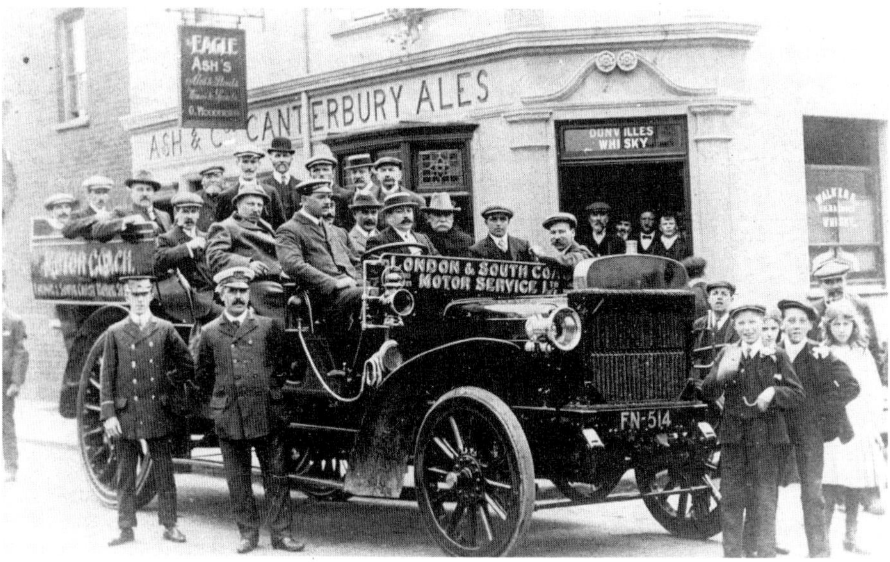

A charabanc outing from the Eagle Tavern between 1907 and 1916. The Eagle Tavern, formerly the Darlington Arms, 89 Guildhall Street, opened in 1855 and traded until 1966 when the premises were demolished.

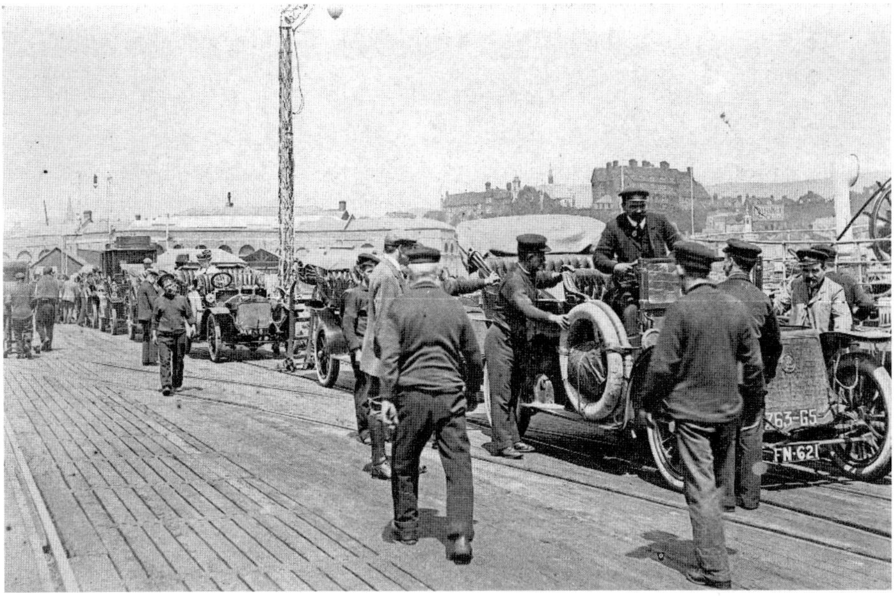

Cars assemble at Folkestone harbour ready to board the cross-channel steamer, *c.* 1910.

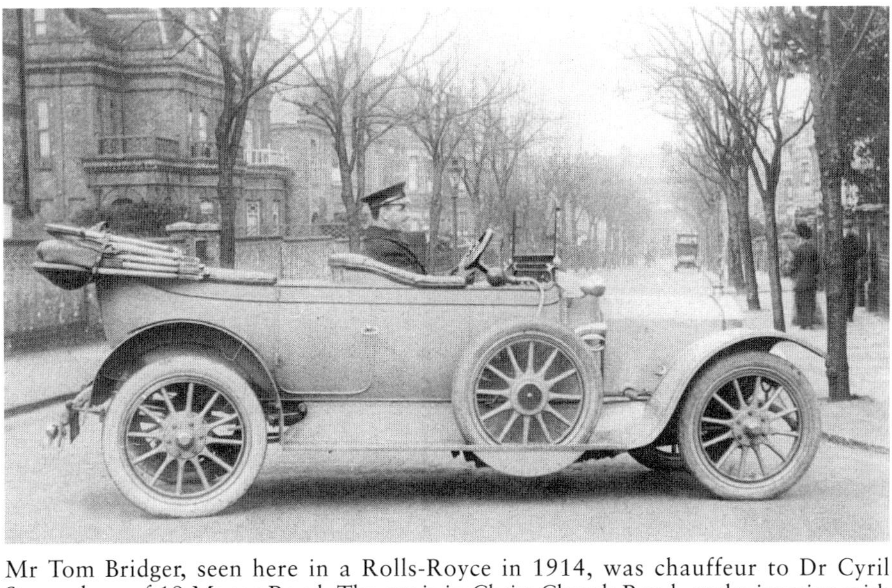

Mr Tom Bridger, seen here in a Rolls-Royce in 1914, was chauffeur to Dr Cyril Stranagham of 19 Manor Road. The car is in Christ Church Road, at the junction with Ingles Road, looking towards Shorncliffe Road.

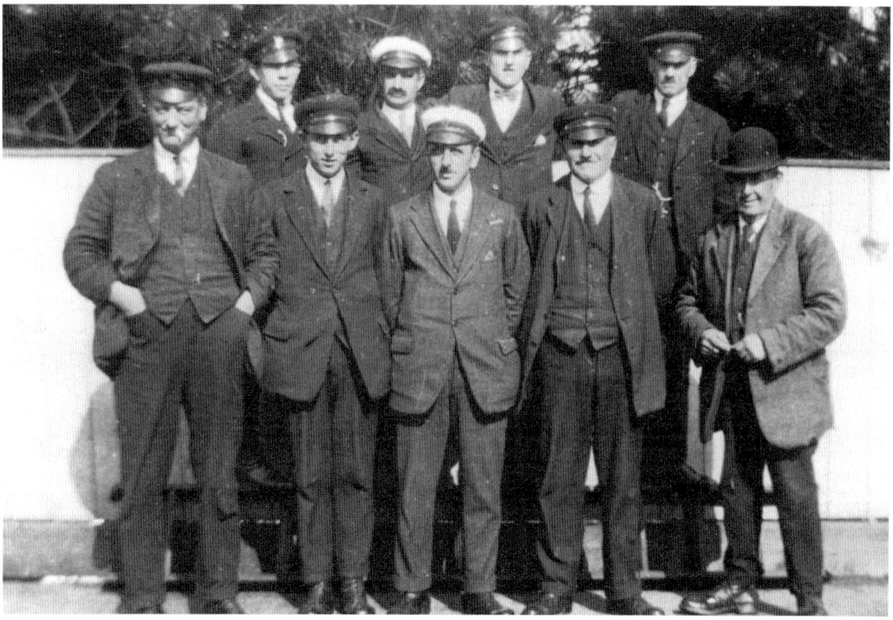

Folkestone taxi drivers, late 1920s. Front row, left to right: Mr Joe Hughes, -?-, Mr Tom Bridger, Mr Alf Grinstead, -?-. Back row: station porter, Mr Freddy Rootes, Mr 'Tich' Grinstead, Mr ? Chandler.

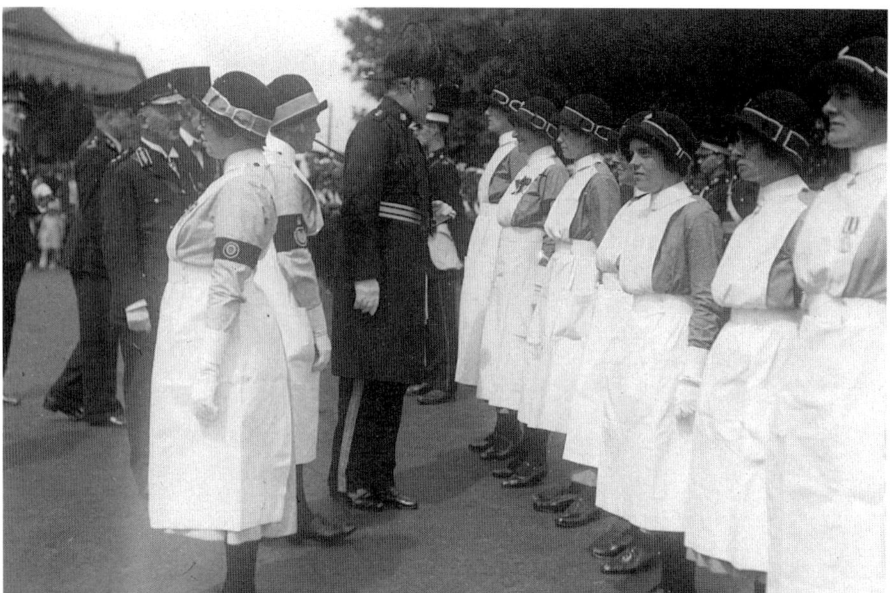

The St John Ambulance Brigade at the Central station, *c.* 1934. The brigade is being inspected by the Chief Commissioner, Sir John Duncan.

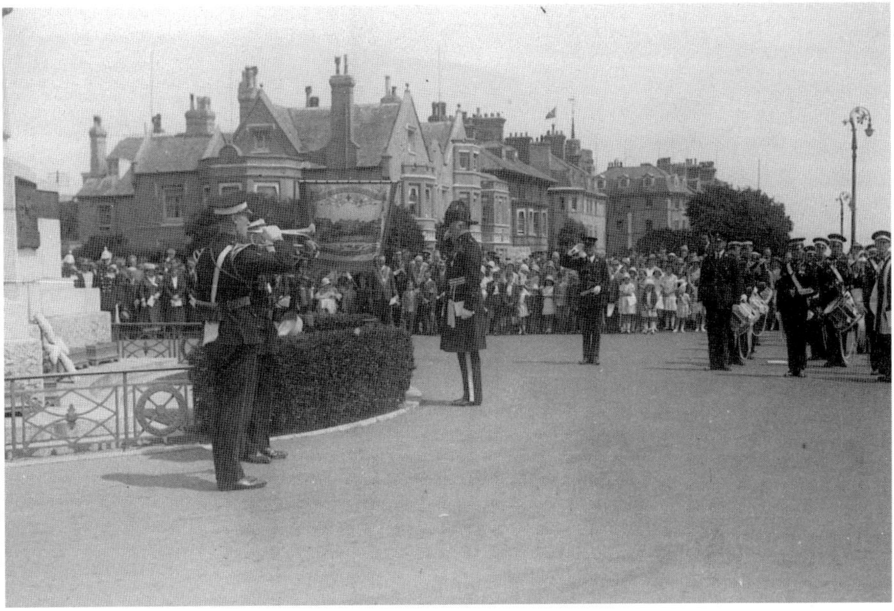

The St John Ambulance Brigade at the War Memorial, East Leas, *c.* 1934. The Chief Commissioner, Sir John Duncan, can be seen saluting.

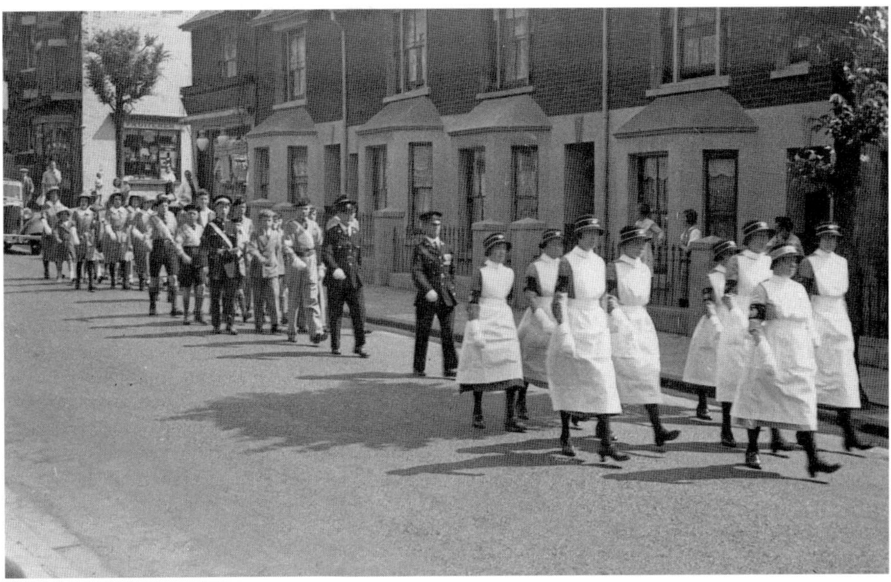

The Folkestone division of the St John Ambulance Brigade marching down Black Bull Road on the way to a church parade, *c.* 1934.

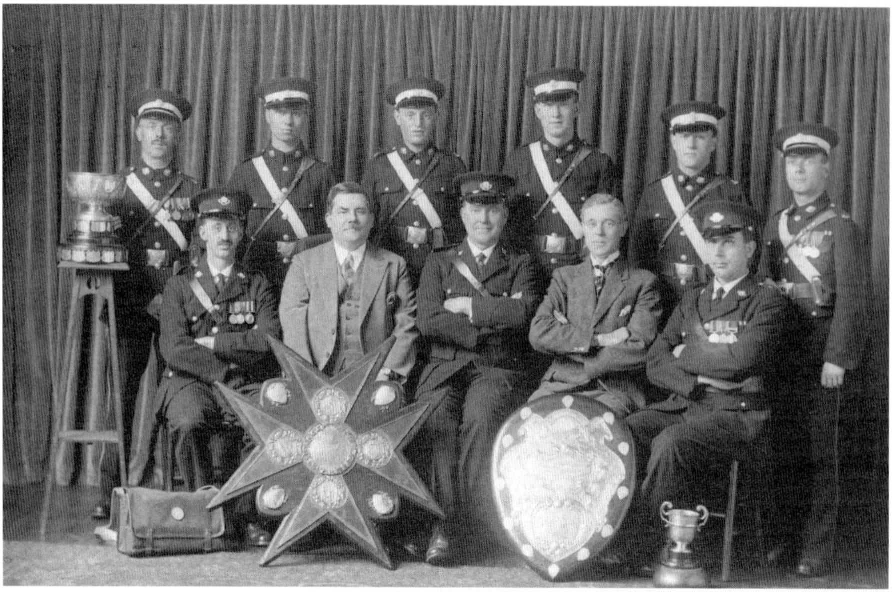

The competition team for the Folkestone division of the St John Ambulance Brigade, 1928. The team is seen here with its trophies.

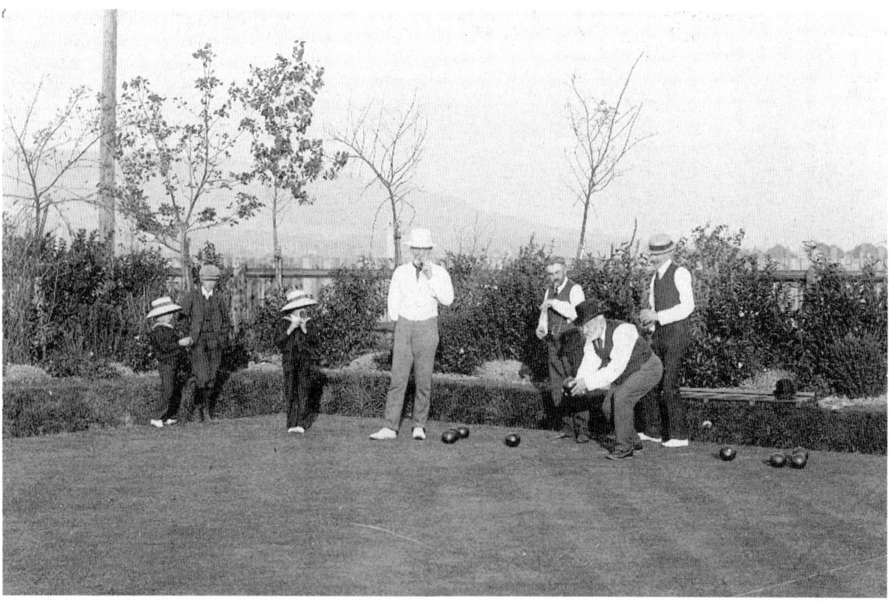

The Folkestone bowling club, Cheriton Road, *c.* 1910. The bowling club was formed in 1906 when the greens were laid.

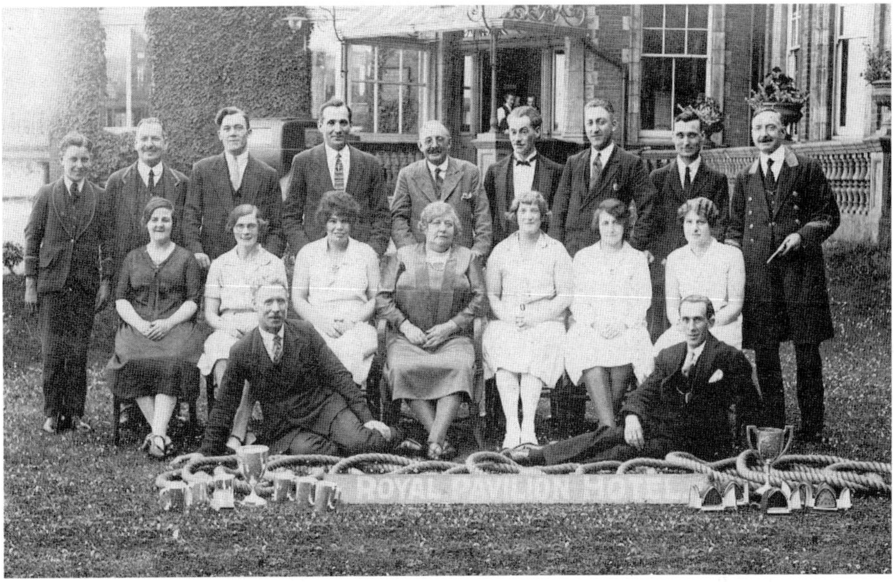

The Royal Pavilion Hotel staff sports day, 1930. The winning 'Tug O' War' teams are seen here with their trophies.

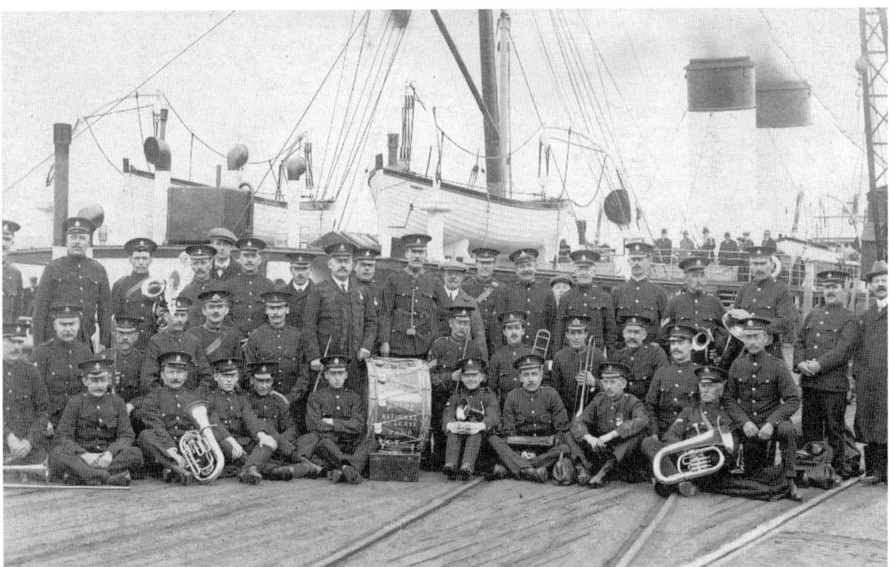

The Hythe National Reserve Band, Folkestone harbour, 1913. They are about to embark on the cross-channel turbine steamer.

Acknowledgements

This publication has been compiled entirely from the collection of Alan Taylor and the late C.P. Davies. I am indebted to those people who, over the years, have given me items or have allowed photographs to be copied, thus helping to build my collection.

I should like to offer sincere thanks to the following people:

Mr R. Adams • Mr G. Ball • Mr P. Bamford • Mr K. Bridger
Mr R. Briggs • Mr J. Carter • Mr M. Fagg • Mr J. Gale • Mr J. Godden
Mr D. Hall • Mrs D. McGuire • Mrs D. May • Mr G. Neal • Mrs S. Pass
Mrs E. Robinson • Mr V. Seymour • Mr J. Slade • Mr K. Smith • Mr C. Wells

I should also like to thank Arthur Bailey from the Guildhall Camera Centre for all his dedicated work in copying photographs.

BRITAIN IN OLD PHOTOGRAPHS

To order any of these titles please telephone Littlehampton Book Services 01903 721596

ALDERNEY

Alderney: A Second Selection, *B Bonnard*

BEDFORDSHIRE

Bedfordshire at Work, *N Lutt*

BERKSHIRE

Maidenhead, *M Hayles & D Hedges*
Around Maidenhead, *M Hayles & B Hedges*
Reading, *P Southerton*
Reading: A Second Selection, *P Southerton*
Sandhurst and Crowthorne, *K Dancy*
Around Slough, *J Hunter & K Hunter*
Around Thatcham, *P Allen*
Around Windsor, *B Hedges*

BUCKINGHAMSHIRE

Buckingham and District, *R Cook*
High Wycombe, *R Goodearl*
Around Stony Stratford, *A Lambert*

CHESHIRE

Cheshire Railways, *M Hitches*
Chester, *S Nichols*

CLWYD

Clwyd Railways, *M Hitches*

CLYDESDALE

Clydesdale, *Lesmahagow Parish Historical Association*

CORNWALL

Cornish Coast, *T Bowden*
Falmouth, *P Gilson*
Lower Fal, *P Gilson*
Around Padstow, *M McCarthy*
Around Penzance, *J Holmes*
Penzance and Newlyn, *J Holmes*
Around Truro, *A Lyne*
Upper Fal, *P Gilson*

CUMBERLAND

Cockermouth and District, *J Bernard Bradbury*
Keswick and the Central Lakes, *J Marsh*
Around Penrith, *F Boyd*
Around Whitehaven, *H Fancy*

DERBYSHIRE

Derby, *D Buxton*
Around Matlock, *D Barton*

DEVON

Colyton and Seaton, *T Gosling*
Dawlish and Teignmouth, *G Gosling*
Devon Aerodromes, *K Saunders*
Exeter, *P Thomas*
Exmouth and Budleigh Salterton, *T Gosling*
From Haldon to Mid-Dartmoor, *T Hall*
Honiton and the Otter Valley, *J Yallop*
Around Kingsbridge, *K Tanner*
Around Seaton and Sidmouth, *T Gosling*
Seaton, Axminster and Lyme Regis, *T Gosling*

DORSET

Around Blandford Forum, *B Cox*
Bournemouth, *M Colman*
Bridport and the Bride Valley, *J Burrell & S Humphries*
Dorchester, *T Gosling*
Around Gillingham, *P Crocker*

DURHAM

Darlington, *G Flynn*
Darlington: A Second Selection, *G Flynn*
Durham People, *M Richardson*
Houghton-le-Spring and Hetton-le-Hole, *K Richardson*
Houghton-le-Spring and Hetton-le-Hole: A Second Selection, *K Richardson*
Sunderland, *S Miller & B Bell*
Teesdale, *D Coggins*
Teesdale: A Second Selection, *P Raine*
Weardale, *J Crosby*
Weardale: A Second Selection, *J Crosby*

DYFED

Aberystwyth and North Ceredigion, *Dyfed Cultural Services Dept*
Haverfordwest, *Dyfed Cultural Services Dept*
Upper Tywi Valley, *Dyfed Cultural Services Dept*

ESSEX

Around Grays, *B Evans*

GLOUCESTERSHIRE

Along the Avon from Stratford to Tewkesbury, *J Jeremiah*
Cheltenham: A Second Selection, *R Whiting*
Cheltenham at War, *P Gill*
Cirencester, *J Welsford*
Around Cirencester, *E Cuss & P Griffiths*
Forest, The, *D Mullin*
Gloucester, *J Voyce*
Around Gloucester, *A Sutton*
Gloucester: From the Walwin Collection, *J Voyce*
North Cotswolds, *D Viner*
Severn Vale, *A Sutton*
Stonehouse to Painswick, *A Sutton*
Stroud and the Five Valleys, *S Gardiner & L Padin*
Stroud and the Five Valleys: A Second Selection, *S Gardiner & L Padin*
Stroud's Golden Valley, *S Gardiner & L Padin*
Stroudwater and Thames & Severn Canals, *E Cuss & S Gardiner*
Stroudwater and Thames & Severn Canals: A Second Selection, *E Cuss & S Gardiner*
Tewkesbury and the Vale of Gloucester, *C Hilton*
Thornbury to Berkeley, *J Hudson*
Uley, Dursley and Cam, *A Sutton*
Wotton-under-Edge to Chipping Sodbury, *A Sutton*

GWYNEDD

Anglesey, *M Hitches*
Gwynedd Railways, *M Hitches*
Around Llandudno, *M Hitches*
Vale of Conwy, *M Hitches*

HAMPSHIRE

Gosport, *J Sadden*
Portsmouth, *P Rogers & D Francis*

HEREFORDSHIRE

Herefordshire, *A Sandford*

HERTFORDSHIRE

Barnet, *I Norrie*
Hitchin, *A Fleck*
St Albans, *S Mullins*
Stevenage, *M Appleton*

ISLE OF MAN

The Tourist Trophy, *B Snelling*

ISLE OF WIGHT

Newport, *D Parr*
Around Ryde, *D Parr*

JERSEY

Jersey: A Third Selection, *R Lemprière*

KENT

Bexley, *M Scott*
Broadstairs and St Peter's, *J Whyman*
Bromley, Keston and Hayes, *M Scott*
Canterbury: A Second Selection, *D Butler*
Chatham and Gillingham, *P MacDougall*
Chatham Dockyard, *P MacDougall*
Deal, *J Broady*
Early Broadstairs and St Peter's, *B Wootton*
East Kent at War, *D Collyer*
Eltham, *J Kennett*
Folkestone: A Second Selection, *A Taylor & E Rooney*
Goudhurst to Tenterden, *A Guilmant*
Gravesend, *R Hiscock*
Around Gravesham, *R Hiscock & D Grierson*
Herne Bay, *J Hawkins*
Lympne Airport, *D Collyer*
Maidstone, *I Hales*
Margate, *R Clements*
RAF Hawkinge, *R Humphreys*
RAF Manston, *RAF Manston History Club*
RAF Manston: A Second Selection, *RAF Manston History Club*
Ramsgate and Thanet Life, *D Perkins*
Romney Marsh, *E Carpenter*
Sandwich, *C Wanostrocht*
Around Tonbridge, *C Bell*
Tunbridge Wells, *M Rowlands & I Beavis*
Tunbridge Wells: A Second Selection, *M Rowlands & I Beavis*
Around Whitstable, *C Court*
Wingham, Adisham and Littlebourne, *M Crane*

LANCASHIRE

Around Barrow-in-Furness, *J Garbutt & J Marsh*
Blackpool, *C Rothwell*
Bury, *J Hudson*
Chorley and District, *J Smith*
Fleetwood, *C Rothwell*
Heywood, *J Hudson*
Around Kirkham, *C Rothwell*
Lancashire North of the Sands, *J Garbutt & J Marsh*
Around Lancaster, *S Ashworth*
Lytham St Anne's, *C Rothwell*
North Fylde, *C Rothwell*
Radcliffe, *J Hudson*
Rossendale, *B Moore & N Dunnachie*

LEICESTERSHIRE

Around Ashby-de-la-Zouch, *K Hillier*
Charnwood Forest, *I Keil, W Humphrey & D Wix*
Leicester, *D Burton*
Leicester: A Second Selection, *D Burton*
Melton Mowbray, *T Hickman*
Around Melton Mowbray, *T Hickman*
River Soar, *D Wix, P Shacklock & I Keil*
Rutland, *T Clough*
Vale of Belvoir, *T Hickman*
Around the Welland Valley, *S Mastoris*

LINCOLNSHIRE

Grimsby, *J Tierney*
Around Grimsby, *J Tierney*
Grimsby Docks, *J Tierney*
Lincoln, *D Cuppleditch*

Scunthorpe, *D Taylor*
Skegness, *W Kime*
Around Skegness, *W Kime*

LONDON

Balham and Tooting, *P Loobey*
Crystal Palace, Penge & Anerley, *M Scott*
Greenwich and Woolwich, *K Clark*
Hackney: A Second Selection, *D Mander*
Lewisham and Deptford, *J Coulter*
Lewisham and Deptford: A Second Selection, *J Coulter*
Streatham, *P Loobey*
Around Whetstone and North Finchley, *J Heathfield*
Woolwich, *B Evans*

MONMOUTHSHIRE

Chepstow and the River Wye, *A Rainsbury*
Monmouth and the River Wye, *Monmouth Museum*

NORFOLK

Great Yarmouth, *M Teun*
Norwich, *M Colman*
Wymondham and Attleborough, *P Yaxley*

NORTHAMPTONSHIRE

Around Stony Stratford, *A Lambert*

NOTTINGHAMSHIRE

Arnold and Bestwood, *M Spick*
Arnold and Bestwood: A Second Selection, *M Spick*
Changing Face of Nottingham, *G Oldfield*
Mansfield, *Old Mansfield Society*
Around Newark, *T Warner*
Nottingham: 1944–1974, *D Whitworth*
Sherwood Forest, *D Ottewell*
Victorian Nottingham, *M Payne*

OXFORDSHIRE

Around Abingdon, *P Horn*
Banburyshire, *M Barnett & S Gosling*
Burford, *A Jewell*
Around Didcot and the Hagbournes, *B Lingham*
Garsington, *M Gunther*
Around Henley-on-Thames, *S Ellis*
Oxford: The University, *J Rhodes*
Thame to Watlington, *N Hood*
Around Wallingford, *D Beasley*
Witney, *T Worley*
Around Witney, *C Mitchell*
Witney District, *T Worley*
Around Woodstock, *J Bond*

POWYS

Brecon, *Brecknock Museum*
Welshpool, *E Bredsdorff*

SHROPSHIRE

Shrewsbury, *D Trumper*
Whitchurch to Market Drayton, *M Morris*

SOMERSET

Bath, *J Hudson*
Bridgwater and the River Parrett, *R Fitzhugh*
Bristol, *D Moorcroft & N Campbell-Sharp*
Changing Face of Keynsham, *B Lowe & M Whitehead*
Chard and Ilminster, *G Gosling & F Huddy*
Crewkerne and the Ham Stone Villages, *G Gosling & F Huddy*
Around Keynsham and Saltford, *B Lowe & T Brown*
Midsomer Norton and Radstock, *C Howell*
Somerton, Ilchester and Langport, *G Gosling & F Huddy*
Taunton, *N Chipchase*
Around Taunton, *N Chipchase*
Wells, *C Howell*
Weston-Super-Mare, *S Poole*
Around Weston-Super-Mare, *S Poole*
West Somerset Villages, *K Houghton & L Thomas*

STAFFORDSHIRE

Aldridge, *J Farrow*
Bilston, *E Rees*
Black Country Transport: Aviation, *A Brew*
Around Burton upon Trent, *G Sowerby & R Farman*
Bushbury, *A Chatwin, M Mills & E Rees*
Around Cannock, *M Mills & S Belcher*
Around Leek, *R Poole*
Lichfield, *H Clayton & K Simmons*
Around Pattingham and Wombourne, *M Griffiths, P Leigh & M Mills*
Around Rugeley, *T Randall & J Anslow*
Smethwick, *J Maddison*
Stafford, *J Anslow & T Randall*
Around Stafford, *J Anslow & T Randall*
Stoke-on-Trent, *I Lawley*
Around Tamworth, *R Sulima*
Around Tettenhall and Codsall, *M Mills*
Tipton, Wednesbury and Darlaston, *R Pearson*
Walsall, *D Gilbert & M Lewis*
Wednesbury, *I Bott*
West Bromwich, *R Pearson*

SUFFOLK

Ipswich: A Second Selection, *D Kindred*
Around Ipswich, *D Kindred*
Around Mildenhall, *C Dring*
Southwold to Aldeburgh, *H Phelps*
Around Woodbridge, *H Phelps*

SURREY

Cheam and Belmont, *P Berry*
Croydon, *S Bligh*
Dorking and District, *K Harding*
Around Dorking, *A Jackson*
Around Epsom, *P Berry*
Farnham: A Second Selection, *J Parratt*
Around Haslemere and Hindhead, *T Winter & G Collyer*
Richmond, *Richmond Local History Society*
Sutton, *P Berry*

SUSSEX

Arundel and the Arun Valley, *J Godfrey*
Bishopstone and Seaford, *P Pople & P Berry*
Brighton and Hove, *J Middleton*
Brighton and Hove: A Second Selection, *J Middleton*
Around Crawley, *M Goldsmith*
Hastings, *P Haines*
Hastings: A Second Selection, *P Haines*
Around Haywards Heath, *J Middleton*
Around Heathfield, *A Gillet & B Russell*
Around Heathfield: A Second Selection, *A Gillet & B Russell*
High Weald, *B Harwood*
High Weald: A Second Selection, *B Harwood*
Horsham and District, *T Wales*
Lewes, *J Middleton*
RAF Tangmere, *A Saunders*
Around Rye, *A Dickinson*
Around Worthing, *S White*

WARWICKSHIRE

Along the Avon from Stratford to Tewkesbury, *J Jeremiah*
Bedworth, *J Burton*
Coventry, *D McGrory*
Around Coventry, *D McGrory*
Nuneaton, *S Clews & S Vaughan*
Around Royal Leamington Spa, *J Cameron*
Around Royal Leamington Spa: A Second Selection, *J Cameron*
Around Warwick, *R Booth*

WESTMORLAND

Eden Valley, *J Marsh*
Kendal, *M & P Duff*
South Westmorland Villages, *J Marsh*
Westmorland Lakes, *J Marsh*

WILTSHIRE

Around Amesbury, *P Daniels*
Chippenham and Lacock, *A Wilson & M Wilson*
Around Corsham and Box, *A Wilson & M Wilson*
Around Devizes, *D Buxton*
Around Highworth, *G Tanner*
Around Highworth and Faringdon, *G Tanner*
Around Malmesbury, *A Wilson*
Marlborough: A Second Selection, *P Colman*
Around Melksham, *Melksham and District Historical Association*
Nadder Valley, *R. Sawyer*
Salisbury, *P Saunders*
Salisbury: A Second Selection, *P Daniels*
Salisbury: A Third Selection, *P Daniels*
Around Salisbury, *P Daniels*
Swindon: A Third Selection, *The Swindon Society*
Swindon: A Fourth Selection, *The Swindon Society*
Trowbridge, *M Marshman*
Around Wilton, *P Daniels*
Around Wootton Bassett, Cricklade and Purton, *T Sharp*

WORCESTERSHIRE

Evesham to Bredon, *F Archer*
Around Malvern, *K Smith*
Around Pershore, *M Dowty*
Redditch and the Needle District, *R Saunders*
Redditch: A Second Selection, *R Saunders*
Around Tenbury Wells, *D Green*
Worcester, *M Dowty*
Around Worcester, *R Jones*
Worcester in a Day, *M Dowty*
Worcestershire at Work, *R Jones*

YORKSHIRE

Huddersfield: A Second Selection, *H Wheeler*
Huddersfield: A Third Selection, *H Wheeler*
Leeds Road and Rail, *R Vickers*
Pontefract, *R van Riel*
Scarborough, *D Coggins*
Scarborough's War Years, *R Percy*
Skipton and the Dales, *Friends of the Craven Museum*
Around Skipton-in-Craven, *Friends of the Craven Museum*
Yorkshire Wolds, *I & M Sumner*